Dan O'Brien

PLAYS ONE

The Body of an American

The House in Hydesville

The Cherry Sisters Revisited

The Voyage of the Carcass

The Dear Boy

OBERON BOOKS
LONDON

WWW.OBERONBOOKS.COM

This collection first published in 2017 by Oberon Books Ltd
521 Caledonian Road, London N7 9RH
Tel: +44 (0) 20 7607 3637 / Fax: +44 (0) 20 7607 3629
e-mail: info@oberonbooks.com
www.oberonbooks.com

A catalogue record for this book is available from the British Library.

PB ISBN: 9781786821744
E ISBN: 9781786821751

Front cover image by Bill Jackson
Back cover author image by Brett Simison

Printed and bound by CPI Group (UK) Ltd, Croydon, CR0 4YY.
eBook conversaion by Lapiz Digital Services, India.

Contents

The Body of an American

Mogadishu, 1993. Paul is a Canadian war reporter about to take a photograph that will win him the Pulitzer Prize. Princeton, the present day, Dan is an American writer struggling to finish his play about "historical ghosts." Though they live worlds apart, a chance encounter over the airwaves sparks an extraordinary friendship that sees these two men journey from some of the most dangerous places on earth to the depths of the human psyche. Flying from Kabul to the High Arctic, *The Body of an American* requires two actors to embody more than thirty roles in an exhilarating new form of documentary theatre, urgently dramatizing these two men's battles—both public and private—against a backdrop of some of the world's most iconic images of war.

The House in Hydesville

In the winter of 1848 the Fox family moves to a bleak cottage in the isolated hamlet of Hydesville, New York. Soon the youngest Fox girls begin to hear strange noises—knocking or "rapping" in the walls—amid rumors of a body buried in the cellar. At once an exploration of familial abuse and the need for spiritual transcendence, *The House in Hydesville* is a compelling "true ghost story," as the Fox Sisters went on to found the Modern Spiritualist movement at a time of great religious, social, and sexual upheaval in America. Were these haunted y young women the products of their time, or the prophets of it?

The Cherry Sisters Revisited

The five Cherry sisters' love of the vaudeville carries them all the way from their snowy farm in Iowa to the bright lights of Broadway, where their egregiously talentless act becomes a smash hit—bringing them fame, and a relentless barrage of rotten fruit and vegetables. Based on a true story, Dan O'Brien's provocative comedy-with-music takes a look at the American compulsion to perform, and our inability to look away.

The Voyage of the Carcass

Bo'sun Smythe is dead. Trapped in the ice at the North Pole, only three members of the doomed *Carcass* crew survive: Bane Barrington, buffoonish explorer; Ship's Chaplain Kane, a rector in drag; and Israel, their mute Canadian first mate. Will they make it home alive? First, they'll take a five-minute break, and explore themselves, their roles, and their predicament as the actors Bill, a struggling mime; his wife Helen, erstwhile actress; and Dan, the passive-aggressive puppet-master, i.e. the writer of this play. Weaving commedia dell'arte with theatre verite, *The Voyage of the Carcass* is a play about dreams, and the aftermath.

The Dear Boy

James Flanagan is not a kind teacher. Is he a good teacher? He likes to think so. On the verge of retirement, a potentially catastrophic argument with a troubled student sends Mr. Flanagan out into the night and New York City to the annual faculty Holiday party where he begins an unlikely romance. The following morning Flanagan must once again confront his student—this time to try to save the boy from himself. *The Dear Boy* is an intimate and stirring character study of a man forced to face his past, his present, and the life he may still yet live.

THE BODY OF AN AMERICAN

Inspired in part by the memoir
Where War Lives by Paul Watson

Characters

Two actors play all the roles here: ideally an actor in his 30s who plays Dan most of the time, and an actor around 50 to mostly play Paul.

The older of these two actors has the first line of the play, and with each new character-heading—even when it's the same character—the actors alternate.

Time & Place

Scenes 1-7: various.

Scenes 8-10: the Arctic, Modern Day.

Notes

In the right-hand column of the script are suggestions of photographs, maps, moving images, etc., to be projected somewhere prominent onstage; as well as suggestions for occasional sound design. All of the photographs listed are by Paul Watson or the playwright or unknown, except where noted.

The Body of an American is winner of the Horton Foote Prize for Outstanding New American Play, the inaugural Edward M. Kennedy Prize for Drama, the PEN Center Award for Drama, and the L. Arnold Weissberger Award.

The World Premiere of *The Body of an American* was produced in 2012 by Portland Center Stage, Portland, OR, Chris Coleman, Artistic Director, directed by Bill Rauch, after having received a workshop at JAW: A Playwrights Festival at Portland Center Stage.

PAUL	William Salyers
DAN	Danny Wolohan

Creative Team

Scenic and Costume Designer	Christopher Acebo
Lighting Designer	James F. Ingalls
Sound and Projections Designer	Eamonn Farrell
Sound Designer	Casi Pacilio
Dialect Coach	Mary McDonald-Lewis
Stage Manager	Jeremy Eisen
Production Assistant	Kailyn McCord

The play was commissioned and developed with support from The Playwrights' Center's McKnight Commission and Residency Program, Minneapolis, MN.

Additional support was received from the Rockefeller Foundation Bellagio Residency, a Future Collaborations Grant from Theatre Communications Group, a Sundance Institute Time Warner Storytelling Fellowship, PlayLabs at The Playwrights' Center, the New Harmony Project, and a workshop at Pioneer Theatre.

The Body of an American received its European premiere in 2014 at the Gate Theatre in London, Christopher Haydon, Artistic Director, in co-production with Royal & Derngate, Northampton, James Dacre, Artistic Director, and directed by James Dacre.

PAUL	William Gaminara
DAN	Damien Molony

Creative Team

Design	Alex Lowde
Lighting Designer	Charles Balfour
Sound Designer	Adrienne Quartly
Video Design	Dick Straker for Mesmer

Premiered off-Broadway in February 2016 at the Cherry Lane Theatre by Primary Stages, Andrew Leynse, Artistic Director, in co-production with Hartford Stage, Darko Tresnjak, Artistic Director.

PAUL	Michael Cumpsty
DAN	Michael Crane

Creative Team

Director	Jo Bonney
Scenic Design	Richard Hoover
Costume Design	Ilona Somogyi
Lighting Design	Lap Chi Chu
Sound Design	Darron L. West
Projection Design	Alex Basco Koch
Casting	Binder Casting/Jack Bowdan, CSA

I do want to hear this because
you're another person in this story.
Um, and each, each person in this story
ends up telling his own story of what
I call – the working title for the book
I'm writing is Where War Lives. From a quote
of Albert Camus when he was keeping
his notebooks pre-World War Two. And a friend
wrote to him saying, you know, I'm grappling
with this philosophical question, Where
does this vile thing, war, live? And Camus said,
he's in Algiers at the time and he says,

I look at the bright blue sky and I think
of the guilt that I feel from not being
in a position where I, I can die
with them, while at the same time wanting to
be as far away as I can from it.

—Paul Watson in conversation
with Dr. Joseph LeDoux, January 2006

for Isobel Kelly

1: FRESH AIR

PAUL My name's Paul Watson.

PAUL I'm Paul Watson.

TERRY GROSS This is *Fresh Air*,

TERRY GROSS I'm Terry Gross. Remember that famous 1993 photo?

PAUL I was a reporter who happened to—

DAN Dear Mr. Watson. I don't usually email strangers like this.

TERRY GROSS This is *Fresh Air*.

DAN I was leaving Princeton.

PAUL New Jersey?

DAN Where I had this fellowship.

PAUL You had a what?

DAN A residency—

PAUL Which means you do what?

DAN Well I was supposed to write a play.

PAUL A play.

DAN Yes.

PAUL About what?

DAN Ghosts.

PAUL Ghosts?

DAN Yeah. Ghosts.

PAUL What kind of ghosts?

DAN Historical, ghosts.

PAUL And they pay you for this?

DAN Sort of. Definitely. I'm really grateful to them—

PAUL Is it scary?

DAN My play? I don't know. I hope so. To me it was.

TERRY GROSS This is *Fresh Air*,

TERRY GROSS I'm Terry Gross. Let's start
with a description of that now famous
Pulitzer prize-winning photo:

PAUL I was
a reporter who happened to carry
a camera, a 35 mm
Nikon I bought because my editors
wouldn't buy me one.

PAUL We were on the roof
of the Sahafi, where the journalists were
staying,

PAUL *if* they were staying.

PAUL You could count
on one hand who was still there.

PAUL I'd have to
count on one hand because my other hand

PAUL isn't really a hand at all.

PAUL I was
born this way.

PAUL A bunch of us were drinking
beer.

PAUL Did you see that light?

REPORTER What light?

PAUL Behind
that chopper there. It just went down behind
that hill.

DAN Chaos ensues.

Image: white light.

PAUL A 16-hour
battle raged through the night between US
Army rangers, special ops, Delta Force
and Somali militias. It started
as an arrest operation trying
to abduct commanders in Mohamed
Aideed's militia. They were trying to
track down Aideed and arrest him for
allegedly organizing attacks
on UN peacekeepers.

PAUL When I woke up
on the hotel floor, still dressed, hung over,
PAUL 18 American soldiers had been killed
and 75 wounded.
PAUL Clouds of smoke
billowing up from burning tire barricades,
dead bodies in the street.
PAUL American troops
were trying to get the rest of their force
back alive, and in so doing they'd killed
more than 600 Somalis so far,
PAUL including women and children, huddled
in the darkness as bullets or shrapnel
pierced the tin walls of their shacks.
PAUL Gutale's
my translator. He hurries through the gate:
GUTALE They are shooting everything that moves now,
even donkeys!
PAUL He gets 30 dollars
a day.
PAUL My driver and bodyguard get
a hundred.
PAUL That's always been the hardest
part of my job: convincing good people
who get none of a byline's ego boost
to risk their lives because I've decided
a story's worth dying for.
GUTALE They're shooting
people on sight! Even people with no
weapons!
PAUL Mogadishu was beautiful
once, white-painted Italianate villas
in the capitol of the most stable
state in Africa.
PAUL Now you see women
grocery shopping with militias firing
machine guns up and down the avenue,

PAUL children playing on the front lines, running
water and bullets beside their mothers
to keep the gunmen supplied.

GUTALE They shot down
a Black Hawk! They are taking a soldier
with them from street to street, perhaps alive,
perhaps dead!

PAUL They threw me in the back seat
of the car,

PAUL a Toyota Cressida
that nobody outside of the safe zone
would recognize,

PAUL and made me hide my face
between Gutale and my bodyguard
Mohamed.

PAUL With another Mohamed
driving, and a gunman in front cradling
an AK-47,

PAUL we drove through
the gates and crawled from street to street. Passing
the corpse-collectors, men carrying bodies
by their hands and feet, glaring at us through
the filthy windshield.

GUTALE Has anyone seen
a captured American soldier?

PAUL Some said,

GUTALE They've seen him. He says he's alive, tied up
in a wheelbarrow.

PAUL A wheelbarrow?

GUTALE No,
this man says he's dead. He's most definitely
dead.

PAUL I took a few pictures of some kids
bouncing up and down on a rotor blade
in the smoldering tail section of that downed
Black Hawk.

GUTALE Have you seen the American
soldier?

PAUL The entire crowd pointed,

GUTALE This way.

PAUL Each time a Black Hawk thundered past people would shake their fists and curse at it.

PAUL We drove all over the city for two hours and were about to give up,

PAUL when the driver makes a u-turn.

GUTALE He sees something.

PAUL A mob of 200 Somalis, moving down an alleyway.

GUTALE What is it?

MOHAMED This is bad, too dangerous.

GUTALE Go slowly.

PAUL What's he saying?

GUTALE He's a coward. He's worried about his car.

MOHAMED This guy's going to get us killed!

GUTALE Shut up!

PAUL Gutale gets out:

GUTALE Gamay's in the car, you know Gamay!

PAUL Gamay is local slang for cripple.

GUTALE Little man! No hand! He's not American, he's Canadian! You know Gamay. He just wants to take some pictures. Can he?

PAUL The crowd parts around me.

PAUL I look down at the street:

PAUL and I meet Staff Sgt. William David Cleveland.

GUTALE Take the picture
quickly.

PAUL I've taken pictures of corpses
before, many of them much more fucked up
than this man.

GUTALE Hurry, Paul!

PAUL I bend over,
shoulders stiff.

GUTALE Take it now!

PAUL With a camera
in front of your eye, you cover your face
and you focus only on the good shot.

PAUL You shut everything else out.

PAUL Everything
goes quiet.

PAUL Despite the noise of the crowd
and the helicopters,

PAUL everything goes
completely silent. And I hear a voice
both in my head and out:

CLEVELAND If you do this,
I will own you forever.

PAUL I'm sorry
but I have to.

CLEVELAND If you do this, I will
own you.

PAUL I've sought psychiatric treatment
in subsequent years. And my psychiatrist
says it's my superego. I believe
it was William David Cleveland speaking
to me.

TERRY GROSS And what did he mean?

PAUL Well, Terry,
I took it as a warning.

TERRY GROSS A warning
of what exactly?

PAUL I have to do this.

PAUL I don't want to do this.

PAUL I don't want to
desecrate your body.

CLEVELAND If you do this
I will own you forever.

PAUL I took his
picture.

Image: Paul Watson's full-length photograph of Staff Sgt. William David Cleveland.

PAUL While they were beating his body
and cheering. Some spitting.

PAUL Some kid wearing
a chopper crewman's goggles shoves his way
into the frame. His face is all screwed up
in rapturous glee while giving the dead man
the finger.

PAUL An old man's raising his cane
like a club and thudding it down against
the dead flesh.

Image: another shot from this series.

PAUL Wind's blowing dirt and the stench
is making me gag.

PAUL For weeks I'd hated
UN peacekeepers like this man, who killed
from the sky with impunity.

PAUL But now
it was us against them.

GUTALE Get in the car,
Gamay!

PAUL The men holding the ropes that bind
the soldier's wrists are stretching his arms out
over his head.

PAUL They're rolling his body
back and forth in the hammering morning light.

PAUL I feel like I'm standing beside myself.

PAUL I feel like I'm somebody else watching
myself take these photographs,

PAUL somebody
named Paul, doing this crazy thing,

PAUL shooting
pictures.

PAUL Asking, Did I put the batteries
in?

PAUL *Click.*

Image: another shot from this series.

PAUL The bullet wounds are in his legs:
did they shoot him in the street, did he die
before he crashed?

PAUL *Click.*

Image: another shot.

PAUL His body's so limp
he must have just died.

PAUL *Click.*

Image: another shot.

PAUL Maybe he's still
alive? Is that why I can hear his voice?
If you do this,

PAUL *Click. Click.*

Image: another shot.

PAUL I will own you.

PAUL *Click. Click. Click. Click.*

Image: another shot.

PAUL You poor man. Who are you?

GUTALE We must go. Let's go. They don't want us here
anymore.

PAUL The car door's shut.

PAUL Soft idling
of the engine. The muffled mob.

PAUL It's like
I've stepped out of Mogadishu into

PAUL a wobbling canoe years ago in
Sudan,

PAUL drifting downriver at dusk with

ANDREW Andrew Stawicki,

PAUL a Polish émigré
photographer who snaps a picture of
boys running naked like a snake along
the river's blood-red spine. That's going to be
a great picture.

ANDREW They won't print it.

PAUL Why not?

ANDREW The kid's dick is showing!

PAUL In my mind's eye

I see Sgt. Cleveland's Army-issue
green underwear, the only clothing left
on his body.

PAUL The underwear's slightly
askew, so you can just make out a piece
of the dead man's scrotum.

Image: Paul's full-body shot.

PAUL Open the door!
Open it!

PAUL This time I framed it better:
the body from the waist up.

PAUL A woman
slapping him with a flattened can.

Image: Paul's famous half-body shot.

PAUL That boy
with the goggles shoveling his face through
the mob,

PAUL laughing at us.

PAUL Men with bloodshot
eyes notice me.

PAUL It would be like squashing
a cockroach to kill me, this infidel
who can't take a hint.

GUTALE Look, he's leaving now!
See? We're leaving for good! Thank you!

PAUL The squeak
of the hotel gate always let me breathe
easier. As if a few sleepy guards could
actually keep us safe from everything
happening out there.

PAUL I take the service stairs
two at a time to my room, stuff the roll
of film between the mattress and box spring,
switch on the broken AC,

PAUL and collapse
on my bed with my eyes closed and I cry
for a very long time.

TERRY GROSS This is *Fresh Air*.
The AP printed it, and so did *Time*
magazine.

PAUL That's right. AP moved the half
-body shots, which appeared in newspapers
all over the world. What *Time* magazine
did, which I find fascinating, is they
digitally altered the underwear
so you can't see any genitals. But
you do see horrific desecration
of an American soldier.

TERRY GROSS This picture
had incredible impact.

PAUL Yes, Terry,
that's right. Because immediately the heat
was on President Bill Clinton to do
something. And that something was to announce
the immediate withdrawal of American
troops. Then, when it became time to decide
whether or not the United States should
lead an intervention in Rwanda,
where 800,000 people were killed
in a hundred days, President Clinton
decided not to use the word genocide
so we wouldn't be *forced* to intervene.
And we know without a doubt Al-Qaeda
was there in Mogadishu. It says so
on indictments in US Federal Court,
bin Laden's bragged about it, his minions
have bragged about it. But what disturbs me
the most is that Al-Qaeda learned a lot
from the propaganda impact of that
photograph. 18 American soldiers
were killed that day. Which is nothing compared
to what used to happen on a bad day
in Vietnam. And it's only relatively
bad compared to what's still happening these days
in Iraq, or Afghanistan. I think
it's safe to say, take all of the events
that happened, but remove the photograph,

and Al-Qaeda would not have chased us out
of Somalia, bin Laden would not have
been able to say to his followers, Look
we're able to do this, we only need
small victories to defeat history's greatest
military. After my photograph:
9/11, and this never-ending
war on terror.

TERRY GROSS My guest today has been
war reporter Paul Watson. His memoir
about reporting from war zones is called
Where War Lives.

TERRY GROSS We'll talk more after a break.

2: WHO WAS HE TALKING TO?

Google map: Princeton, NJ.

DAN I was listening to this podcast. Writing
my play about historical ghosts. Packing
up all our things. It was the very end
of August. It was the end of New York
for us. It was the end of something else,
what? our youth? In Princeton. Which is just so
beautiful this time of year. Every time
of year, really. All the trees and leaves. All
the squirrels. All of the privileged children,
including myself, in some ways. I was
sad to leave. It had been a rough few years.
I'd walk around the campus late at night
and feel almost good about myself. Smart.
Of value. And of course I felt guilty
too, to have had this library. These trees
and squirrels. The beautiful young women
to watch. Unlimited laser printing.
While you're off in Iraq, Paul. Or Kabul.
Or Jakarta, that's where you live, Paul, right?
And Jakarta's in Indonesia. Right?
There was this hangar-sized Whole Foods nearby,
lots of Priuses, and bumper stickers
celebrating the date when Bush would leave

Google map: Jakarta.

Video image: verdant window in Princeton.

office. I'd go running in thunderstorms
sometimes. I'd sit on the back porch sipping
vodka, cooking meat on a charcoal grill.
Watching swallows swoop out of a twilit
sky into my maple tree. And your voice
got to me. It's your voice:

PAUL I tend to be
solitary.

DAN This is you speaking, though
it might as well be me.

PAUL I like to stay
home with my wife and son.

DAN Dinner parties?

PAUL I tend to stay away. I've spent enough
time around people who do what I do,
and in my opinion, and I include
myself foremost in this group, we're a bunch
of misfits, people who are seeking self
-esteem through risk.

DAN I felt you could have been
talking about playwrights. Without any
real risk. You were mad:

PAUL I'm sick of being
lied to. And I take it as a challenge
to make sure nobody's lying to me.

DAN I felt like I knew you. Or I was you
in some alternate reality.

PAUL Men
start wars because it helps them to make sure
that women aren't laughing at them.

DAN You
were funny. Sort of.

Image: Paul Watson preparing to take a photo; his deformed hand is prominent. (Andrew Stawicki)

PAUL I'm more comfortable
with the weak than I am the powerful,
growing up in this condition.

DAN We should
talk about that, your hand.

PAUL Should we?

DAN Why not?

PAUL It's helped me out a lot. In Kosovo
in food lines, they'd think I was a wounded
war vet and give me all kinds of free stuff.

DAN And as I'm packing and listening to you
I'm wondering if I feel so moved because
you sound so messed up,

PAUL If something's risky
and we probably shouldn't do it, I'll say,
Don't worry about me, I'm already
dead.

DAN Or because you scare me. The haunted
often sound like ghosts, in my experience.

PAUL I just have this sense I've already lived
much longer than I should have.

DAN You poor man,
who are you?

3: Q&A. OR, GOT TO GO

Photo: Watson Family photo, 1960; Paul is in the baby stroller.

PAUL I have no idea who my father was.

DAN He was a soldier, right?

PAUL I've got to go.
Take care. Paul.

DAN I just wanted to say thanks
for writing me back. I got your email
on my wife's BlackBerry halfway across
the country, at this tumbleweed rest stop
on an Indian reservation somewhere
outside Tulsa.

PAUL Dear Dan, I just got back
from Kabul. Where I found out it's easy
to buy stolen US military
flash drives at an Afghan bazaar outside
Bagram air base. And these flash drives are full
of classified information, social

Google map: Kabul.

Images: ID photos of US soldiers,

security numbers of soldiers, maps
of Taliban and Al-Qaeda targets
in both Afghanistan and Pakistan.

maps of air strikes in Afghanistan and Pakistan, 2008.

DAN Wow.

PAUL Sorry, what were we talking about?

DAN Your dad.

PAUL Stormed the beach at Normandy. Died
a few days shy of my second birthday.

DAN And you were born when?

PAUL 1959.
How old are you, Dan?

DAN I'm younger than you.
I could be your nephew, or a younger
brother maybe.

PAUL My father didn't die
in the war though.

DAN Of course not. How did he?

PAUL He had PKD, or Polycystic
Kidney Disease.

DAN Which is what?

PAUL Like it sounds:
cysts start growing all over your kidneys
till eventually you die. I have it
too.

DAN Will it kill you?

PAUL I've got pills for it.

DAN So, what you mean when you say you don't know
who your dad was, is you don't remember
him?

PAUL Do you?

DAN Do I remember my dad?

PAUL Do you know who he is?

DAN What do you mean?

PAUL What did you think I meant?

DAN He was around.
I mean my father was always around,

every day. He never spoke to us. If
he did, well then it was just to tell you
how fucking stupid you were.

PAUL Is he dead?

DAN I don't know.

PAUL You don't know?

DAN Wait why are you
asking *me* questions?

PAUL I've got to get back
to Kabul. I'll email you.

DAN I'm staying
in this condo in a renovated
schoolhouse. Sometimes I hear ghostly children
laughing. This gland in my neck is swollen
and aches. I'm Googling the symptoms. Let's Skype
or Facebook. Are you on Facebook?

PAUL I don't
know why but I'd rather keep emailing
like this. I don't know why. But it's almost
like a conversation.

DAN Yeah but it's not
a conversation.

PAUL Yeah but it's almost.
Are you in LA?

DAN I'm in Madison,
Wisconsin.

Google map: Madison, WI.

PAUL What? Why?

DAN Teaching.

PAUL And writing
about ghosts?

DAN Sure. Still.

PAUL Is it snowing there?

Moving image: falling snow.

DAN It hasn't stopped snowing since I touched down
in January. Cars are abandoned
in the middle of highways. I don't leave
the condo much.

PAUL I'm home in Jakarta,
in case you're wondering. There's a thunderstorm
and my little boy's asleep. He's always
asking me, How long will you be gone, Dad?
He's seven, so he doesn't understand
time just yet. Few weeks back we were lying
in bed together and he asked me, When
you're dead will you still be watching me? Where
were we?

Moving image: lightning, rain.

DAN We were talking about fathers.

PAUL So then Ray enlisted at 17,

DAN You call him Ray?

PAUL faked his eye test. He was,

SOMEONE Tall. Splendid physique.

PAUL That's what someone wrote
about him, in one of his files. It said,
Ray is:

Image: family photo again; Paul's tall father.

SOMEONE Frank. Pleasant manner. Decisive
style of thinking.

PAUL This one story I know,
there's only one story I know for sure,
they were taking a medieval city
in France, twisted streets, churches and houses
made of stone. My father takes a bullet
in his thigh. Watches one of his soldiers
trapped in the long grass. Ray can't do a thing
but watch his friend die. Each time this man cries
out for help, a Nazi sniper shoots him
till he's dead.

Map: Villons-les-buissons, France, 1944.

DAN How do you know this?

PAUL Research.
My mother told me.

DAN Yes. Good. What's she like?

PAUL She's the strongest woman I know.

DAN Okay,
fine. What else?

PAUL They were sitting together
on a streetcar. The bang of a pothole
and he's gone. She gets off at the next stop
and walks home, and sits down on the front step.
And waits for him.

DAN Sounds like PTSD.

PAUL I've got to cut this one short.

DAN Can we talk
about your hand again?

PAUL My hand?

DAN You know,
your lack of a hand.

PAUL I'll be in Sulu,
in the Philippines.

DAN Outside my window
a freight train rolls past every night. Its bell
tolls over and over again,

Moving image: snow falling.

PAUL Seven
civilians have been killed by Philippine
troops, including two children.

DAN as the snow
piles higher on Lake Monona, burying
the sign Obama stuck in the ice: *Yes
We Can!*

PAUL Reading glasses, check. Sensible
shoes, check.

DAN Spring break.

Image: bright light.

PAUL —Hey, Dan! You were asking
about my hand. It doesn't bother me
much. My mother used to always tell me,
Nobody's perfect!

DAN How'd it get that way?

PAUL The kids would crowd around me at recess
and the bravest ones would reach out and touch
my stump,

KID How'd it get that way, Paul? Huh? Huh?

PAUL This was when I remember first thinking:
This is not me.

PAUL This, that body belongs
to somebody else.

PAUL The day I was born
I had these nubbins instead of fingers

PAUL and the doctor just snipped them off.

PAUL The hand's
attached to a wrist that bends, with a palm
no bigger than an infant's.

Image: that picture again of Paul preparing to take a photograph. (Stawicki)

DAN Did your mom
take thalidomide?

PAUL Everyone thinks that,
but no she didn't. It's a mystery,
something in the DNA.

DAN Is that why
you're like this?

PAUL Like what, Dan?

DAN Oh I don't know,
a war reporter?

PAUL iPod, check. Satellite
phone, check. Laptop, check. Endless tangles of
cable, check.

DAN Two people have been murdered
near where I'm staying,

PAUL Some bars of Dettol,
disinfectant soap for microbes.

Image: Joel Anthony Marino.

DAN a man
my age. A girl. On different days.

PAUL Check.

DAN Both
were stabbed repeatedly. In the middle
of the day, at home. I go out running
on the icy roads past their stained faces
on telephone poles. Just like I used to
jog past the makeshift morgue outside Bellevue
that long-ago September.

Image: Brittany Zimmermann.

PAUL Sorry, Dan,

I've been out of touch. I was in Christchurch
on vacation. Where were we?

DAN Your perfect
childhood.

PAUL Yes, my street was Princess Margaret
Boulevard, my school was Princess Margaret
Public School.

Google map: Princess Margaret Blvd., Etobicoke, Ontario, Canada.

DAN Who's Princess Margaret again?

PAUL We had a milkman, mailman, paperboy.

DAN How many siblings did you have?

PAUL Four. You?

DAN Five.

PAUL Wow, you really are Irish!

DAN Nothing
bad happened in your childhood? other than
your absent father and your absent hand
that never bothered you?

PAUL My brother Jim
liked to take my father's old Lugar out
of hiding. Sometimes he'd let me hold it
and I'd imagine myself as the man
who'd once held his finger on that trigger.

DAN You mean your father?

PAUL No, the dead Nazi
he got it from!

DAN Did you have friends?
You sound lonely. You sound kind of like this
really lonely kid.

Music: Pink Floyd's "Brain Damage."

Image: Paul Watson as a teenager in the '70s: plaid bow tie, plaid pants. Long hair.

PAUL I was in a band
called Eruption? I was the manager
of the band, because of my hand. We did
a shitload of drugs: Purple Microdot,
California Sunshine—

DAN What's that, acid?

PAUL My best friend Richard and I listening
to *Dark Side of the Moon* in the middle

of this circle we'd burnt into a field
of grass behind my house, high as two kites.
Richard turned me on to Camus. We'd chew
peyote before gym class

PAUL and get off
on the psychedelic rainbows trailing
behind high-jumpers and kids doing flips
off balance beams.

PAUL Oh, I remember one
thing that was somewhat disturbing: our friend
Andy blew his brains out at his parents'
summer cottage.

DAN Just somewhat disturbing?

PAUL It was hardly surprising. He was stuck
outside himself.

DAN Were you, Paul?

PAUL I hung out
with this dealer, he must've been 30.
At a motel he pulls out a bottle
and a baggie full of pills. Up or down,
my choice. I wash down a few with a belt
of whiskey.

DRUG DEALER You took some heavy downers,
man.

PAUL Who cares?

DRUG DEALER That's the trouble with chicks, right?

PAUL Right!

DRUG DEALER Hells yeah!

PAUL An hour later he's carving
his arm with his knife.

DRUG DEALER Bitches always want
perfection!

PAUL Then he's slinging my body
over his back like I'm some medevaced
soldier on TV in Vietnam. Dumping
me in a taxi.

DRUG DEALER He's my little bro,
man. Just take him home.

PAUL Alone and puking
through the chain link of a construction site
as the taxi spits gravel.

DAN You were fucked
up, Paul. Maybe you were depressed. Maybe
you were low on some brain chemical like
serotonin, dopamine, whatever,
and this kind of crazy behavior was
your way of feeling normal.

Image: close-up of that photo of Paul as a teenager in the '70s.

PAUL But I was
also having fun. Didn't you have fun
in high school, Dan?

DAN Sorry, I've got to go
teach. My students are trying to learn how
to write with conflict and stakes and something
remotely real.

PAUL I had this one teacher
I loved. He took us all on a field trip
once. There we were floating in our canoes
in Algonquin Provincial Park, under
a canopy of stars. With my classmate
Stephen Harper, future Prime Minister,
no kidding, paddling behind. Thinking, Who
could *not* love Albert Camus? And that's how
I ended up winning the Pulitzer.

Moving image: river at night. Stars.

DAN Wait. What? I don't get it—

PAUL I've got to go,
this time it's an emergency. Turn on
your TV and you'll see.

Google Map: Burma.

DAN I've got to say,
Paul, I can't help feeling you're not being
entirely honest with me here. I mean,
I don't mean that you're lying, per se. But
everything has this kind of Hemingway
patina to it. This kind of old school
journalistic swagger. It's like you're trying
to impress me.

PAUL I got into Burma

on a tourist visa. With the Tribune
execs measuring the column inches
we produce, not getting into Burma
to cover the cyclone devastation
would've been career suicide. Hiding
by day in the hull of a riverboat
in the Irrawaddy Delta. Among
the hundreds of corpses bobbing at dusk
in the sea-soaked paddies is the body
of a child. In pajama bottoms with
teddy bear cartoons on them. The bleached skin's
like rotting rattan. The leg bones are green.
The stench is unbearable, but the people
on shore don't seem to notice. My fixer
explains that Buddhists believe the body

Image: this image, perhaps.

FIXER is nothing more than an empty vessel,
and the soul has already been reborn
as someone new.

Moving image: river at night. Stars.

PAUL After several stiff drinks
that night I lay on the roof of our boat
staring up at the universe,

PAUL listening
to Laura Bush give forth with earnest pleas
to the junta on Voice of America,

PAUL and I imagined myself as nothing
more than a passenger on this rotting
vessel of my body. And it felt good,
I felt free.

DAN That freight train's approaching fast,
its headlamp swallowing the churning snow.
The chiming bell, the shrieking horn—

PAUL Dear Dan,
I've been meaning to say: you sound kind of
depressed. Don't let that get ahold of you.
Trust me. Maybe you should talk to someone
besides me? Or take a pill. Has it stopped
snowing yet?

Moving image: falling snow.

DAN Nope.

PAUL Medication. Calculate
estimated time away, multiply
by seven pills a day for depression,
blood pressure, PKD. Toss in extra
in case I get kidnapped. Check.

DAN Where are you
going this time, Paul?

PAUL A few chocolate bars:
85 percent cocoa, for the dose
of flavonoids the TV doctor says
will give me an extra 3.5 years
and fight heart plaque.

DAN Where are you now?

PAUL My son
is sleeping. It's the rainy season here
again and lightning's lighting up his face
like a strobe. I lean in close to his ear
and whisper,

PAUL Don't be afraid.

PAUL I'll come back
home soon.

PAUL Do not be afraid.

PAUL Japanese
green tea for the antioxidants. Corkscrew
for the cheap Bordeaux I'll purchase en route
at Duty Free,

DAN I've got some more questions
for you, Paul—

PAUL more antioxidants and
some liquid courage to help ease the pain
of these five-star hotel room blues.

4: THE GHOSTS ARE GETTING CLOSER

But I'm whining, Dan.

DAN Okay, let's get back
to the story. You win the Pulitzer
Prize.

PAUL I was in Rwanda when I heard
the news. As everybody's aware now,
300 Tutsis an hour were being
beaten to death with these large wooden clubs
with bent nails and heavy spikes sticking out
of them. Real prehistoric shit. Homemade
machetes. Just a few thousand UN
soldiers with air support could've washed all
those maggots away.

PAUL We were getting high
on the bridge over Rusumo Falls.

Moving image, sound: waterfall.

PAUL We
is not the royal we, we is someone
I don't want you to meet just yet.

PAUL Khareen
and I watching refugees spill over
the border to Tanzania. Watching
corpses spill over the waterfall down
into this brown whirlpool, smashing against
the rocks.

PAUL In a house we found children piled
like sandbags on a bed.

Sound: flies buzzing.

PAUL There's a baby
down at the bottom. Its tiny hand is
bloated, its severed head cracked open like
an eggshell. Did the older children try
to hide him in here?

PAUL Outside the back door
I slipped on a bunch of school books. One book
had been covered neatly with a color
publicity shot of the *Dynasty*
TV show cast. With John Forsythe's fucking
grinning face.

PAUL The ghosts are getting closer.

PAUL In Gahini, a 16-year-old named
François Sempundu sat on the grimy
brown foam of his hospital bed.

TRANSLATOR He says
Hutus hacked up his mother and siblings.
He says he hid beneath the kitchen sink
for a week, beside his family's rotting
corpses.

PAUL François Sempundu was speaking
so calmly.

TRANSLATOR He says, By then if someone
had come to kill me I wouldn't have cared
much.

Sound: cicadas, crickets.

PAUL At a church near Nyarubuye
we pushed open a gate on a courtyard
like Auschwitz. Like Sarajevo. They'd come here
hoping God would protect them somehow, but
it only made things that much easier
to get butchered.

PAUL In Zaire a girl stands
at the roadside. Rows of buzzing corpses.

PAUL At a Rwandan refugee camp.

PAUL She's
looking for the toilet,

PAUL which was a field
where a hundred thousand people would shit
and piss and die.

PAUL This girl stumbles barefoot
into a ditch of bodies, some rolled up
in reed mats. She's looking everywhere and
now she begins to cry.

PAUL As if hoping
somebody will help her.

Sound: this child crying, as if far away.

PAUL But nobody's
coming.

PAUL I thought to myself, This would make
a great picture.

PAUL This is a beautiful
picture, somehow.

PAUL I raised my camera, stepped backwards to frame her with more corpses and I stepped on a dead old woman's arm.

Image: this child lost among corpses of Rwandan refugees in Zaire.

PAUL It snaps like a stick.

PAUL Then a few days later
I'm at Columbia University's
Low Memorial Library. In this room
like the Parthenon and the Pantheon
confused. Cornucopias of hors d'oeuvres
on aproned banquet tables, wearing tight shoes
and a navy blazer, wool slacks picked out
this morning at Brooks Brothers. John Honderich,
my boss at the *Star*—

HONDERICH Watson, you don't look
so hot.

PAUL I guess I just feel bad about
that soldier's family.

HONDERICH Have you thought about
finding his wife, or his mother? hunting
them down?

PAUL Had I?

PAUL Had I?

PAUL I win
A Pulitzer in the category
of Spot News Photography.

PAUL Collecting
my Tiffany crystal paperweight at
the dais. Shaking hands.

PAUL Kevin Carter,
who just last month was snorting Ritalin
off the floor of my apartment before
rocketing off into the townships,

PAUL wins
for Feature Photography:

PAUL a vulture
waiting for a Sudanese girl to die.

PAUL Always a popular category.

PAUL Carter comes back to the table:

CARTER Hear that
applause, Watson? I kicked your arse!

PAUL Two months
later I'm back in Rwanda. Honderich
calls me on my satellite phone:

HONDERICH Carter
killed himself last night. Parked his pickup truck
in Johannesburg, duct-taped a garden hose
to the tail pipe. Left a suicide note

PAUL that I'll paraphrase:

CARTER I have been haunted so
now I'll haunt you.

HONDERICH Paul?

HONDERICH Paul?

PAUL I don't care about
him.

PAUL —Who cares?

PAUL I don't care!

PAUL With so many
people suffering all over the world
who want nothing more than to live— ?

PAUL That man
is a coward!

PAUL If you can't do your job
then get out of the way so someone else
can.

PAUL Of course I've wanted to kill myself
before. But the truth is I've always lacked
the courage.

PAUL So I tell myself:

PAUL Just go
someplace dangerous. Let somebody else
kill you.

5: SHRINKING

GRINKER O-kay. So. You are 35 years old,
you are male. You are a reporter for
the *Toronto Star*, and you're stationed here
in Johannesburg.

PAUL You have a real talent
for stating the obvious.

Image: dark bookcase.

GRINKER Are you shaking?

PAUL Am I?

GRINKER You have sweat all over your face!

PAUL Let me catch my breath.

GRINKER O-kay.

PAUL It's just that
I've never been to a psychiatrist
before.

GRINKER And what are you scared will happen
to you?

PAUL I'll lose my edge.

GRINKER What does that mean,
your edge?

PAUL Being crazy.

GRINKER You think I could
cure you of that?

PAUL Being somewhat crazy
is a requirement in my line of work.

GRINKER If you leave I won't charge you anything.
You wouldn't be the first to change his mind
about therapy. But you called me, Paul,
and told me you've been feeling paranoid—

PAUL That's not a psychiatric disorder,
in my opinion. People don't deserve
to be trusted.

GRINKER You are irritable,
small things will make you cry. Interestingly
you deny nightmares. No psychiatric
history prior to this. Congenitally

deformed arm. Don't smoke. Self-medicating
with lots of alcohol, marijuana—

PAUL Look
all I want from you is some feel-good pills
to patch me up. "O-kay"?

GRINKER O-kay. We can
find you something, I'm sure.

PAUL Thank you.

GRINKER But first
you'll need to talk to me. Medication
targets symptoms: we will need to target
your soul as well. You find that funny?

PAUL Yes

GRINKER What's your mother like, Paul?

PAUL She's the strongest
woman I know.

GRINKER And have you known many
women?

PAUL One.

GRINKER You've known only one woman?

PAUL I've been in a relationship with one
woman. On and off. Khareen.

GRINKER Careen?

PAUL Ha!

GRINKER What a name! Tell me, what's this Careen like?

PAUL She loves rococo art. Homemade knödles
and beer for dinner.

GRINKER Ha ha ha! Sounds nice!

PAUL Her father is this German bureau chief,
and one time she was sitting on his lap
in front of me, smiling, with her bare arm
up around his neck, like this. She's the one
who needs some therapy, don't you think? She flashed
her tits at me once down this long hallway
in her father's condo —I don't know why
I feel the need to keep talking about
her father. She's blonde. Great body. Sexy

voice. Calls me Paulie. She doesn't let me
have sex with her though. We share a house but
I pay the rent. I live in a closet
-sized room off the kitchen. I'm happiest
on her leash, so to speak. I like to sit
with her when she takes a bath or lying
in bed with candles lit, drinking wine or
smoking a joint, while she gets herself off
beneath the covers. It's not sex, she says.
It's only for comfort, Paulie. She likes
to tell me that. One time she let this guy
into our yard to watch through the window
while she fucked this other guy. She described
this at breakfast, in great detail. She wants
to be a war reporter, so we went
to Rwanda where we met this handsome
aid worker named Laurent. Who was building
latrines for refugees. And there I was
with my camera in my one hand. Shooting
pictures. By that evening she was lying
in his tent, under his netting, writing
in her diary. He got a hotel room
underneath ours. With grenades exploding
in the shanties and the death squads spreading
through the streets, I call downstairs. She answers
laughing,

KHAREEN Paulie?

PAUL We have to go.

KHAREEN Not now,
Laurent.

PAUL They're killing people outside.

KHAREEN Get
off me please, Laurent!

PAUL He's living with us
here in Johannesburg. They fight and then fuck
all the time.

GRINKER Why don't we stop for the day.

I'm going to write you a prescription for
450 milligrams of
moclobemide.

PAUL Okay. Is that good?

GRINKER No,
that is bad. You're clinically depressed and
you have post-traumatic stress disorder.
It's good that you've come. Do you have someone
at home? Besides that sick woman, of course.
These drugs will take some time to change your brain
chemistry, and we don't want you killing
yourself in the meanwhile.

PAUL —Do you believe
in ghosts, Dr. Grinker?

GRINKER Well, I believe
people are haunted.

PAUL What if I told you
I came to you in the first place because
I'm haunted. Cursed.

GRINKER I'd ask you some questions
to rule out schizophrenia.

PAUL I told him
about the picture.

GRINKER It's famous. It's yours?

PAUL Then I told him what Cleveland's voice told me.

CLEVELAND If you do this,

CLEVELAND I'll own you forever.

GRINKER That was your superego. Your mind was
simply speaking to itself.

PAUL I know what
my own mind sounds like. This was somebody
else.

GRINKER The soldier?

PAUL I've felt him next to me,
feared his presence.

GRINKER Is he here with us now?

PAUL He is. He's here when I wake up, he's there

when I'm asleep. He's with me whenever
I'm happy, when I'm having fun or sex
or watching TV, as if he's saying,
This can not last. And of course he's with me
whenever things go wrong. He's happiest
when I'm in pain. He'll never go away
till he gets what he wants from me.

GRINKER And what
does he want from you, Paul?

6: IRAQ

PAUL This was in Mosul in Northern Iraq
at the beginning of the war. A boy
was throwing some pebbles at a marine
humvee, whose .50 caliber machine gun
was whipping and twisting like a fire hose
spraying death. And as I'm taking pictures
a gang of students comes rushing by with
another student bleeding from a deep
gash in his face. Somebody makes that sound,
you know, *click,* like, Take his picture! And while
I'm switching lenses you can see the switch
go on in somebody's head. Like, He's white,
what the hell's he doing here? I'm lifted
off the ground, tossed around, stoned. Somebody
slides his knife in my back and I'm feeling
the blood pooling in my shirt. I'm holding
onto my camera while they're stretching out
my arms, like this, till I'm floating on top
of the mob. And I'm not trying to be
cinematic here, but it was like Christ
on the cross. Cause I had absolutely
no sense of wanting to live. Or fighting
back. Protesting my innocence. Crying
out for mercy. I had this sense of, Well
we knew this was coming. And here it is.

But the truth of these places is always
the same. A dozen people, a dozen
against a multitude, formed a circle
around me. And we were close to this row
of shops that were closing, and these people
simply pulled the shutters up and shoved me
under. That's when I realize my camera's
gone, the hand's empty, the mob is pounding
on metal. The tea shop owner says, Look
you know I'd really like to help you but
would you mind leaving my tea shop soon? So
I end up in the street again kneeling
in the dirt at the order of some pissed
-off marines, and somehow I convince them
to take me back behind the wire. That's why
I know it's not just my brain, Doctor. Or
my father dying when I was two. Or
this hand. It would be poetic justice to
get ripped apart by a mob. Remember
what Cleveland said to me: If you do this
I will own you. I just have this feeling
he's thinking, You watched my desecration,
now here comes yours.

7: SOME EMBARRASSING THINGS. OR, THE PLAN

DAN Dear Paul. It's been a while. Apologies.
I've finally escaped from the Wisconsin
winter, and I'm back in my strange new home,
LA. And I'm hoping you're still willing
to write this play, or whatever it is,
with me. I know it's been a long time since
I first reached out to you. Maybe sometime
I could give you a call?

Google map: Los Angeles.

PAUL I have to go
to the Philippines, where Abu Sayyaf
the local Al-Qaeda affiliate
is on the march once again. I'm worried

my editor, who hates me for reasons
I can't even pretend to comprehend,
won't like it. It's not the sort of story
that tends to garner those coveted clicks
on the *Times'* website.

DAN It's 75
degrees here and sunny. Women's faces
are slick masks, thanks to Botox. Some men look
embalmed and tan also. I walk my dog
four times a day. The only helicopters
I see here are LAPD circling
over Brentwood like they're still looking for
OJ's white Bronco. While I'm running up
Amalfi to Sunset the Palisades
look more like the hills of South Korea
on MASH. Or Tuscany. Where are you now,
Paul? What's your cell number? Can I call you?
Can I come visit you in Jakarta
soon?

PAUL I thought you might enjoy hearing this
sound bite directly from the fetid mouth
of our paper's new owner, Sam Zell. Here's
a link: http://gawker.com/
5002815/exclusive
-sam-zell-says-fuck-you-to-his-journalist

Moving image, silent: http://gawker.com/5002815/exclusive-sam-zell-says-fuck-you-to-his-journalist

ZELL My attitude on journalism is
simple: I want to make enough money
so I can afford you!

PAUL And while it's true
I like a gutter-talking billionaire
as much as the next guy, I do wonder
what he's up to. Especially after
publishing a new employee manual
telling us all to question authority
and "push back."

ZELL I'm sorry, I'm sorry but
you're giving me the classic what I call

journalistic arrogance of deciding
that puppies don't count!

PAUL With all the chaos
building at the gates in Afghanistan
and Iraq, he's just the sort of leader
I'm not willing to die for.

ZELL Hopefully
we'll get to the point where our revenue
is so significant we'll be able
to do both puppies *and* Iraq. Okay?
—Fuck you!

PAUL So if ghostly voices ever
figure into this script, maybe this clip
will make a good one.

DAN Don't you think it's strange
you've never heard my voice, Paul? I've heard yours
on *All Things Considered*, the *LA Times'*
website. Let's set this trip up now! I won
a grant to come visit you.

PAUL Hey, congrats
on the grant! I've got a rusted RV
in Bali, we can watch the surf and drink
and discuss genocide. Only problem is
I finally got fired. And my RV
just got crushed by a tree. But have no fear!
I've got an idea.

DAN My wife's an actress
on a TV show that flopped. We're not sad
about it at all, but everyone thinks
we should be. It's winter, but it's sunny
and warm. Every season's the same: sunny
and warm. I have trouble remembering what
season it is without thinking. The days
get shorter or longer but the sun stays
the same. I go out running on the beach
at dusk. It's beautiful. It's beautiful.
It's beautiful.

Moving image: water at mid-day.

PAUL I'm going to move back home
to Canada, where the plan is I'll work
for the *Toronto Star* again. Covering
the Arctic aboriginal beat. Shooting
pictures, writing stories, blogging about
life in the midnight sun. Or the noontime
moon. In any case I've been waking up
thankful each morning I won't have to write
another sentence about Al-Qaeda
ever again. Unless Zawahiri's
hiding in some ice cave.

Google terrain map: Canadian Arctic.

DAN You have no clue,
Paul, how happy this makes me! You have no
idea how much the ice-and-snow-and-wind
speaks to me, so much more so than the sun
of LA, or Bali. My entire life
I've been obsessed with nineteenth-century
polar exploration. Trapped in the ice
for months, sometimes years. Scurvy, insanity,
cannibalism. It helps me relax
and fall asleep. So maybe I could come
visit you there this winter? And who knows
maybe the Arctic will be the second
act of our play? Cause I have this deadline
coming up—

PAUL What kind of deadline?

DAN It's mine
and it's soon. The end of winter. So when
will you give me your God damned phone number
so I can plan this trip?

PAUL What are they like,
Dan?

DAN What?

PAUL Your plays.

DAN I don't know. Historical,
like I said. I prefer things in books.

PAUL Why?

DAN I like things that have already happened
to other people, a long time ago.

PAUL Why?

DAN I don't know. I have some ideas but—

PAUL Like what?

DAN Well the truth is I'm insecure
around you, Paul. You intimidate me
terribly. You're like this mythic figure,
with your hand, your constant returning to
the underworld of the most nauseating
things in history. Recent history. You've looked
at that which the rest of us won't look at,
or can't look at. You're the type of writer
I've always wished I were. Engaged with life,
people.

PAUL You don't engage much with people?

DAN No. I like to seclude myself. Like you
I like to stay away. Sometimes I lay
my head against my dog's head and I think,
You're my best friend. You're my only friend. If
you get sick I'll get a second mortgage
for you. Even though we don't have a first
mortgage yet. We're just renters. I even
like my obsessions but I don't know why
I do. Like I said, I have my theories
but I think they'd be boring to someone
like you.

PAUL Try me.

DAN I'm like you, like I said.
Like you I'll sometimes cry for no reason
at all. Or I don't cry for months and months
and months. Like you I see flashbacks. I'm scared
to change that part of me that's craziest,
because if I'm not crazy anymore

how will I do what I do? I'm the same
age you were in Mogadishu, the same
age Sgt. Cleveland was that day. I'm cursed
too, just like you are.

PAUL But you won't tell me
what's cursing you?

DAN Because it can't compare
to what you've been through!

PAUL After my memoir
came out, I'd hear from strangers who'd tell me
the most intimate things about themselves.
Embarrassing. About their lives. They saw
that just like them I had these internal
conflicts. Except you, you didn't confess
anything. Which is probably why I wrote
you back. Do you know that quote of Camus'
where he says he's solved the mystery of where
war lives? It lives in each of us, he said.
In the loneliness and humiliation
we all feel. If we can solve that conflict
within ourselves then we'll be able to
rid the world of war. Maybe. So tell me,
Dan: where does war live in you?

DAN My family
stopped talking to me, several years ago,
and I have no idea why. That's not true,
I have many ideas but none of them
make sense. I was about to get married
but it wasn't like they didn't approve
of my wife. It had something to do with
the fact that nobody would be coming
from my family because they have no friends.
I mean literally my parents don't have
any friends. They can barely leave the house
and whatever's left of their own families
won't speak to them for reasons I've never
understood. And I'd just written a play

that was the closest I'd come to writing
autobiography. And my brother
was in the hospital again, for God
knows what exactly, depression mostly.
He hadn't spoken to any of us
in years. Which was mostly okay with me
cause like everyone else in my family
I suppose I just wanted to forget
he'd ever existed at all. Maybe
this was all because of him? reminding
my family of what happened years ago
when I was 12 and he was 17,
one Tuesday afternoon in February
walking up the driveway when I noticed
him coming around the house with his back
all pressed with snow, the back of his head white
with snow, and I thought it was so funny
he wasn't wearing a jacket or shoes.
He was barefoot. And by funny I mean
disturbing. I've told this story thousands
of times, I hardly feel a thing. He'd jumped
out of a window, was what I found out
later, and fallen three stories without
breaking a bone. That night my mother cried
in my arms and said, This is a secret
we will take to our graves. I developed
innumerable compulsions, including
counting, hand-washing, scrupulosity
which is the fear that one has been sinful
in word or deed or thought. I was afraid
to leave the house, to touch any surface,
but I hid it so well that nobody
noticed. I was class president. I played
baseball, soccer. I wrote secret poetry.
And eventually I got out and went
to college. And things went coasting along
as well as things can in a family with

Moving image: snow falling.

an inexplicably cruel father and
a masochistic mother who can't stop
talking about nothing. Logorrhea
is the clinical term, I think. Until
I came home one weekend for a visit
just before my wedding and my father
said I looked homeless. My beard and hair. When
in fact I looked just like other adjunct
professors of writing. But they told me
I looked like a man who'd slit his own throat
soon. They said I looked just like my father's
brother, a man who disappeared after
I was born. He was tall, he was funny,
long hair and barefoot in jeans, a hippie
and some kind of artist. The opposite
of my father. I'm the spitting image
of this man, they said. They were terrified
for this reason. There are things you don't know!
my father kept saying, without saying
what it was exactly I didn't know.
My mother and father were both screaming
together, it felt almost sexual.
There are things you don't know! I drove away
and haven't heard from them since. They are dead
to me. And I don't mean that in the way
it sounds, melodramatically. I mean
I can't remember them. And by memory
I mean I can't feel. I have no pictures
of my childhood. It's like my entire life
up until I was 33 happened
to someone else. Someone who's haunting me,
who makes me feel cursed. Makes me feel certain
that yes, they're right, I've failed, something is wrong
with me. I don't know what it is but yes
something is wrong. I've failed, I've failed, I've failed,
I've failed. Only writing and running helps
some. I sit at my desk like a lab rat

clicking on a button that shows me who's
visiting my website. And it doesn't
tell me who's visiting exactly but
it shows your city or town on a map
of the entire world. When I said they don't
talk to me, that wasn't true. I can tell
my mother checks my website at least once
a day. Sometimes twice. It's a compulsion,
I know, but still I like seeing those dots
on the map. But it's nothing! it's nothing
to complain about, it's the sort of thing
everybody has. And nothing compared
to the unspeakable acts of cruelty
you've seen, Paul.

PAUL Let's get together somewhere
in the Upper Arctic, in 24
-hour darkness, this winter. The hotels there
are like dorms for racist construction crews
from the south, and the costs run high because
everything's flown in. But the ambience
will be just perfect. So let me know when
you'd like to come, and I'll put together
some kind of plan.

8: HI WHAT'S YOUR NAME WHEN ARE YOU LEAVING?

DAN Sand snow sand snow sand snow sand snow sand snow
snow snow snow.

DAN LAX to Vancouver,
Vancouver to Yellowknife.

Google Earth: Yellowknife, Northwest Territories, Canada.

DAN What the hell
kind of name is Yellowknife? I've read that

DAN copper in the ground turned the Inuit's
knives yellow.

DAN Yellowknife to Kugluktuk
by twin turboprop. How do you say that
name again?

Google Earth: Kugluktuk, Northwest Territories.

DAN Kugluktuk. But I don't know
Inuktitut.

DAN What's that?

DAN Their language.

DAN Whose?

DAN The Inuit. Which means simply people
in Inuktitut.

DAN I'm getting all this
information off Wikipedia
on my new iPhone.

DAN The flight attendant

DAN is an Inuit kid, gay, goth, nose ring
and an attitude.

ATTENDANT Does anyone want
this last bottle of water?

DAN The pilots
are supposedly Inuit too, though
the cockpit door's closed the whole way. No one
speaks over the intercom. A black guy
dressed all in white shares the aisle with me:

BLACK GUY What brings you to the North, my mon?

DAN His voice
sounds almost Jamaican.

BLACK GUY True dat, true dat.
Are you done with your paper, mon?

DAN Later
I'll find out his name's Isaac, from Ghana,
when Paul's interviewing him.

DAN: His family
immigrated to Yellowknife after
some coup in the '80s.

DAN An old woman
in traditional clothes, like calico
fringed with coyote fur, her hood hiding
her face,

DAN doesn't say a word.

DAN A teenaged
girl with an iPod as we're descending
into Kugluktuk

DAN taps me on the arm

DAN and asks me, smiling wide,

INUIT GIRL Hi what's your name
when are you leaving?

DAN Grandma and the girl
shuffling across the ice of Kugluktuk
while Isaac and I fly two more hours north
to Ulukhaktok.

Google Earth: Ulukhaktok.

DAN Where the airport is
a room,

DAN the cab's a van gliding across
a desert of snow.

DAN Sand snow.

DAN The cabbie's
white, from Newfoundland, a newfy.

DAN Which means
he's some kind of Canadian redneck,

DAN according to Wikipedia.

TAXI DRIVER Why
don't you drive the taxi eh? Joe asks me.
You know where everyone lives. Everyone
lives in the same flipping place!

DAN Then he asks
Isaac, probably because he's black:

TAXI DRIVER Are you
here to teach basketball eh?

ISAAC No, soccer.

TAXI DRIVER That'll be ten dollars eh?

ISAAC I got it, I got it
—welcome to the North, my mon!

DAN The hotel's
a prefab one-storey house, corrugated
tin roof, windows for like six rooms.

Image: hallway of hotel in Ulukhaktok.

DAN Inside
it smells like Clorox. Inuit women
scrubbing the deep fryer.

INUIT WOMAN Hi what's your name
when are you leaving?

DAN I'm filling out forms
at the front desk, which is just a closet
with a desk inside it. Paul had emailed
we might have to share a room. Please God don't
make us share a room. What if he tries to
get in bed with me? What if he kills me
in my sleep? in his sleep? What happens if
he hangs himself in our shower? At least
then I'll have my second act.

PAUL Are you Dan?
I'm Paul.

DAN His hair's messed up. He needs a shave.
His thick wool socks are sloughing off.

DAN Pink eyes,
unfocused.

DAN There's a deep crease in his face,
between his eyes like it's carved.

DAN He's wearing
an old sweatshirt with a red maple leaf
on it.

DAN Who does this man remind me of?

DAN He's somebody I should know.

DAN Paul's left hand
is a stub. Like his arm simply runs out
of arm. But he's still got some kind of thumb
at the end. He's rubbing his furrowed brow
with it.

PAUL How was Eskimo Air?

DAN Don't look,
Dan.

DAN Not now.

DAN Show what kind of man you are

DAN by not looking at Paul's hand.

DAN I wonder
what I look like to him?

PAUL You look a lot
like Jesus. You know that?

DAN Thanks?

PAUL You're a real
tight packer.

DAN I brought dehydrated
food. You wrote me the food sucked so I bought
dehydrated organic lasagna
at REI in Santa Monica?

PAUL Ooh, I love that stuff!

DAN Let me just finish
with this form, and I'll swing by your room.

PAUL Our
room. Door's always open.

DAN —Hey!

PAUL Come on in,
Dan, have a seat.

Moving image: gently snowing window.

DAN So.

PAUL So.

DAN So here we are
finally!

PAUL Finally! I know it's not that much
to look at. But these beds are pretty firm.
They keep the heat so high you'll want to sleep
on top of the blankets, but it's better
than bunking in here with some drunk racist
construction worker from Edmonton, right?

DAN Right!

PAUL And cell phones don't work. But the wireless
is free. In case you want to Skype your wife.
I Skype my wife pretty much every night,
if you know what I mean. Ha ha ha. —So
what do you want to do this week? Because
we never really decided, only
that you'd come.

DAN And watch you work.

PAUL And watch me
interview people. You're going to get bored.

DAN I could interview you. You know, research
for the play. If you want.

INUIT GIRLS Hi what's your name
when are you leaving?

DAN Two Inuit girls
appear in the doorway. Like *The Shining*
or something. Selling key chains and lanyards
made of sealskin.

PAUL Not now. Go away.

DAN Why
are they all asking that, Hi what's your name
when are you leaving?

PAUL They're just assuming
we're leaving soon. Like every other white
person they've ever met.

DAN Is it okay
if I record this?

PAUL Guess so.

DAN Do you miss
Afghanistan, Paul? places like that?

Image: bright light.

DAN Sand
snow snow.

DAN Do you feel you've made a mistake
leaving war reporting behind? It's like
you've been sent away to Siberia
literally. Or is it like a respite?
a reward for everything before?

DAN But
I don't ask him any of that. Instead
I ask:

DAN Do you ever get bored up here,
Paul? It must get kind of lonely.

PAUL That's right,
but I learn a lot of things too.

DAN Like what?

PAUL Like you shouldn't ask too many questions
about polar bear hunts, for example.
It's shamanistic. The Inuit still
believe shamans can turn themselves into
spirits, into animals like muskox
and seals and bears. That shamans can become
other people too. All in the pursuit
of exorcising ghosts—

Moving image: falling snow.

DAN Should I tell him
that for weeks I've been having this feeling
when I run that somebody is running
with me?

DAN: Sand sand sand.

DAN: Over my shoulder
in the sun and the sand.

DAN Who is that man
who's running after me?

DAN Which reminds me
of that story of Ernest Shackleton
down at the opposite pole, staggering
through a blizzard with his fellow travelers
starving, delirious,

DAN how they kept seeing
someone with them,

DAN how they kept asking,

DAN Who
is that man who walks always beside you?

DAN Is Staff Sgt. William David Cleveland
following me? And what could he possibly
want from me? I don't say any of this
to Paul.

DAN Snow snow.

DAN I don't want him thinking
I'm too crazy.

PAUL Hey, want to watch TV?

DAN We could try to track down a shaman.

PAUL Who?

DAN That's something we could do. This week. Maybe
he could try to heal you. Ha ha ha.

PAUL Oh
that reminds me: I'm trying to set up
this dog sled ride with these two Inuit
hunters named Jack and Jerry. 500
dollars but I'll pay them, the *Toronto
Star* will I mean. Do you hear those huskies
howling? They're chained on the ice all their lives.
I don't know how they take it, the boredom
I mean. Because you're right, there's definitely
a lot of boredom up here. It's supposed
to snow tomorrow, but we'll go sledding
if the weather's any good.

Sound: dogs howling far away, chains, wind.

Moving image: more snow falling, becoming a blizzard of white.

9: BLIZZARD

Light: dark Arctic noon.

Moving image: window full of snow.

Sound: Ryan Adams singing "Rescue Blues" low.

Where's the remote? Do you like John Mayer?
I like John Mayer. And Ryan Adams
too. And Queen Latifah. I like to watch
TV with the sound off and just listen
to my iTunes. This okay with you? This
sucks. This sucks. There's nothing good on TV!
I usually watch just like sports, hockey
and football, sometimes entertainment news
because it's stupid but I love it when
celebrities do stupid things. It helps
me relax. And I like watching curling
as an Olympic sport. I love hearing
the women's curling team screaming, Harder!
Faster! All of these women with their brooms
that look more like Swiffer WetJets rubbing
some kind of path in the ice for the weight
or the pot or the stone or whatever
screaming, Harder! Faster! As if that does
anything, really! What about this show,
The Bachelor? Have you seen *The Bachelor*? Look,

she's pretending to cry. She's pretending
to cry! What are all these people, actors?
Strippers? She's trying so damn hard to cry
real tears! Harder! Faster! How's it look?

DAN Looks
bad.

PAUL It must be gusting up to like, what,
65 an hour?

DAN My iPhone says that
it's negative 50 out there.

PAUL Wind chill
included?

DAN I'm not sure, let's see.

PAUL Celsius
or Fahrenheit?

DAN I'm Googling it.

PAUL I think
Celsius and Fahrenheit become the same
at minus 40 anyway.

DAN Earlier
Jack the Inuit hunter woke us up
with some coffee.

Light: dark dawn.

JACK Morning, Paul. Morning, Dan.
Looking really bad out there.

DAN Almost ten
and it's basically sunrise.

JACK The next time
you come up here you bring me a brand new
skidoo. Okay? Maybe helicopter.

DAN Before the ban on polar bear hunting
businessmen from Texas would come up here
and Jack would help them track down a mother
bear to shoot. And mount. These rich guys would leave
enormous tips, like snowmobiles.

JACK Bad news:
can't go out sledding this morning. Jerry's
got the dogs and Jerry's at the doctor's
because he's got like this titanium plate?

in his forehead, from a real bad sled crash
few years back. Ha ha ha. And anyway
Elder says this snow's no good. GPS
can't see shit today. We'll go tomorrow
at nine, Inuit time.

DAN Inuit time
means what, Paul?

Light: mid-afternoon.

PAUL At least we've got the wi-fi,
and this six-pack of Bordeaux I picked up
in Yellowknife.

Back to the soundless TV screen.

DAN I didn't bring any
alcohol. How could I forget to buy
alcohol?

PAUL You're not bored are you?

Sound: John Mayer, "Stop This Train (Acoustic) (Live)."

DAN I was
hoping at some point we might get back to
interviewing you?

PAUL I'm an open book,
Dan. Blank slate. No secrets.

DAN You want to read
our play? I've got a first act but—

PAUL I can't
figure out my story. Global warming
or the arts. Or corruption. There's something
shady going on here, I can feel it
with the white guys running this place. Kickbacks
or something. Maybe it's better not to
stir things up too much? don't want to end up
dead in a snowdrift, right?

DAN Paul's popping pills
out of his many-chambered plastic pill
organizer—

PAUL Depression, blood pressure,
Polycystic Kidney—

DAN Which reminds me
to take my Zoloft.

Light: evening.

PAUL Oh God I love this
movie.

DAN That evening it's *The River Wild.*

PAUL Meryl Streep's on the run, on the river
actually ha ha ha, in a rafting
boat trying to escape from this psycho
-killer Kevin Bacon. Is this movie
good? or shit. It's shit but Jesus Meryl
Streep is so gorgeous.

Laptop plays Queen Latifah's "Lush Life" low.

DAN Paul, can I ask you
some questions, maybe during commercial
breaks?

PAUL Sure. Shoot.

DAN I'm thinking it would help me
finish our play. Which you're welcome to read
at any point, by the way—

PAUL Do you want
a glass of Bordeaux?

DAN Yes please.

PAUL Go ahead.
Blank book, open slate.

DAN What is it about
the Arctic— ?

PAUL I guess I'm just happiest
when I'm unhappy. When I'm on the phone
with one of my brothers and he's talking
about, you know, problems at work. I say,
How long we been talking? 15 minutes.
I say: Now you're 15 minutes closer
to death.

DAN I'm sure he loves that.

PAUL It bugs me
to the core though! that people don't notice
how quickly we die. Whether you're driving
home from work, or suntanning on a beach
in Phuket and this wave comes in and just
keeps on coming—

DAN How can you live like that?
I mean, how can you walk around living

like you're going to die? Like back in LA
you can't be worried about the earthquake
that could erupt any second. You can't
ride the New York City subway thinking
about the likelihood of a terrorist
bomb exploding. Like on 9/11
I woke up—

PAUL You were there?

DAN And actually
I saw a ghost in our bedroom. Covered
in dust. Carrying his briefcase. He looked
so confused! He disappeared and I heard
the sirens. I went downstairs to find out
what was going on, and to hit Starbuck's
too. All these papers were spiraling down
from the sky. And I remember thinking
for a minute, Now all the bankers will
be humbled. I got my venti latte
and came back out in time to see the plane
hit the second tower. An old woman
sat down on the pavement and just started
sobbing. I went upstairs to get my wife
though we weren't married yet, and we joined
a river of people like refugees
walking uptown. While all the working men
and women were jumping. I never saw
my brother jump out the window. Maybe
there's something in that? A radio outside
a hardware store in Chinatown told us
the South Tower had come down. In a bar
somewhere in the East Village we watched as
the North Tower sank out of the blue sky
on TV. People were almost giddy
with panic, and grief. Some guys were tossing
a Frisbee in the street. I told myself,
If there's going to be a war, I will go.
I saw myself holding a machine gun
in my mind's eye, someplace bright and sandy

like Afghanistan, or maybe Iraq.
But I didn't go. Because I didn't
consider it the right war. Or because
nobody made me.

PAUL And are you hoping
I'll forgive you?

DAN My point is maybe not
everyone's meant to be as courageous
as you are.

PAUL It's not courage—

DAN It's also
altruistic. Necessary. If you
don't do what you do then none of us will
ever have any idea what's really
going on.

PAUL When I started out it was
all for self-esteem. I'm sure you started
out the same way too. I wanted people
to say I was brave, and heroic. Then
I began to hate it but I needed
that fix of adrenalin. The third stage,
where I am now? I don't really need it
anymore. But now I see the lies, now
I see how the people doing my job
don't get it. Or if they get it they don't
talk about it. They want success, they want
a seat at the Sunday morning talk show
round table. They want their own cable show.
I just want to chip away at those lies
now. But that's a losing game. Most people
don't care what's going on, or they don't know
what they're supposed to do. So we just stop
listening to the litany of evidence
of the coups we're pulling off, the phosphorus
bombs dropping on Fallujah in '04
that melted the skin off children —I could
go on and on and on and on. That's why
I object to the word altruistic.

DAN Why? Because you're too angry?

PAUL I see it
as a labyrinth: if you can find the truth
you get out. But you don't, it just gets worse,
you get more lost. And the harder you try
the darker it gets. As opposed to what,
being like you, I guess. Right, Dan? Who cares?
Let's watch some more TV. Let's drink more wine.
As long as I'm safe I don't need to do
a thing!

DAN I guess that's fair.

PAUL Sorry. See? This
is why I don't like to talk to people
besides my wife. People ask me questions
they don't want the answers to.

DAN Do you want
to unmute the movie?

JACK Morning, Paul. Dan,
the next time you come up here from LA
you bring me back a black twenty-year-old
girl. Okay?

Light: dim sunrise.

DAN Next morning Jack says maybe
we'll go out on the land. Till an elder
stands up and peers out the kitchen window
at the snowflakes floating in a milky
morning light.

JACK Elder says,

ELDER Earth is moving
faster now.

JACK He means this weather's messed up
cause of climate change. Says we'd better wait
until tomorrow.

Moving image: blizzard in the window.

DAN The snow is moving
faster now, I can't tell if it's falling
out of the sky or up from the treeless
lunarscape. Jack, do you happen to know
any shamans around here?

PAUL Dan's thinking
it'll make a good story.

DAN It might be,
I don't know, entertaining.

JACK A shaman?

DAN You know, a medicine man. A healer
of some kind.

JACK Sure. Roger.

DAN Roger?

JACK Roger
Umtoq. He's a storyteller? Makes stone
sculptures, junk like that. He lives out beyond
the trap lines in Minto Inlet. Don't know
if he's still alive.

DAN Could you ask around
for his number? or email?

PAUL Jack told me
last winter one of these blizzards lasted
fourteen days.

Light: evening.

Moving image: blizzard in the window.

DAN Fourteen days!

PAUL That's a fortnight
to Canadians.

DAN Later that evening
we're getting into bed, snow is whispering
beneath the windowpanes.

PAUL I wouldn't mind
staying here for a while. Just between me
and you, my confessor. They're refusing
to send me anywhere interesting
anymore. I don't know why.

DAN Are you scared
you'll be fired?

PAUL Of course. Nobody's reading
anything anymore. Are you?

DAN Reading
newspapers?

PAUL And nobody's clicking on

these Arctic pieces either. My expense
reports are obscene.

DAN Why not do something
else then?

PAUL Like what? Maybe I could become
a wedding photographer.

DAN Why don't you
write a book?

PAUL I already wrote a book.
Remember? I think I sold like maybe
six copies in the US. One review
on Amazon said:

AMAZON The lesson we learn,
that war lives in all of us, is neither
original nor particularly
helpful.

AMAZON Author Watson is at his best
whilst giving us the sights and sounds of war,

AMAZON but his memoir suffers when he aspires
to some kind of poetry whose only
loyalty is to the truth.

PAUL I'm paraphrasing
now, of course, but what kind of an ass-jag
uses the word whilst?

DAN Your book had no point
for me actually. To be completely
honest with you. I would read a chapter
or two, then have to put it down. And go
wash my hands. Because—it was all too much!
And repetitive. All these horrible
things you've lived through, I still don't understand
how you don't just surrender to profound
despair.

Light: lights out.

Sound: wind howling.

PAUL Have I ever told you about
the time I met Mother Theresa?

DAN No.

PAUL I was stuck in Calcutta—

DAN I'm going to
record this, okay?

PAUL So I went over
to Mother's House. Which was this heavily
trafficked place, full of these shady-looking
characters wearing Rolex watches and
Italian business suits. There was a chair
by the door, and a sister said:

SISTER Sit down,
and if she's willing she will come.

PAUL Maybe
two or three days passed like this, till someone,
some sister comes downstairs and says,

SISTER Mother
will see you now.

SISTER Only for a short while,

SISTER a moment if you're lucky.

PAUL I turn on
my tape recorder and race up the stairs
where she's hobbling around in her knobby
crippled kind of bare feet in this small room
of hers with no doors,

PAUL just some curtains and
I'm watching her shuffle back and forth from

PAUL one doorway to the other,

PAUL appearing
and then disappearing in the sunlight
and then shade.

PAUL Never once looking at me.
Because I'd been to her treatment centers,
she didn't call them that, they're basically
places to go and die, right?

DAN Right.

PAUL Full of
row upon row of starving AIDS victims
and others,

PAUL lying on these sorts of cots
very low to the ground.

PAUL And they don't get
a lot of medical care, they get cleaned
and they get fed.

PAUL They don't get fed a lot.

PAUL And I was trying to be this heavy
on Mother Theresa, you know, saying,
Don't you think you should feed them some more food?

PAUL Don't you think maybe you should be doing
this or that?

PAUL And she said, They don't need food.
They need love. And she kept on saying that.

MOTHER THERESA They need love. They need love. That's all. That's all.

PAUL I was thinking, Wow, this is like shooting
ducks in a pond! This woman's a moron,
right?

DAN Ha ha ha, right!

PAUL So I go and write
my hit-piece about Mother Theresa.
It wasn't this blatant, but basically
what I said was that she was this harpy,
this, you know, cold-hearted nun mistreating
all these poor people. Well —bullshit. She's right.
What they *did* need was love. Because it was
respect. Either they die in the street or
they die in Mother's House. And if you die
in Mother's arms then at least you've died with
somebody loving you. And not because
they owe it to you, or because they feel
some familial obligation —they're just
doing it because they know you deserve
to be loved. You know? Maybe I'm a fool
but I think that was the point of my book
that no one bought.

DAN So what you're saying is
war would disappear if we could all just
hold each others' hands?

PAUL Why are you trying
to turn me into some kind of guru?

DAN Am I?

PAUL Like I've got some kind of answer
for you.

DAN I don't know.

PAUL That thing you wrote me
about your family, Dan. They disowned you
for no reason.

DAN Right.

PAUL And how your father
kept saying, There are things you do not know!
And how you look just like your dad's brother,
I keep thinking about that.

DAN I do too.

PAUL Did your father mean he's not your father?

DAN I don't know. It's crazy, but—

PAUL Why don't you
start asking some questions? That's what I'd do
if I were you.

DAN Paul's laptop starts ringing.

PAUL It's Skype. It's my wife. Stay here.

DAN No I'll go
sit in the kitchen.

PAUL No stay here. Hello?
Sweetness?

DAN I hear Paul's wife's voice. I don't look
at the screen. I go out to the hallway
and sit by the pay phone. And try calling
home on an empty calling card.

Light: dawn, no storm.

PAUL Sweetness,
I miss you so badly.

DAN The next morning
things look different.

JACK Next time you come up here,
Dan, you bring me back a bag of cocaine
and an AK-47.

DAN We step
outside.

DAN Snow snow.

DAN Jerry's down on the ice
with his sled and his dog team. The sky is
bright, snow's drifting like pollen.

PAUL Would you mind
riding with Jerry, Dan? Jack can pull me
behind his skidoo and I can shoot you
and the dogs that way.

DAN Jerry's middle-aged
and mildly hunchbacked. I think I can see
that titanium plate in his forehead.

JERRY Guys!
Guys! We're losing our sunlight here!

DAN I snap
some pictures before my camera's frozen.

PAUL Put it inside your coat! Put it next to
your skin!

DAN I can't hear you!

JERRY Hoot, hoot!

Moving image, no sound: Dan's footage of the dogs.

DAN Jerry's
beating his dogs' muzzles with a short stick.

JERRY No, Ghost! Bad Ghost!

DAN You call your dog Ghost? Why?

JERRY I'm training him to lead. I had to sell
my old leader. But Ghost's a real scaredy
-cat.

DAN The dogs are tangled in harnesses
of yellow nylon cords.

JERRY Misty wants to
lead instead.

DAN Who's Misty?

JERRY The one in back.

DAN She's cute. Smelly. Hyper. A bit dangerous.

JERRY Real bitch.

DAN They can't stop barking.

JERRY Hoot! Hoot!

DAN High
-pitched yelps. They seem insane. Like a savage
race of idiot wolves.

JERRY Hoot! Hoot!

DAN I'm missing
my dog now. She's a miniature schnauzer
these huskies would eat for breakfast. A few
of them are eating their own shit. Tearing
at hunks of meat.

JERRY Hoot! Hoot, hoot!

DAN Who knows what
Jerry's trying to say?

JERRY Sit your ass down,
Dan! —Hoot, hoot, hoot!

DAN And we're off. I'm sitting
down, on my ass, on a blue plastic tarp
with my rubber boots splayed in front, inches
above the ice above the sea—

JERRY Hold on
to these ropes down here, Dan!

DAN Jerry's kneeling
behind my ear.

JERRY Gee! Gee! Zaw!

DAN Gee means right,
I think. I've heard mushers say Haw! for left
but Jerry says

JERRY Zaw! —Hoot!

DAN means faster. Paul's
riding in a box on skis.

DAN Jack's pulling
him with his skidoo.

DAN Red taillights dancing
in a whorl of snow.

JERRY Hoot, hoot!

DAN You feel it
in your spine, your neck, your skull. The grinding
of the rusted runners on ice crystals
like sand.

Moving image, silent: this dog sled ride, Dan's POV.

DAN Snow snow snow snow snow snow.

DAN Cresting
another invisible ridge, the dogs
fan out to shit in streaks.

JERRY Misty, no! Gee!
Gee!

DAN We're moving onto the Arctic Sea,
and if we could only change direction
and head that way—

JERRY Zaw! Zaw! Zaw!

DAN If we could
only get the dogs to turn to the left
instead,

DAN we'd be in Minto Inlet.

DAN Where
Roger Umtoq the shaman lives.

JERRY Misty,
no! Zaw!

DAN We stop at the floe's edge. The sea
is an undulating eternity
of black slush a few feet away. Seal heads
breaking through the new ice, their spectral eyes
on us.

PAUL My feet are completely numb, Dan.

DAN I think I bruised my tailbone.

JERRY Hey guys! Guys!
Theose dogs aren't tired enough! Got to
keep going!

More footage, no sound: dogs barking in harness on the ice.

DAN The dogs keep barking,

DAN while Paul
sets up his tripod and shoots Jack kneeling
at the waterline,

DAN tossing a snowball
onto the thin veneer of ice forming
on the water. It sounds like a pebble
bouncing off glass.

PAUL Have you ever seen it
this melted before?

JACK Usually ice floes
come down from the hill, usually springtime
like April May June?

JERRY Hey guys! Guys! These dogs
are real worked up! Going to have to run them
some more!

JACK Because that's when we get the winds?
But I've never seen it this warm before
in wintertime.

JERRY Hey Dan.

DAN Yeah.

JERRY Put your weight
on this anchor.

DAN What for?

JERRY Just stand on this
and don't go anywhere. I need to go
drain my dragon.

DAN The anchor's a steel claw
dug in the ice. Tied with a yellow cord
that's tied to the very last barking dog
in the team. Named Misty.

JERRY Misty! shut up!

DAN Jerry!

JERRY Huh?

DAN You don't know Roger Umtoq
the shaman in Minto Inlet?

JERRY Old guy?
Told kids bullshit stories?

DAN He's a healer
too.

JERRY I don't know nothing about all that.

DAN Can you take us out to Minto Inlet
to see him? Of course we'll pay you something,
Jerry.

JERRY I'd like to take you to Minto
but the Roger I know out in Minto
died of heart attack last winter—

DAN Misty
takes off,

JERRY Misty no!

DAN pulling the whole team,

DAN and the sled starts sliding sideways,

DAN I start
laughing, like I'm embarrassed,

DAN as my boot
slips off the anchor,

DAN as the anchor slips
out of the ice—

JERRY What are you doing, Dan!

DAN Me?

JERRY Ghost! Ghost!

DAN And for an instant I see
the top of the world from above,

PAUL Hey Dan,
are you okay?

DAN as the steel anchor wraps
around my ankle and whips me up off
my feet,

PAUL I'm so sorry.

DAN and the seal heads
duck back under the new ice.

Light: Arctic night.

PAUL I'm feeling
so guilty.

DAN We're back in our hotel room
and I can't move.

PAUL How's your head?

DAN It's all right.

PAUL Do you need any more ice?

TV on, no sound: entertainment news.

DAN It's my groin
that's killing me.

PAUL We're out of wine. You sure
you didn't bring anything?

DAN I forgot,
I told you. I'm sorry.

PAUL —You should've seen
yourself, you were sideways! You were almost
inverted! I don't know how that happened,
the physics of it, I mean. You don't have
anything to drink? no vodka?

DAN I wish
I had some right now.

PAUL This reminds me of
Abdul Haq —you know who he is right?

DAN No.

PAUL He was this mujahedeen famous for
defeating the Soviets in the '80s
with the CIA's help, of course. After
9/11, I went to interview
him in Peshawar.

DAN Pakistan?

PAUL —Here here here
record this.

DAN Okay.

PAUL I mean this guy looked
exactly like Rob Reiner with a tan!
and a bright white shalwar kameez. He hugged
me! without knowing me! He was limping
around on his prosthetic foot. I'm sure
that's why he liked me.

DAN Why?

PAUL He was going
back to Kabul so that when the US
invaded he'd be an alternative
to the Taliban. I'm sure he wanted
revenge also, cause Talibs killed his wife

and son a few years before, or maybe
it was ISI—

DAN ISI is what
again, Paul?

PAUL I was eating and sleeping
on the floor, outside Kabul. With dried blood
in the corner, bullet holes in the wall.
Bathing in a bucket, with one toilet
all plugged up with shit. Everybody there
had dysentery. And somebody asked me,
Have you heard what happened to Abdul Haq?
He came over the Khyber Pass last week
with 25 men, and Taliban troops
ambushed him. He hid all night in the rocks
calling the CIA for air support
but no one came. Taliban captured him
the next morning and hanged him from a tree
with a metal noose. Cut off his dick and
stuffed it in his mouth. Shot up his body
till he was just this hanging piece of meat.
I'm sorry, Dan. Sorry. I don't know why
I'm thinking of him now. I don't know why
I'm crying either! Maybe it's just cause
you got tangled up in all that cord?

DAN Paul's
staring straight ahead. He's not here. Paul's not
here anymore. I get up, head spinning,
groin aching.

Moving image: snow falling

PAUL Sorry, Dan. Sorry.

DAN I see
who he is now, finally: sitting there
in his socks, his filthy sweatshirt, his eyes
are like looking down a well. His greasy
hair's all messed up. He's my older brother
sitting at the kitchen table, the day
they brought him back home from the hospital.
I was standing in the doorway watching
him pretend to eat something. Nobody

was saying a word. I could have sat down
with him. I was scared I'd catch his disease.
I thought, Sadness is an illness you catch
if you aren't careful enough. I ran
outside to play with friends. Are you hungry,
Paul? They've left some dinner on the table
for us.

10: YELLOWKNIFE

PAUL It's like this French bistro called *Le Frolic*
I think? just down the hill from the hotel
in Yellowknife.

DAN That whole flight from Ulu
Paul's pitching me a TV show about
life in the Arctic:

Google directions: Ulukhaktok to Kugluktuk, Kugluktuk to Yellowknife.

PAUL *Fawlty Towers* meets
White Fang!

DAN I'm not really writing TV
shows, Paul.

PAUL Then your wife, your wife could write it
for you!

DAN I'm worried about the play, how
to end it.

PAUL I'm not saying it's a good
French bistro. It's decent. I had dinner
here on my way up. I'll get a bottle
of their finest Cabernet. Do you want
some beer, vodka?

DAN How'd you meet your wife, Paul?

PAUL My wife?

DAN You never mention her. Except
to say she's "changed your life," in your memoir.
Just like you've only told me your mother
is the strongest woman you've ever known.

PAUL She's Chinese.

DAN Your wife?

PAUL No my mother. Yes
my wife's Chinese.

DAN She's a photographer,
right? I read that in your book.

PAUL I don't talk
about her for a reason.

DAN Is she why
you're doing better?

PAUL Am I?

DAN I don't know
what I thought would happen up here. I'm not
saying I think I failed. Maybe I did,
maybe I failed to get a story, but
I don't know yet. Because in many ways
you're just as fucked up as I'd imagined—

PAUL Thank you.

DAN In other ways you seem better
than I could ever hope to be.

PAUL You sound
kind of disappointed, Dan.

DAN What happened
to the ghost of William David Cleveland?
I kept meaning to ask—

PAUL What do you mean
what happened to him?

DAN Are you still haunted
by him? Does he follow you? Is he here
with us now? Or was that all a story
to sell books.

PAUL He's here. He's gotten quieter,
that's true. It could be the meds. I worry
about my son, cosmic retribution
of some kind. I don't think about myself
anymore.

DAN When did that change?

PAUL I don't know
exactly. I know you were hoping for
an epiphany of something. Maybe

an exorcism. I know you wanted
to visit a shaman and have my soul
cleansed—

DAN And cleanse myself.

PAUL That's not how it works.
You get used to it. It just turns slowly
into something else. It's like when I called
Cleveland's mother—

DAN Right that's in your book—

PAUL No
that's just book-bullshit. When I wrote that book
I didn't understand it. I didn't
understand the conversation. You should
hear it sometime, remind me to send it
to you when I get home.

DAN You recorded
the phone call?

PAUL That's right.

DAN Why?

PAUL Flew to Phoenix,
rented a car. At the Ramada Inn
turned on the AC

PAUL and pulled the blinds down
and picked up the phone:

Sound: answering machine beeping.

PAUL Um yes hello ma'am
my name's Paul Watson. This is difficult
for me to say. But I took that picture
of your son that day in Mogadishu.
I've wanted to meet you for years, to speak
to you about what happened. And I hope
you might be willing to give me some time
in the next couple of days—

PAUL Had some dinner
at the mall, back in the room the phone was—

PAUL Hello?

BROTHER This is William David Cleveland's
brother.

PAUL Oh. —Hi, sir.

BROTHER Hi. Can I ask you
never to call my mom again? She called
me crying her eyes out cause you threw her
into a really bad relapse.

PAUL Well, sir,
it's just that I've been living with this thing
for more than a decade now—

BROTHER You're talking
about that picture you took of my brother
drug through the streets?

PAUL That's right. And I'm hoping
if I can understand my place in time
and his place in time, then maybe we could
bury a few things.

BROTHER Well, he was no different
than all the people over there right now
in Iraq and Afghanistan. Fighting
for something they believe in, even when
nobody else does.

PAUL That doesn't help me
understand him as a person.

BROTHER That's him,
that's him as a person.

PAUL I know him, sir,
only from that moment. And for my own
mental health—

BROTHER He was a kind of weird kid
who didn't match in with nobody. But
he always knew he wanted to protect
people.

PAUL Was your father in the navy,
sir?

BROTHER He was an engine mechanic.

PAUL And
did your brother have a wife?

BROTHER Well he had
a couple of them.

PAUL And you wouldn't know how
I might go about trying to track down
these women? Or other relatives?

BROTHER Nope.

PAUL He had some kids I understand.

BROTHER Sorry?

PAUL He had a few kids.

BROTHER —Now are you looking
to do some kind of story again?

PAUL Sir,
I just wish we could meet—

BROTHER I don't care to
meet you at all.

PAUL Do you hate me, sir?

BROTHER What?

PAUL You hate me, sir, I know it!

BROTHER I don't hate
nobody, man!

PAUL But —but I dishonored
your brother, that's what haunts me—

BROTHER His honor
wasn't tarnished in the least.

PAUL Well, sir, see
there's a lot of people who would argue
with you on that point.

BROTHER They must not've been
one of the 3,000 people crowding
into a church that could hold only like
a hundred for his funeral. Must not've
been one of the 32 cars following
us all the way to the cemetery,
or the four helicopters with gunships
giving him an escort all the way. They
didn't feel he'd been dishonored.

PAUL Others
who know him from my picture—

BROTHER I don't care
about your picture! I'm not interested
in discussing it, I'm not interested
in meeting you, and I do apologize
if that offends you, sir—

PAUL Could we do this
over email, sir?

BROTHER No.

PAUL Can't we just meet,
and you can see who I am— !

BROTHER Once again
negative.

PAUL Sir I have begged, I, I, I
don't understand why—

BROTHER You're going to have to
deal with this on your own time.

PAUL Your mother
hates me, sir. I read this interview about
that thing in Fallujah where they strung up
the American contractors from that bridge?
And your mother broke down crying and told
the reporter she hated the person
who did it then, like she hates the people
who do it now.

BROTHER She was talking about
the people desecrating all of them
bodies.

PAUL —No, sir, she was talking about
me, sir! I know it!

BROTHER The thing of it was,
when David got shot down and went missing?
since our mom had remarried and taken
a different name, they told his stepmother
he'd been killed in action. We found out while
watching Peter Jennings. When my mother

recognized David's feet. Cause they looked like
his dad's. If it weren't for your picture
we might've never found out.

PAUL You must blame
me for that much, sir—

BROTHER Man, you don't listen
very well, do you?

PAUL Do you want to know
why I did it?

BROTHER No.

PAUL Why not?

BROTHER Explaining
don't change the fact a thing got done.

PAUL A week
before, another Black Hawk got shot down,
and kids were parading the body parts
of servicemen through the streets like pennants
at a baseball game. And the Pentagon
denied it. They said it didn't happen.
Because I didn't have a picture.

BROTHER Right.

PAUL I wasn't a machine, I cared.

BROTHER Right.

PAUL And
honestly, sir, I believe your brother
would still be alive today if people
had known the truth.

BROTHER From my own life I'd say,
and I was in the Air Force for ten years,
I volunteered to go to Somalia
but they wouldn't let me go, cause of work,
where I was. But I can honestly say
I'd have no problem if I'd been the one
in my brother's shoes.

PAUL You would've wanted
that picture taken?

BROTHER I would've.

PAUL Why, sir?
for the reason I just explained or?

BROTHER Both,
for the reason you just said and because
you're just doing your job.

PAUL Well I'm grateful
to you for saying that.

BROTHER Not a problem.

PAUL It takes a large weight off. I only wish
the rest of your family felt the same way.

BROTHER You're going to have to take my word on that
unfortunately.

PAUL Oh yeah no, I won't go
down that route, sir.

BROTHER I appreciate that, sir.

PAUL I'm just talking about the larger world
here.

BROTHER Well the world's fucked up.

PAUL Sure.

BROTHER Short and sweet,
the world's a fallen place. Ha ha ha.

PAUL And
I hope this won't upset you but one thing
that still haunts me is that I heard a voice
when I took that picture. And your brother
warned me: If you do this I will own you
forever.

BROTHER Well how do you know David
meant something bad?

PAUL He said I will own you
forever—

BROTHER Maybe he meant you owe him
something now.

PAUL Like what?

BROTHER Look, I've got to go
pick up my boy.

PAUL Okay sir, I forgot
to ask you your name.

BROTHER Ray.

PAUL Ray, that's my dad's
name.

RAY Ha ha ha.

PAUL Sir, please apologize
to your mother for me?

RAY Good night.

PAUL Good night.

DAN The phone's hung up. The hum fades out.

DAN Footsteps
on hotel carpeting. The zipping up
of a bag.

DAN After dinner we're struggling
through blistering wind,

DAN sand snow,

DAN to the Hotel
Explorer, this strangely lavish, somewhat
Soviet, high-rise hotel for diplomats
from the south.

PAUL I'm going up to Resolute
soon. Where the American scientists hang out
all summer long.

DAN —I can't hear you!

PAUL I said
I'm doing a story about robot
submarines!

DAN That's awesome! Maybe I'll try
for a grant to go with you!

PAUL Great!

DAN We step
inside the elevator.

PAUL I'm leaving
first thing in the morning. Fuck me.

DAN My flight's
in the afternoon. So I guess this is
goodbye.

PAUL Here's my floor. So.

DAN Hey Paul, thank you
for writing back to me for three years now.
For writing back in the first place. It's hard
to explain everything it's meant to me,
to be able to leave my home and go
someplace like this, with somebody like you,
even for a short while.

DAN But I don't say
any of that. I say:

DAN Paul, I don't know
if this play's going to be any good. But
I'll email it to you when I'm done.

PAUL Don't
bother, I won't read it. I can't look back
on all this old stuff anymore, Dan. But
I'm happy you're the one writing it. Bye
now. Safe flight.

DAN The elevator closes
and I wonder if I'll ever see him
again.

Moving image: snow falling.

PAUL My deepest apologies, Dan,
for not writing sooner. I'm in Resolute
where I've just destroyed all my computer
equipment, by accident, by dropping
my bag off the side of an icebreaker .
I simply lost my grip! as we broke through
miles and miles of ice near Taloyoak.

Google terrain: Resolute.

DAN I'm working on our play at a theater
in Minneapolis, in a neighborhood
called Little Mogadishu. Somali
refugees everywhere. Girls in hijabs
walking down the sidewalk. It would be strange
to have you with me here, Paul. I don't know
whether you'd hate it. Or love it.

Google map: Minneapolis.

PAUL Dear Dan,
just between me and you, my confessor:
the big news is I'm back in Kandahar.
It's summer again and the Taliban's
itching for a fight. The *Toronto Star*
wants its pretty thin coverage here beefed up,
and if I want to keep my wife and son
in new snow boots I need to make myself
valuable to the *Star*. And Canada's
still responsible for Kandahar. Truth
is I'm no different than those Americans
driving their trucks in near suicidal
conditions in Iraq, just to pay off
mortgages in Florida. This is what
I've come to: I'm a mercenary and
a desperate one at that. Just between me
and my confessor. But there's something else:
I feel like Cleveland's happy I've come back,
though I don't know why yet. Maybe you'll come
visit me here sometime? Someplace relaxing
like Kabul. Maybe there's a book in it,
or a play. So what do you say? Will you
come, Dan? I promise to keep you as safe
as I can. Though of course nobody knows
what can happen out here. Talk to you soon,
your friend Paul.

Google Earth: Kabul.

END OF PLAY

THE HOUSE IN HYDESVILLE

Characters

The Fox Family:

MAGGIE, 14	
CATHIE, 11	sisters
MARGARET, 51	their mother
JOHN, 59	their father
DAVID, 28	their brother
LEAH, 34	their sister
LIZZIE, 17	Leah's daughter

Time & Place

A small one-and-a-half story frame house in Hydesville, New York, at the crossroads of Hydesville and Parker Roads, beside the Ganargua River.

The first act begins with the Fox family's arrival at the Hydesville house on December 11, 1847, and continues in the months leading up to March 31, 1848.

The second act takes place over the course of a day, a night, and a morning, a little over a month later in early May, 1848.

Notes

Scenes occur in the different rooms on the house's ground floor, and one scene takes place outside the back door, so the house might revolve on stage, or transform in some other, simpler way. A distinctly physical, cramped, oppressive sense of the house is what's important here.

Also, a sense of simultaneity in the house is intended, in that characters not directly involved in a scene in the kitchen, for example, might be visible sleeping, resting, reading, or listening in another room, in the dark or not.

The actors playing Leah, Lizzie, and David all have considerable offstage time; they might act as foley artists, as it were, creating the various haunting sounds called for throughout the script. The spirit, and the presence of the spirit via sound, is central to the play. Regardless of its agency, this rapping is a human sound.

The House in Hydesville was commissioned by Geva Theatre Center, and supported in part by the 2006-7 Hodder Fellowship at Princeton University, the 2008 Djerassi Fellowship at University of Wisconsin-Madison, and a residency at the 2006 New Harmony Project.

The play received subsequent development at Geva Theatre Center, Lark Play Development Center, and in the 2007 PlayLabs at the Playwrights' Center. *The House in Hydesville* premiered in 2009 at Geva Theatre Center, Mark Cuddy, Artistic Director, directed by Skip Greer.

MAGGIE	Annie Purcell
CATHIE	Lauren Orkus
MARGARET	Kristin Griffith
JOHN	Michael Rudko
DAVID	Garrett Neergaard
LEAH	Lanie MacEwan
LIZZIE	Rachel Rusch

Creative Team

Scenic Designer	Patrick Clark
Costume Designer	B. Modern
Lighting Designer	Matthew Reinert
Sound Designer	Lindsay Jones
Dramaturg	Marge Betley
Stage Manager	Marianne Montgomery
Assistant Stage Manager	Janine Wochna
Production Assistant	Jenny Daniels
Casting Directors	Elissa Myers & Paul Fouquet, CSA

Yes, these eyes are windows, and this body of mine
is the house.

—Herman Melville

Part One: The Rapping

1A. DARKNESS.

(Two girls speaking:)

CATHIE

Mr. Splitfoot?

MAGGIE

—Don't say that.

CATHIE

Why not?

MAGGIE

What if it's true?

CATHIE

Mr. Splitfoot? Do as I do:

(CATHIE claps her hands three times. Pause.

The sound of someone rapping, as if their knuckles on wood, in response three times.

The girls cry out.

Rapping continues: staccato, eerily, growing less mysterious, as if someone's knocking at the door ...)

1. KITCHEN.

(Lights rise on the inside of a kitchen: dreary, dark, empty but for a table and some chairs.

Mid-afternoon in mid-December.

Everything's covered in what appear to be filthy bed sheets.

The floor is bare: a warped patched planked floor. Outside the sun off snow is near blinding but fails to brighten this room.

Someone's knocking at the kitchen door.)

CATHIE

(Outside.)

—Just go in!

(Slowly the door opens, and MAGGIE, 14, attractive but plain, steps inside in an old, ill-fitting coat; looking around disappointedly:)

MAGGIE

(To herself.)

... This is the house?

(Enter CATHIE behind her, her sister: 11, reed-thin, bird-like; there's something electric, ethereal, almost frightening about her.

She strides past MAGGIE and circles the room.)

CATHIE

Hello?

MAGGIE

There's no one in here, Cathie ...

CATHIE

Who's here?

MAGGIE

Nobody, Cathie—it's empty.

CATHIE

It's not: I saw a face.

MAGGIE

Where?

CATHIE

At that window there. Looking out at me ...

MAGGIE

That was only your own reflection you saw ...

CATHIE

These windows are filthy. —Look at my hands!

MAGGIE

We'll clean them then—

CATHIE

Hello? —Echo!

MAGGIE

Stop it or they'll hear you!

CATHIE

So? —What's that sound?

MAGGIE

Where?

CATHIE

There's a fly in here, at that window ... That's strange, in winter ...
Maybe there's something dead in here?

(CATHIE sniffs the air.)

MAGGIE

(Looking.)

It's not a fly, it's a moth ...

CATHIE

I smell peppermint. Do you?

(CATHIE smiles. MAGGIE sniffs the air now too.)

MAGGIE

No.

CATHIE

"No." —This won't do at all. —It's much too small for us!

MAGGIE

We've lived in smaller before ...

CATHIE

We'll go home today ...

MAGGIE

This *is* our home, Cathie ... For now.

(CATHIE peers round the door, into the pantry.)

MAGGIE (cont'd.)

It's only for the winter they said ...

CATHIE

I'm not sleeping in that pantry. I can tell you that much.

MAGGIE

Why not?

CATHIE

—It's the pantry!

MAGGIE

We'll sleep in the bedroom then.

CATHIE

There's only one room, in front. —*They'll* sleep in there.

MARGARET

(Outside.)

—Girls?

(CATHIE grabs MAGGIE's hand and they run through the open door—into the pantry.

As MARGARET enters, their mother, 51: stout, grim, voluble, silly, it would seem. Her hair is a mess of white.

She carries an old rocking chair, loaded up with supplies; and balanced there on top: a bushel of bright red apples.

She drops the chair—it rocks, and a few things spill out across the floor, some apples ... Winded, but with great determination, she begins unpacking, sweeping the dust-filled sheets off of the disappointing furniture.

There's something uncannily childlike in her voice:)

MARGARET (cont'd.)

Where are you girls hiding now? You know your father needs our help outside, carrying all our things down into that cellar ... Can't you hear him now? he's opened up the cellar door—on my word! this house is well kept up ... Have you seen? They've left some fresh linens over all the things, their furniture, it's warm in here, such bright windows! and cozy, yes, with a view of the river and snow beyond and the sun and smell of peppermint somehow ... This will be a very good home, for the time being, don't you think?

(She kills a moth on the wall with her hand. Wipes her hand off on her coat, cheerfully.)

MARGARET (cont'd.)

—Girls? There's a butterfly in here!

(Now she hears a thump or rustle—doesn't know where from. She creeps about, as if a girl herself, looking for them.)

MARGARET (cont'd.)

... Margaretta? Catherine? —Don't you play games with your mother now!

(She's about to peer into the pantry when—)

CATHIE

—Help us Mother, please!

(CATHIE shrieks, MAGGIE squeals in sympathy and excitement, as both girls burst from the pantry and spill out around the room.)

MARGARET

—Oh!

(Their mother falls back in her chair, heaving, frightened, delighted, rocking ...

MAGGIE stands next to her mother, patting her forearm gingerly, as CATHIE circles the room again:)

MAGGIE

We're sorry, Mother ...

CATHIE

(Mimicking.)

"We're sorry, Mother" ...

MARGARET

(To Cathie.)

—I knew where you were this whole time!

CATHIE

You were scared! I could tell!

MARGARET

You mustn't do that! You mustn't scare your mother like that! —I could belt you for that one, you know!

CATHIE

But you won't.
We're not sleeping in that room, Mother, by the way.

MARGARET

(Standing up.)

Oh, are we not now?

CATHIE

No.

MARGARET

And why, may I ask our little princess ... ?

MAGGIE

She wants to sleep in the other room with you. With all of us, together.

CATHIE

You want that too.

MAGGIE

Why would I?

MARGARET

We won't be doing that no ...

CATHIE

Why not?

MAGGIE

Why do you want that so badly, Cathie?

MARGARET

Yes, why, Catherine?

CATHIE

Other families do it.

MARGARET

Not Methodist families ...

CATHIE

We used to sleep together. We've done it before.

MARGARET

We don't have to anymore. Not out here.

CATHIE

"In the sticks" ...

MARGARET

You watch your tongue, young lady.

CATHIE

I can't: see, my tongue's too short. *(She sticks out her tongue at her mother while speaking:)*

Can you watch my tongue? What's it saying?

(MARGARET has busied herself unpacking.)

MARGARET

... Your father likes it here, all this quiet ... He likes the quiet, don't you? I like the quiet too ... Though not so much as others ... Don't you like it out here, so quiet, all the time? and the snow in all ways, all around us ... Some people like the quiet, and others they do not. —Your older siblings, now, they *all* like quiet ... very much so, like their father does—

MAGGIE

I like the quiet too, I think.

CATHIE

You don't.

MAGGIE

—I might!

CATHIE

You're quiet, but you don't like it.

—I'm not going to sleep in that room, Mother. And nothing you can do or say will make me!

(Pause. Mother and daughter square off.)

MARGARET

Go ask your father then.

CATHIE

"Go ask your father then."

MARGARET

You're a very good mimic. You ought to be an actress.

CATHIE

"All actresses are whores."

MARGARET

—Filth!

CATHIE

Father says that: Father says filth sometimes!

MARGARET

You watch your tongue, young lady.

CATHIE

You watch it! —I can talk without moving my lips, see?

MAGGIE

No you can't, Cathie ...

CATHIE

You're not even watching!

Mother, can't we all sleep together in the very same room tonight, please?

MAGGIE

It's only for the winter ...

(CATHIE sticks her tongue out at her sister.)

MARGARET

You listen to your sister, she's got more sense than you. One day you'll find yourself alone in this world, and then all you'll have is family ... And Maggie here will save you.

Now help me with these things. Be careful, they are delicate ...

(MAGGIE helps: unpacking chipped cups and saucers, some glasses and well-worn plates, unwrapping the newspaper from around them ...

CATHIE sulks.)

MAGGIE

... We could sleep in the attic, could we not?

CATHIE

"Could we not?"

MARGARET

The attic is for storage. You mustn't play up there. This house is much too small, for everything we own ... We've left a lot in town. But we've brought so much with us here! too much for this small house ... So we'll have to leave it all unpacked, upstairs. For the time being. —Don't you think that's best? The attic, until springtime comes and we can move again ...

CATHIE

What about the cellar?

MARGARET

You mustn't play down there either. Or your father will get cross.

MAGGIE

She means for sleeping, in the cellar.

MARGARET

Don't be stupid! You can't sleep underground.

CATHIE

Ghosts do.

(Short pause.)

MARGARET

You're not a ghost you're a girl.

(MARGARET continues to unpack.)

MARGARET (cont'd.)

My mother saw ghosts. You never met her. —In another age, she'd have been thought a witch, I'm sure of it.

CATHIE

We all know about your mother, Mother ...

MARGARET

I dreamed of her last night. I don't know why that is. She had that gift, of second sight. Or *future* sight, as the Scots say. —I wonder what's the difference?

MAGGIE

(Quietly.)

Who knows?

CATHIE

"Who knows."

MARGARET

Who knows. That's right. She came from France originally. She was a Huguenot, and prosecuted—

MAGGIE

"Persecuted," Mother.

MARGARET

I'm sure she was that too ... She would have these *premonitions* ... where she would rise up out of her bed, walk out into the road—where she'd *swear* she was seeing a funeral procession, right there in front of her eyes! passing by our home ... And she'd follow them down to the graveyard ... where she'd cry, alone, watching the phantom burial occur.

My father used always to go find her, somewhere in that very large cemetery, in Rockland, late at night. —And sometimes he'd find her elsewhere, walking the streets, shouting out at neighbors' homes the names of those she knew would pass away that night.

He'd have to quiet her sometimes. He'd have to drag her home. He'd have to lock her up, sometimes ...

But always—she was correct! In the morning, whomsoever she had seen in her vision would be stiff. As wood.

(She knocks on wood, crosses herself.

CATHIE shivers.)

MARGARET (cont'd.)

Are you cold, dear? That's natural, after a story like that. —You're a Sensitive! that's what you are. My mother was one too. You've been that way since birth. We'll get that stove working soon, you'll see ...

CATHIE

It's cold here. *(She steps or leans:)* But not here.

MARGARET

(Pleasantly.)

Yes now why do you think that is?

MAGGIE

Who knows?

CATHIE

"Who knows?"

MARGARET

I don't think it's cold. Do you? You have to keep yourself moving. You're much too thin. You don't see Maggie shivering, do you?

CATHIE

I think that it's the river ...

MARGARET

What's the river? all this damp?

MAGGIE

It's a creek.

CATHIE

What's its name again?

MAGGIE

It's called Mud Creek by some ...

CATHIE

(Recalling; as if mesmerized.)

"The Gargantuan"—

MAGGIE

But it's real name is the Ganargua.

CATHIE

Sounds like a throat's been cut.

MARGARET

—Catherine Fox!

(MARGARET has slammed a bowl, or a stack of plates, down to the table. They've made a clatter, but nothing's broken.)

MARGARET (cont'd.)

... Go outside and help your father please.

CATHIE

(Resolutely.)

No.

(MARGARET backs down. As she cleans, unpacks:)

MARGARET

... I don't know why you're all so afraid of him ... If you think he's so bad then you ought to have met my father ... My father didn't like your father—not one bit! I come from good stock ... We had to run away, and it was like a novel. —Now, my father—

(CATHIE takes an apple.)

MARGARET (cont'd.)

Is that him I hear downstairs? —He must have opened up the cellar door, from the outside, he's storing up the apples, amongst other things. —It was so nice of the Posts to give us their apples, don't you think? What do you think of the Posts, are they kind? —I like apples when they are cold, don't you?

(CATHIE bites into her apple now.)

MAGGIE

I'll help you help Father, Cathie ...

CATHIE

I can't go. I break things.

MARGARET

That's true. Why is that? your grandmother was *just* like that!

CATHIE

My hands are too small, I drop things. See? You go, Maggie. You've got big hands, for a girl ...

(Pause. MAGGIE looks at her hands, almost suspiciously ...

She goes out: snow-bright white out there.

The not-too-terribly-secure back door shuts.)

MARGARET

Isn't that so? a very cold, crisp apple? in the very dead of night? I mean winter ... Makes one feel hopeful ... I feel hopeful naturally. Don't you?

CATHIE

Can't we go home now please, Momma?

MARGARET

We've only just arrived!

CATHIE

When can we go, then?

MARGARET

When the winter's done.

CATHIE

In May?

MARGARET

If we're lucky it will be April ...

CATHIE

"This winter lasts the whole life long" ...

MARGARET

Who said that, some poet?

CATHIE

It just came into my head ...

(MARGARET continues to unpack.)

MARGARET

Help me, Cathie, help your mother please ... You won't drop them now with your hands all sticky from that apple ...

(CATHIE helps, reluctantly: unpacking more glasses, cups, saucers, etc.; dusting them off, lining them up on the tabletop in order of size and utility ...

It's not a very impressive collection.

MARGARET moves to the stove, opens it, cleaning ash, on her knees with her head and hands inside.

After a moment:)

CATHIE

Why did Poppa sell our furniture? ... I saw him in the street.

(MARGARET rises from the stove, looks at her daughter as if startled, then confused ... Some ash on her face.

She turns away again, bustling about the kitchen, opening up drawers and cabinets, slapping them out with a rag.)

MARGARET

It was good of the Posts to give us those apples. Don't you think? after all? —And so many! They are kind souls, if they are Quakers ... And Hicksites to boot. —Even though they think so much of themselves sometimes, their *knowledge* ... Even if they think they know God, or that Negroes are like normal men—

(A teacup from the table next to Cathie appears to fall, as if by itself—

CATHIE catches it.)

MARGARET (cont'd.)

—Careful!

CATHIE

Sorry, Momma. It was an accident. Almost.

(CATHIE smiles. MARGARET goes back to work.

As CATHIE sets the teacup carefully on the tabletop again.)

CATHIE (cont'd.)

Momma?

MARGARET

You talk too much, you know that?

CATHIE

Mrs. Weekman had help. Had she not?

MARGARET

Of course. Mrs. Weekman. Who's she?

CATHIE

The family that lived here before us. Before the family before. A renter, like we are.

MARGARET

Do I know her?

CATHIE

She's alive now still. In Macedon. She had help with her four children, did she not?

MARGARET

I presume so.

CATHIE

She saw a ghost here once.

(MARGARET stops working.)

MARGARET

Mrs. Weekman did ... ?

CATHIE

The help did. Jane Lape was her name. Still is, she's alive now too, I think. This was only last year this all occurred. Or the year before that. — Jane Lape told Mr. Hyde's boy who told *me* ... that Jane Lape saw a man.

MARGARET

In this house?

CATHIE

In that pantry. At the top of the stairs down to the cellar.

(MARGARET sits down, across the table from her daughter.

She may even reach out and touch her daughter's hand—a glancing numb touch.)

MARGARET

... What did he look like? did she say?

CATHIE

Tall, and thin ... He wore gray pants and a long black coat, black hat, wide brim—you could scarcely see his face! ... He held this bag in his hands, a sack full of bottles of—very small vials of scent ... You could smell the peppermint, Jane said. You could hear the bottles clinking in the bag, like chimes ...

MARGARET

Like chimes? ... She told all this to you?

CATHIE

She told Mr. Hyde's boy, who told me: the man stood in the doorway, and watched her.

MARGARET

And what did he say?

CATHIE

Nothing.

MARGARET

Why not?

CATHIE

His throat been cut.

(MARGARET gasps. She crosses herself. Thrilled:)

MARGARET

—You mustn't tell this to anyone, ever!

(Footsteps come knocking up from the cellar, into the pantry. MARGARET and CATHIE start mildly in surprise at:

JOHN Fox, who enters the kitchen from the pantry.

He stands in the doorway, soft black hat on head, a dirty, deflated sack in his hands ... He looks at his wife and daughter.

He's an old man almost, late 50s, not aging well. His face is pale, gaunt, vacant; but he's still powerfully built: the arms and shoulders and hands of a blacksmith.

He doesn't say a word. He's holding the empty bag.)

JOHN

Help your sister.

CATHIE

Yes, sir—

JOHN

And I'll brook no more complaints from you. —Understand?

CATHIE

Yes, sir.

MARGARET

—Complaints, John?

JOHN

I heard everything. I was downstairs. *(Pause.)* Outside. Go.

(JOHN drops the empty sack to the table, as—

CATHIE exits. But she grabs another apple from the bushel, deftly, without being seen.

She's gone.

MARGARET continues to unpack and clean and stow, nervously, as if cheerful ...

JOHN sits down at the table.

He looks around him at the small, dark room, the dirty windows, the blinding white light outside ...

He stares ahead into nothing.

MARGARET, unpacking, unwrapping, glances at the empty sack.)

MARGARET

Have you stored all the apples in the cellar?

(He doesn't answer.)

MARGARET (cont'd.)

It was kind of the Posts—

JOHN

Can't you ever shut your mouth?

(She continues to work, busily, seemingly unperturbed.

In one of the upstage windows we see the top of CATHIE's head, outside, as if she's standing on something unsteady, a rock or log; now we see her face, peering at her parents through the dirty glass ...

MAGGIE's face appears in the other window, watching much more furtively, guiltily. She's watching her sister at the other window as much as she's watching her parents inside. Both their faces appear warped in the glass.

MARGARET finds a box of matches, moves to the stove and strikes a match, bends to the grate. JOHN stares at the back of her.

A knocking sound is heard, but not from either window—a loud report. The parents respond with some surprise, if not alarm, as the girls duck down out of view.

Lights out.)

MARGARET

—Oh!

2A. DARKNESS.

CATHIE

Ask him a question, Momma.

MARGARET

Ask him?

CATHIE

Anything you've always wanted to ask a soul ...

MARGARET

Anything?

MAGGIE

Something only a spirit would know, Momma.

CATHIE

A secret.

MARGARET

Secret?

CATHIE

Only a spirit would know ...

MARGARET

... How many children have I, Spirit?

(Slowly, we hear six knocks. The sound of MARGARET *gasping.*

Then: a seventh knock.)

MAGGIE

There aren't seven of us. *(Short pause.)* ... Momma?

2. PANTRY.

(Lights up on the sisters in their one small bed together. It's the middle of the night.

No candlelight, just moonlight off snow and the black shapes of branches in the room's one, tall, narrow window.

The walls and floor are bare.)

CATHIE

Margaretta. Margaret. Maggie.

MAGGIE

I'm sleeping.

CATHIE

No you're not.

MAGGIE

Not now ...

CATHIE

Listen:

(They listen.)

MAGGIE

... What is it?

CATHIE

Somebody's downstairs, in the cellar.

MAGGIE

No there isn't ...

CATHIE

—There is!

MAGGIE

—There's no one down there, Cathie!

CATHIE

I hear him. Shuffling.

MAGGIE

Shuffling?

CATHIE

Like an animal does ...

MAGGIE

It's only Father.

CATHIE

Doing what do you suppose?

MAGGIE

Whatever it is he does down there.

CATHIE

What *does* he do? Do you know? —I've gone down there—

MAGGIE

You shouldn't, Cathie—

CATHIE

You've gone down there too: I've seen you.

(A pause.)

CATHIE (cont'd.)

And I found the bottles ...

Do you remember Jane Lape said the ghost had been a pedlar, in life? That's why he held that bag in his hands, full of bottles ...

MAGGIE

Those were perfume bottles—

CATHIE

The ones I found were empty. The glasses were all green. Underneath an old stinking tarp ... The labels had all been scratched away.

—And when I held them to my nose they smelled like peppermint.

(Pause.)

MAGGIE

It's the fields.

CATHIE

What's the fields?

MAGGIE

All these fields around here are full of peppermint, in the spring. You'll see. That's what's farmed out here mainly.

CATHIE

It's not springtime now.

MAGGIE

It will be soon. You'll see.

CATHIE

"The snow is deep, and falling ever faster" ...

MAGGIE

Who said that?

CATHIE

I don't know. Some poet.

(CATHIE starts with fear.)

MAGGIE

It's nobody, Cathie—

CATHIE

—It's Nobodaddy!

MAGGIE

Who's that?

CATHIE

Just another name for Splitfoot.

MAGGIE

Who's Splitfoot?

CATHIE

You know ...

MAGGIE

You mustn't say those names— !

CATHIE

You mustn't say mustn't because it makes you sound like Mother! Mother's crazy!

MAGGIE

That's not true!

CATHIE

She can't stop talking about nothing! That's crazy!

(A quiet, single knock, from somewhere down below. They both hear it this time.)

CATHIE (cont'd.)

You pretend like you don't hear it but you do ...

MAGGIE

It's Father, I know it is—

CATHIE

It's not!

MAGGIE

How do you know?

CATHIE

If he went down there while we were sleeping we would've seen him pass through. He would've stepped on us.

MAGGIE

He got in from the outside then. Through the cellar door.

CATHIE

If you listen you can hear him breathing, through the wall ... He's asleep, on the other side, with Momma.

(Another knock, somewhat louder.)

CATHIE (cont'd.)

He's walking up the stairs now—

MAGGIE

It's the house.

CATHIE

How the house?

MAGGIE

It's an old house—houses make sounds—

(Another knock, louder. Like a footfall on the cellar stairs.)

MAGGIE (cont'd.)

—It's all in your imagination!

CATHIE

Are we imagining this together then?

(MAGGIE fumbles for her box of matches, strikes a match—about to light the candle:)

CATHIE (cont'd.)

—Don't!

(CATHIE waves or claps or blows the match out.)

CATHIE (cont'd.)

You'll scare him off that way ...

(Another knock, louder.

CATHIE gets out of bed.)

CATHIE (cont'd.)

Maybe he's one of those men, who go fishing in the creek at night ...

MAGGIE

A man?

CATHIE

Who chop holes in the ice with their axes and saws ...

MAGGIE

It's too late for night-fishing, Cathie ...

CATHIE

That's why it's called night-fishing!

MAGGIE

—It's nature I bet.

CATHIE

What kind?

MAGGIE

Outside. Just sounds like it's in. The trees, there's so many of them overhanging the house— !

CATHIE

Trees don't walk around the cellar, up stairs.

MAGGIE

Trees have branches.

CATHIE

You mean arms that hold things ... like axes!

MAGGIE

—Stop it!

CATHIE

Because it *is* a man. I can feel it ...

One of those fishermen from the Ganargua ... When all his friends have gone home, to their families ... This one has nowhere to go. He watches us, through that window there ...

And he's crept into our house, through the cellar door—

MAGGIE

What for?

CATHIE

What all men want: to kill us.

(They listen.)

MAGGIE

It's rats, probably.

CATHIE

—We have rats?

MAGGIE

I don't know, maybe.

CATHIE

That's what Mrs. Bell told Lucretia.

MAGGIE

Who's Mrs. Bell?

CATHIE

Who lived here before us. Before the Weekmans too, long time ago, maybe four, five years ... Nobody likes the Bells around here. I don't know why that is. They live in Lyons now.

MAGGIE

Who's Lucretia?

CATHIE

Pulver. The girl who told the girl who worked for the Weekmans, Jane Lape, after the Bells, who talked to Mr. Hyde's boy, who told me:

How one night Lucretia Pulver went down to the cellar for some things, some jam maybe, and she fell down! the dirt was so loose and choppy down there ... Like someone been digging ... She fell down on her knees. She came upstairs and told Mrs. Bell in the kitchen who said those was only just rat holes the rats had made. She gave Lucretia Pulver a spoonful of jam ...

MAGGIE

Why ... ?

CATHIE

And before that—Lucretia said she saw the pedlar here the night he disappeared, with his bag full of perfumes and buttons and ribbons and thimbles ... They asked him to spend the night, if he cared to. Then they sent Lucretia away—for three whole days! and when she came back ... Mrs. Bell wore that pedlar's thimble on her finger.

MAGGIE

His thimble?

CATHIE

Made of silver ... And there were those rat holes down below!

(Silence. They listen.

A long pause ... Is he gone?

A very loud knock, this time as if coming from the other side of the door.)

MAGGIE

—It's nobody!

CATHIE

—It's Nobodaddy!

(Another knock: twice.)

MAGGIE

—Don't open it, Cathie! Please!

CATHIE

You believe in him now?

(Pause. CATHIE opens the cellar door.)

MAGGIE

Who is it? Who's there?

(CATHIE turns to her sister, smiling:)

CATHIE

Nobody.

(Blackout.)

3A. DARKNESS.

MARGARET

How many years ago were you murdered, Spirit? Count the years for me, please.

(Five raps.)

CATHIE

—The Bells!

MARGARET

And where are you now? I mean, of course, where is your body buried?

(Knocking: an urgent rapping from below, almost an arrhythmic crackle along the floor.)

3. KITCHEN.

(Steel gray morning. MARGARET is busy in the kitchen, though doing what is anyone's guess.

MAGGIE enters, looking tired, heads straight for the apples on the table in the bowl.)

MAGGIE

Where's Father?

MARGARET

Can't you hear? he's outside, chopping wood ...

(A distinct chopping sound, not far off, continues sporadically throughout the scene, except where noted.)

MAGGIE

Why isn't he out building our new house?

(Her mother watches her. MAGGIE turns away.)

MARGARET

You've seen the snow ...

MAGGIE

It snows all winter long ...

MARGARET

Everyone knows that!

MAGGIE

"The snow is deep, and falling ever faster" ...

MARGARET

What is that, a song?

MAGGIE

Can't you build a house in winter?

MARGARET

Not easily. Not well. You look ill.

MAGGIE

I'm tired. I don't sleep well here ...

MARGARET

You're reading again, at night. I told you not to.
... What are you reading?

MAGGIE

I'm hungry.

MARGARET

Make yourself some oats then, if you're so hungry ...

MAGGIE

I'm not a horse ...

(MAGGIE bites into an apple.)

MARGARET

That's right. You're a pig, with that apple in your mouth. I find these apples tart, don't you? It's a wonder you're so stout when I never see you eat.

MAGGIE

It's cold in here, all the time ...

MARGARET

I'm not cold. Are you? I keep myself moving. You should keep yourself moving more. That way you would be trim, like Cathie is. You may add some more wood if you like.

MAGGIE

There isn't any wood.

MARGARET

That's because your father's outside chopping it, now isn't he. Move your chair closer to that stove if you're so cold ...

(MAGGIE moves her chair closer to the dim stove—with a grating sound that irritates her mother.)

MAGGIE

Where's Cathie?

MARGARET

You slept late. She's at school. I let you. —You were very pale last night!

MAGGIE

I told you I can't sleep.

MARGARET

Is it your headaches again ... ?

(MARGARET studies MAGGIE's face.)

MARGARET (cont'd.)

It's the fault of those books. It will ruin your eyes, it will age you. Boys don't like girls who read books. What are you reading again?

(MARGARET has returned to her work: though it's still not clear if she's cleaning, cooking, or just moving things around.

MAGGIE watches her mother closely.)

MARGARET (cont'd.)

Because some books are good, and some are bad. Within reason. All my children are intelligent! I'm intelligent, for a girl. I was told so in my youth. My school. My father did not care. My mother laughed and laughed—

MAGGIE

I wish we had a cow.

MARGARET

—Don't be stupid.

MAGGIE

I could milk it.

MARGARET

We're not dairy farmers. —Thank goodness for that!

MAGGIE

I wish I could go to school, then. Still.

MARGARET

You're too old. You'll stay home with me now. Don't you want that? Don't you want to stay home with your father and I?

Soon you'll have your *own* house, when you're married ... and then we'll never see you again ... We want you to stay with us, as long as we can keep you. Don't you want that too?

(Short pause.)

MAGGIE

I think I'll get married soon because I'm so bored.

MARGARET

—You don't know any boys!

MAGGIE

I do.

MARGARET

Name one!

MAGGIE

Nobodaddy.

MARGARET

Who's that?

MAGGIE

In the city I knew lots of boys. At school. Not out here, in the sticks ...

MARGARET

You'll go to church on Sundays.

MAGGIE

—I hate church.

MARGARET

You mustn't say that. You mustn't let your father hear you!

MAGGIE

You don't like it there.

MARGARET

I'm not a Methodist ...

(She crosses herself.)

MAGGIE

Everyone sits around all day, so sad for what they've done ... Nobody ever says what they've done!

MARGARET

Why should they tell you? You're not God.

MAGGIE

Do you like it here in Hydesville?

(Pause.)

MAGGIE (cont'd.)

You look like you hate it here. All the time.

MARGARET

Are you watching me ... ?

MAGGIE

You stare out that window there like you're looking down into a bucket. An empty one.

MARGARET

It's quiet. Your father likes the quiet. I like the quiet too.

(MARGARET stares out the window while she works.)

MAGGIE

I could get a job ...

MARGARET

Doing what, do you suppose?

MAGGIE

Like Leah does. In Rochester.

(MARGARET takes the apple core from MAGGIE. Returns to her busy activity.)

MARGARET

Your sister has to work. She hasn't got a choice, she hasn't got a man.

MAGGIE

She used to have one.

MARGARET

Leah married far too young. —I told her!

MAGGIE

You married young. Didn't you?

(MARGARET won't turn around, continues working.)

MARGARET

You have my name, but I swear you look just like her, the *body* ...

MAGGIE

(Quietly, as if to herself.)

I wish I was a man sometimes. Because men can disappear ...

(MARGARET turns around, deeply agitated.)

MAGGIE (cont'd.)

Or—I wish I'd never need a man!

MARGARET

—You *sound* like Leah now, too!

MAGGIE

Like a teacher?

MARGARET

A *piano* teacher ...

MAGGIE

I wish I could play the piano ...

MARGARET

—And a Hicksite to boot! An agitator ... She thinks she knows so much! She and that brother of yours, all those *books* ... At least your sister has religion, some kind ... I think your brother is a free-thinker—

MAGGIE

No he's not— !

MARGARET

In *secret* ... I don't know why he thinks so much of himself. His mind ... He's dull! That's what I think. Sanctimonious! that's the word. They're both so sanctimonious it hurts my teeth sometimes!

MAGGIE

Don't you miss her though?

MARGARET

I miss my granddaughter. Lizzie. I miss her every day.

MAGGIE

Won't you write them a letter then?

MARGARET

Why should I? Why don't they! They can write. Leah wants silence now, I don't know why that is ... Do you? I don't know why we can't all be friends.

Forgive and forget, that's what I've always said. Isn't it? —Isn't it? Though I don't know what she thinks I've done. Do you?

MAGGIE

No.

MARGARET

It was your father ... A disagreement. —Of the slightest kind! I don't know where it comes from. I don't know why that is ... Do you?

MAGGIE

No.

MARGARET

I think she's rather crazed. I think her soul's been soured. Won't you write a letter for me to her please?

MAGGIE

Saying what?

MARGARET

That she really must apologize. That I miss my granddaughter Lizzie. That soon we'll all be dead and then won't she be sorry? Because life is so terribly short ... and family is so precious. There's nothing more precious than that. You see, family is like this knot, made of blood, that must never come untied. And if you untie it, well then: we bleed. The whole family does.

And in the end all you have is who you come from, there's no escaping that.

(Pause.)

MARGARET (cont'd.)

Will you write that for me please?

MAGGIE

All right. I'll try.

MARGARET

You mustn't let your father know.

—She's untied it anyway, as have all your other sisters ... I don't know why that is. Only David likes us now. Do you know why?

MAGGIE

Did we move because of Leah?

(MARGARET gives her daughter a bowl and a spoon to mix.)

MARGARET

Mix this for me please, while you're busy asking questions ...

(MARGARET keeps herself busy, back turned, rearranging still to no apparent purpose. MAGGIE mixes and mixes.)

MAGGIE

I could live with Leah. Like we did last summer. On Sophia Street. I could get a job, and send home money—

MARGARET

What have you been reading?

(MAGGIE doesn't answer her.)

MARGARET (cont'd.)

Because I know what you've been reading. I don't want you reading that book. Understand me? —I don't approve of such books!

Because some books are shameful. You know that. Otherwise you would not have felt the need to hide it.

(MAGGIE doesn't respond.)

MARGARET (cont'd.)

You'll return it to your brother please. Understand me? Otherwise I'll have to tell Father ... Do you want that?

What you've been up to, that book ...

(Another long pause.)

MARGARET (cont'd.)

Are we done here? let me see ...

(MARGARET takes the bowl back from MAGGIE, mixes it herself furiously ...

She returns, herself and the bowl, to her business.

Outside the sound of JOHN chopping wood is particularly strong.)

MAGGIE

Momma ... this morning I stained the bedclothes some ... Some got on Cathie: she's not angry.

(Long pause.)

MAGGIE (cont'd.)

I'm out of rags now. That's all.

MARGARET

Rinse this for me please, Margaretta ...

(MAGGIE gets up, moves to the basin. Rinses the bowl out, as:

MARGARET puts on her coat.)

MARGARET (cont'd.)

I'll up to Newark then. I'll be home ere long. If your father wants his supper then you'll fix it for him please.

(MARGARET exits by the back door.

After a moment alone, washing ...

MAGGIE hurls the bowl against the wall. Where it shatters in a cloud.

Long pause. The sound of her father chopping wood has stopped.

Terrified, MAGGIE rushes for the broom.

On the floor, sweeping up the shards and dust, she pricks her finger slightly:)

MAGGIE

Ow—

(She sucks her finger ...

Some gentle rapping at the kitchen door now. She stands, her clean-up interrupted. She tries desperately to hide the broom.

As DAVID Fox, 28, enters, hat and coat dusted in snow. He's tense, distracted.)

MAGGIE (cont'd.)

I thought you were Father.

DAVID

I'm not.

MAGGIE

I know that ...

DAVID

I didn't mean to frighten you ...

MAGGIE

You didn't.

DAVID

You looked afraid. *(He smiles.)* —You look scared right now.

MAGGIE

So do you.

(MAGGIE gets back to sweeping. As DAVID takes off his coat and hat, brushing off more snow.)

DAVID

Where is he?

MAGGIE

Outside, chopping wood.

DAVID

He's not.

(It's true: the chopping sound has stopped.)

MAGGIE

... He's in the cellar then. I don't know. Wait here.

(She disappears into the pantry. A moment of DAVID alone, looking suddenly quite pained, exhausted.

He's cold; he moves to the stove: it makes no difference ...

He moves to the table and the apples. He rearranges them in the bowl.

MAGGIE reappears with a large, black, worn book. DAVID recomposes himself.)

DAVID

Did it help?

MAGGIE

With what?

DAVID

Whatever it was you needed it for ...

MAGGIE

I'm curious, that's all.

DAVID

It's a good book for that ...

(He sits down at the table.

MAGGIE places the book on the table. He slides it closer to himself.)

DAVID (cont'd.)

There's nothing shameful about the body, Maggie. When I was a kid I wanted to be a doctor.

MAGGIE

Why aren't you?

DAVID

We could use it at home now, actually ...

(He takes an apple from the bowl.

Gesturing to the shards on the floor, perhaps the spot on the wall:)

DAVID (cont'd.)

What happened here?

MAGGIE

(Shrugging.)

Accident.

DAVID

Looks like it ... *(He eats his apple.)*
You sure you're not spooked?

MAGGIE

By you?

DAVID

The "spook-house" ... That's what people call it around here.

MAGGIE

I know. Why?

DAVID

Well, it's ugly. For one. And small. Poor people live here.

(MAGGIE sits down across from him.)

MAGGIE

What happened with the Bells, Dave?

DAVID

Who?

MAGGIE

The Bells. Who lived here before the Weekmans. He must have been a bad man.

DAVID

What makes you say that?

MAGGIE

No one liked him. Or they don't remember him at all. He must have not spoken much, like Father. He must've been a bad man.

DAVID

I don't know much about the Bells ... I'd see him in the road sometimes to say hello. They live in Lyons now. *(Eats his apple.)*
These are good!

MAGGIE

Cathie's heard stories about them too.

DAVID

The Bells?

MAGGIE

She scares herself sometimes.

DAVID

She doesn't scare you? *(He smiles.)* I wouldn't let it bother me none ... Every house around here's supposed to be haunted ...

(He looks preoccupied; eats his apple.)

DAVID (cont'd.)

I mean, enough bad things happen out here, Maggie. —Terrible, sick-making things!

MAGGIE

Like what?

DAVID

Well. Last winter Mrs. Iverson killed herself, and her baby boy.

MAGGIE

Why ... ?

DAVID

Slit her throat. After doing it to her baby first.

MAGGIE

How could she ... ?

DAVID

With a shard of glass. A mirror. *(He shrugs.)* She got deranged. It's the winter.

(Eats his apple.)

MAGGIE

The Iversons live down the road ...

DAVID

Some do.

That's not counting typhus, malaria, diphtheria ... There's plenty of perfectly natural reasons to feel scared out here ...

(He finishes his apple—or as much of it as he cares to.

He stands, moves the chair a few times, trying to find just the right placement for it ...)

DAVID (cont'd.)

Where's she gone to?

MAGGIE

Up to Newark.

DAVID

For the doctor?

MAGGIE

I'm not sick. Are you? —What do you need a doctor for, Dave?

DAVID

No, no, the baby does. I'm tired ... I thought, for a moment ... She doesn't know Ella's sick.

MAGGIE

—What's wrong with Ella, Dave?

(DAVID shrugs.)

MAGGIE (cont'd.)

Does Elizabeth need help— ?

DAVID

She can't stand it down here ...

MAGGIE

Let me come up there and help you then—

DAVID

She's not going to die, I've read about this—in that book. She's throwing up. I can't stand the *sound* ... I'm not—women are stronger ... If she dies it won't bother me none ...

Some women have a baby each spring and each winter they plant him in the ground ...

(Pause.)

DAVID (cont'd.)

Not everybody's as lucky as our parents.

MAGGIE

Lucky how?

DAVID

Six kids! and not one of them died ...

She's only our first ...

MAGGIE

One died.

DAVID

Which one?

MAGGIE

The one with no name.

DAVID

Don't be so dramatic—you sound like Cathie now!

MAGGIE

I don't know its name. A girl. She died before Leah was born.

DAVID

—*Before* Leah?

MAGGIE

I heard them once, talking—

DAVID

I don't think that's so ...

MAGGIE

At Leah's house last summer. After Ella was born.

(Short pause. DAVID stares ahead into nothing.)

MAGGIE (cont'd.)

Momma must have been very young to have had a baby before Leah ...

DAVID

—Do you think she went to heaven, that girl? Or any child that dies unbaptized?

Do you think they go to heaven, or to hell?

MAGGIE

Who knows?

DAVID

Who knows ... Do they go nowhere then?

MAGGIE

They're innocent, so—

DAVID

They *have* to go to heaven.

MAGGIE

I think so ...

DAVID

I don't believe in either.

MAGGIE

That's what Mother was sad about, when we heard her crying, in the dark. They were shouting at each other, but in whispers ... That baby hadn't been baptized and she said it was all his fault somehow ...

... Ella's baptized, right?

DAVID

Why would she be?

MAGGIE

Oh, David. Everyone does.

DAVID

I don't believe in it. I don't think it matters.

MAGGIE

Why don't you do it then, just in case?

DAVID

I'm not like Father claims to be ...

MAGGIE

You don't think he means it?

DAVID

Who knows?

MAGGIE

He wasn't always like that, was he? He didn't always have God.

(Pause.)

MAGGIE (cont'd.)

—What happened in our family, Dave? when we weren't born yet. In the years between you four and we two?

DAVID

... Why, is something happening now?

MAGGIE

All I mean is, there was this time. When father wasn't here. In the family ... Where was he? I'm old enough to know now.

DAVID

You don't know?

(She shakes her head "no.")

DAVID (cont'd.)

I'm not the one who should be telling you this—

MAGGIE

How long was he gone, Dave?

DAVID

You promise me you won't tell anyone?

(She nods her head "yes.")

DAVID (cont'd.)

Twelve years. I don't know what he got up to. Mother knows, maybe. I wouldn't ask her if I were you.

—You can't ask her about this, okay? It's a secret.

MAGGIE

I won't.

DAVID

I thought he was dead. Mother let me think so.

MAGGIE

Why did he leave us in the first place?

DAVID

He didn't leave us. He left Momma.

MAGGIE

Why did he come back?

DAVID

Who knows? You'd have to ask her that too ...

If you ask her, you figured this all out on your own. Okay?

(MAGGIES nods.)

DAVID (cont'd.)

It was because of the drinking ... You know, whiskey.

MAGGIE

I know what drinking is—

DAVID

How do you know?

MAGGIE

Why did he drink?

DAVID

Some people do. They like it. Makes me sick, just the smell of it ...

(He sniffs the air absently ... Rearranges the apples in the bowl.)

MAGGIE

What did he do when he was drunk?

DAVID

He wasn't kind.

MAGGIE

What did he do?

DAVID

Nothing. He's like he is now. Doesn't look at you, God help you when he does.

Once, we were eating. Mother was asking me those questions, you know, about nothing? and I said under my breath, Don't you ever stop talking? I was your age, maybe. And Father grabbed a rolling pin and broke my arm. *(Pause.)* I don't know if he was drunk when he did it.

I deserved it, in some ways.

MAGGIE

... Why do you even talk to him now ... ?

DAVID

What else can I do?

MAGGIE

Are you scared of him? You're as strong as he is now— !

(Pause.)

MAGGIE (cont'd.)

You're paying the rent on this place, aren't you?

(DAVID stands.)

DAVID

He's fine, he's ashamed. —He's a Methodist, he's taken the pledge. He carries that paper in his pocket.

MAGGIE

It must taste good to drink ...

(DAVID looks askance at her.)

MAGGIE (cont'd.)

Otherwise why do it?

(The sound of someone entering the house through the front door.)

DAVID

You mustn't say that ever.

MAGGIE

You mustn't say mustn't because it makes you sound like Mother.

(CATHIE comes rushing in from the sitting room, having entered through the front door.

She's splashed up to her chest in snow.)

CATHIE

—Davey!

DAVID

My little snow fox!

CATHIE

I knew I'd find you here—

DAVID

I saw you in the fields this morning—in the snow, with a sparrow in your mouth! —My littlest snow fox—you must've been so hungry!

(He tickles her.)

CATHIE

—Get off me!

MAGGIE

You mustn't come in through the sitting room, Cathie. You've tracked snow all throughout the house ...

CATHIE

So? —I met someone, Davey—

DAVID

"So?"

CATHIE

A woman. In the fields. —She was beautiful!

DAVID

What's she like?

CATHIE

A bird. Like a sparrow, like you said. She wore gray clothes, like a Quaker. Like Leah does. She stopped me in the fields ... Her legs were so bare.

I couldn't see her feet, they disappeared down into the snow ... I asked her if she was cold. And she said, "One of your family will die soon. Mourn not for her. She will be happy with the angels."

(DAVID looks at CATHIE, with hurt, confusion.)

MAGGIE

... Who is she, Cathie?

CATHIE

She said she was the spirit of the infant Ella Fox.

(DAVID is suddenly quite angry. He might shake CATHIE, or strike her.

Instead, he puts on his coat. He picks up his book. And exits quickly, by the kitchen door.

A long pause. CATHIE stifles a sob.)

CATHIE (cont'd.)

... But I *did* see her ...

(As CATHIE moves to her sister, she steps in the leftover dust and shards of the bowl.

MAGGIE stoops and picks up a shard:)

MAGGIE

It shattered. By itself.

(CATHIE smiles at that, MAGGIE smiles in return. Blackout.)

4A. DARKNESS.

MARGARET

Were you killed by a shotgun blast?

(Nothing.)

MARGARET (cont'd.)

Were you poisoned in your food?

(No raps.)

MARGARET (cont'd.)

Were you stabbed by a butcher's knife?

(Two raps. The girls and their mother gasp.)

MARGARET (cont'd.)

Was your throat slit by a butcher's knife like a pig while you slept as a guest in this house?

(As moonlight rises on:)

4. PANTRY.

(Late at night, the girls out of bed, barefoot.

They face each other across the floor, in moonlight.)

MAGGIE

I'm cold.

CATHIE

You must be brave.

MAGGIE

Can I put my stockings on?

CATHIE

No.

(They wait expectantly; MAGGIE perhaps less so.)

MAGGIE

What should I do now?

CATHIE

That I can not say.

MAGGIE

Why not?

CATHIE

—If I tell you then it won't happen for me anymore.

MAGGIE

Can't you show me?

CATHIE

You must use your imagination, Maggie. *(Pause.)* Watch.

(MAGGIE watches everywhere.)

MAGGIE

What's going to happen?

CATHIE

Just wait. You'll see.

MAGGIE

What am I waiting for?

CATHIE

For something to *come* to you ...

MAGGIE

Like an idea does?

CATHIE

Or *through* you.

MAGGIE

Like electricity?

CATHIE

Like a *spirit* does ...

MAGGIE

—Like a telegraph!

CATHIE

Or like lightning hits a house.

MAGGIE

—And you're the house?

CATHIE

Like a guitar is played ...

MAGGIE

And you're the guitar. —I wish I could play the guitar. Or any instrument, for that matter ...

CATHIE

You will: one day: I see it.

MAGGIE

Like a piano, and Spirit plays the keys. —And we're the keys!

CATHIE

We both are—

MAGGIE

You're the black keys, and I'm the white—

CATHIE

I'm the left hand, and you're the right—

MAGGIE

We're rhyming now! We're rhyming! —Is it happening? is it happening now for me?

CATHIE

Who knows?

MAGGIE

"Who knows?"

CATHIE

"Who knows?"

(They listen.)

MAGGIE

Are we witches then, Cathie? ... Like Momma's momma was?

CATHIE

I hear him sometimes, in my ear.

MAGGIE

What's he saying to you ... ?

CATHIE

I don't know what he wants from me ...

(CATHIE shivers.)

MAGGIE

I'll help you, Cathie. I'll protect you. I won't go away.

(MAGGIE reaches out her hand to CATHIE. They touch fingers across the floor. As if completing an electrical circuit between them.

Suddenly a distinct, if quiet, rapping sound from the floor beneath CATHIE.)

MAGGIE (cont'd.)

—Is it happening?

CATHIE

—Mr. Splitfoot!

MAGGIE

—Is it happening now for me?

CATHIE

Open your eyes, Maggie! —Look!

MAGGIE

You mean listen— !

CATHIE

No—open your eyes!

(Again: a distinct rapping sound from the floor beneath CATHIE, louder.

Pause.

Then: weakly, faintly, a rapping on the floor under MAGGIE's feet.

The girls run to each other, squealing. They embrace.

Another knocking sound, this time from the wall of their parents' bedroom.)

MARGARET

(Off.)

—Girls?

(The girls jump into their bed and pull the blankets over their heads, squealing with a barely suppressed joy.)

5. SITTING ROOM.

(A windy night. The sounds of wind and the occasional, muted whine and squeak and knocking sound.

JOHN, kneeling backwards on his chair. This chair has been brought with them: its deep cushion is mostly threadbare. But it's clearly the best piece of furniture they still own.

JOHN's praying now, brow tight, face turned upward, eyes closed. A tall candle burns beside him, beside his open Bible.

This is the first time we've seen the sitting room: it's meant to be cozy, but it's not.

The stove beside John burns warmly, surprisingly; a round table has been pushed aside, still covered in its dirty cloth. Some things piled on it.

CATHIE enters barefoot in her nightdress. Silently. She watches, from just outside this cone of candlelight, as her father prays ...

JOHN opens his eyes, backing off his chair with surprise.)

CATHIE

You heard it.

(JOHN looks at her, confused.)

CATHIE (cont'd.)

On the chair, while you knelt. You heard the rapping. Did you not?

(Another pause.)

CATHIE (cont'd.)

You backed away. I saw you—

JOHN

Go to bed now, Cathie ...

(She steps into the candlelight.)

CATHIE

I can't.

JOHN

Why not?

CATHIE

Mr. Splitfoot keeps me up at night. —Have you really never heard him?

JOHN

I don't know who that is ...

CATHIE

He makes the sounds you hear.

(JOHN sits down.)

JOHN

It's a windy night tonight ...

CATHIE

Not every night.

JOHN

This is an old house, Cathie ...

CATHIE

When was it built, Father?

JOHN

Thirty years ago, at least.

CATHIE

That's not old. David's almost that old, and he's still a boy, in many ways. Have you seen Ella? Doctor says she's mending, but you never know ...

JOHN

No, you never know ...

CATHIE

"Who knows?" ...

JOHN

She was born too soon. Sickly. Too small. Like you. That's life.

CATHIE

"That's life" ...

JOHN

Where's your sister now?

CATHIE

Which one?

JOHN

You know which one I'm talking about, Catherine ...

CATHIE

I have so many sisters: Beth, who lives in Consecon, in Canada. With her family. Marie, who lives nearby yet we never see her. I don't know why that is. Do you? They never write us letters, like Leah doesn't anymore ...

(CATHIE sits down on one of the chairs.)

CATHIE (cont'd.)

Maggie's got one of her headaches again ...

JOHN

Sit with me.

(He pats his thighs. She won't move.)

JOHN (cont'd.)

What's wrong?

CATHIE

You smell.

JOHN

What do I smell of?

CATHIE

Something bad.

JOHN

I'm a man, men smell bad. It's bad, maybe, to a girl like you ... But one day you'll marry, and he'll smell like me ... And then it won't seem so bad anymore.

(He pats his thighs again; reaches out his hand.

She gets up and moves to him. Leans onto his lap. She's uncomfortable.

Gently, he begins stroking her back ...

She closes her eyes, as if against her will, with the pleasure of it.

He smokes his pipe. Stops caressing her, momentarily, when she hears something.)

JOHN (cont'd.)

It's nothing. It's the wind.

(He continues to caress her, distractedly.)

JOHN (cont'd.)

It's the house at night. —A window sash, like this one.

(He reaches out to the window pane, pushes on the sash: knocks it twice.

Distinctly: two soft taps are heard, as if in response.)

CATHIE

You see?

JOHN

It's nothing.

CATHIE

—Do it again!

JOHN

It's the wood.

CATHIE

How the wood?

JOHN

Expanding and contracting—

CATHIE

Like breathing?

JOHN

Maybe it's the Dueslers, across the field, dancing ...

CATHIE

Dancing?

JOHN

You shouldn't listen so much.

CATHIE

You've heard it. I know you have.

JOHN

I've heard your sister and you, scaring your mother half to death.

CATHIE

She scares us!

JOHN

I've heard trees, and wind. And rats.

CATHIE

—I'm not afraid of rats.

JOHN

I've heard foxes.

CATHIE

We're the Foxes!

JOHN

I know.

... I've heard all of these things, Cathie ... But I've yet to hear the sound of your Mr. Splitfoot.

(CATHIE listens.)

JOHN (cont'd.)

Ghosts aren't real. You know that.

CATHIE

What about the Holy Ghost?

JOHN

All right, there's one.

CATHIE

Ghosts are in the Bible: there are angels, and devils. —God speaks to men all the time! And women.

JOHN

These were prophets. Are you one?

CATHIE

I think I may be.

(JOHN stops caressing her altogether.)

JOHN

That is a blasphemy, my dear.

CATHIE

Where do we go then, if we die? if there are no spirits?

JOHN

Heaven, if we're lucky.

CATHIE

And good.

JOHN

Yes. If we are good.

CATHIE

And hell?

JOHN

If we die unsaved.

CATHIE

You mean not sorry.

JOHN

... That is what I mean.

CATHIE

Are you sorry?

(He doesn't answer her right away.)

JOHN

For what?

CATHIE

Whatever it is you've done.

(Short pause.)

JOHN

—Why do you call him "Mr. Splitfoot," do you suppose?

CATHIE

I don't know his Christian name.

JOHN

He doesn't have one.

CATHIE

I haven't asked him yet, I'm frightened to!

JOHN

You should be. A split-foot is a cloven hoof, Cathie. What else has a cloven hoof?

CATHIE

A girl.

(Pause. JOHN is obviously discomfited, confused by this response.)

JOHN

The Bible says that ghosts are but demons in disguise—

CATHIE

That's not so!

JOHN

And you must never talk to demons. They'll talk to you, sometimes, one way or another. They'll whisper in your ear. They'll ask you so many questions, like your mother does—and you must never answer them. Do you understand? They'll confuse you. They'll lead you astray. They'll destroy you, if you let them.

CATHIE

Is that how it is with the other kinds of spirits?

(He doesn't answer.)

CATHIE (cont'd.)

I've heard Mother call it that, the devil drink ...

(He pushes her off his lap, as he stands.)

JOHN

You'll stop scaring her now.

CATHIE

—But she's scaring me!

JOHN

You will not raise your voice to me! —Do you understand?

CATHIE

(Quietly.)

Yes, sir ...

JOHN

You are deceiving her! with your tales. You'll stop it. Now.

CATHIE

—I'm not deceiving!

JOHN

You'll not answer me! You'll say nothing when spoken to—do you understand?

(She doesn't answer. But slowly nods her head. Then quietly:)

CATHIE

"Nothing" ...

(MAGGIE appears, in the shadows of the kitchen through the doorway, listening, unseen.)

JOHN

Go to bed now, Cathie ...

CATHIE

Mr. Splitfoot—

JOHN

(Shouting.)

Enough of Mr. Splitfoot! There's no such thing as "Splitfoot"! You're imagining—

CATHIE

I'm not!

JOHN

—You're *lying!*

CATHIE

You don't hear it because you won't listen! Everybody hears him now—Mother, Maggie!

JOHN

Catherine—

CATHIE

It's happening in the pantry, while we sleep—it's happening right now, if you listen! I hear him all the time, scratching his fingernails on the wall—that's why I left! I can't stand it in there—he's waiting!

JOHN

For you?

CATHIE

—He knows things I shouldn't, about you. He says things I don't think are true—

(JOHN slaps her face, hard. She's too stunned to cry at first.

MAGGIE, hidden in the kitchen, hears the slap and shudders, as if her own face were struck.

JOHN moves to leave the room—for the kitchen?—he doesn't seem to know where to go in this very small house ... MAGGIE scurries back into the pantry to hide.

But now, behind him, in the sitting room, a knocking sound: three distinct, loud raps from somewhere in the room.

JOHN can't tell where it comes from. It stops him cold.)

CATHIE (cont'd.)

(Through tears.)

I swear it is not me ...

(The sound again: two knocks.)

JOHN

There's nothing in that sound but the Devil ...

CATHIE

It's not the Devil, Father. It's the spirit—of a man.

JOHN

Go to bed now ... No more lies ...

(He sits again.

Takes up his heavy Bible to read. Fumbles for his spectacles.

A knock upon the wall, as if behind his chair, louder than before: like someone's kicked the wall, violently.

He stands.)

CATHIE

—Where's it coming from now, Father? Can't you tell?

(Another knock, somewhere else, louder.)

JOHN

You'll stop it now! Do you hear me?

CATHIE

I swear it is not me!

(JOHN reaches for her, but she slips away, as—

MARGARET enters from their bedroom, candle in hand.)

MARGARET

What's going on out here, John?

JOHN

—Go to bed.

MARGARET

—What have you done, Catherine?

CATHIE

Me?

(Another loud rap.)

CATHIE (cont'd.)

—Momma!

MARGARET

John?

JOHN

It's the girls—

CATHIE

—It's not!

JOHN

It's Cathie and Maggie together ...

MARGARET

Where's Maggie now?

CATHIE

She's sleeping.

MARGARET

In this noise ... ?

JOHN

—She's banging the walls with her fists!

(JOHN bangs the wall with his fist.

Pause. Another loud thump, in response, very strong.)

MARGARET

... I hear it every night. You know I can't sleep either—

JOHN

You're always hearing things ...

(She tries to catch his gaze:)

MARGARET

John ... ? Are you well— ?

(JOHN moves quickly as if to seize or strike MARGARET—

A loud, angry report of rapping on the walls. CATHIE screams.

JOHN's candle has somehow been knocked to the ground. He rushes to stamp out the flame—he snaps his candle underfoot.)

MARGARET (cont'd.)

Careful!

CATHIE

—He's angry with us!

MARGARET

What for?

MAGGIE

Momma ... ?

(MAGGIE has appeared in the doorway from the kitchen.

The rapping continues—lower in volume—from random points in the room now, it seems.)

CATHIE

Where's it coming from now, Father? —If Maggie's doing it—

MAGGIE

Doing what?

CATHIE

Where's it coming from *now*?

JOHN

Shh ...

MAGGIE

—Momma?

MARGARET

Quiet now, girls, listen ... It's over there now, John.

CATHIE

On the floor ...

MAGGIE

He's angry with us ...

MARGARET

Why would he be?

CATHIE

—Mr. Splitfoot?

MARGARET

Where's it coming from *now*, John?

JOHN

Shut your mouth! All of you!

(A series of knocks, as if receding, as if footsteps walking off.)

MAGGIE

—He's going into our room!

(JOHN takes MARGARET's candle, exits into the kitchen for the pantry.

As MAGGIE rushes to her mother, in the now darkened room. The only light is moon- and starlight through the window, off snow.)

MARGARET

It's all right now, girls ... Shh ... Be quiet ... Quiet ...

(CATHIE joins them, embracing her sister and mother. MARGARET strokes CATHIE's hair, absently.

CATHIE closes her eyes, as if peacefully.)

MARGARET (cont'd.)

What is it, John? some animal?

JOHN

(Off.)

—It's no one!

(More rapping, on the floor.)

MARGARET

He's in the cellar now, John! I hear him—downstairs!

(The sound of JOHN descending the stairs to the cellar—in a hurry, a bit dangerously.

After a pause:)

MARGARET (cont'd.)

—John?

JOHN

(Off.)

There's no one down here! —The outside door is locked!

(The sound of someone rapping on the walls now, as if all around the outside walls of the house.

The girls, and their mother, shriek in terror.

MARGARET races to the front door, locks it.)

MARGARET

—He's outside now, John! —Someone is!

(The sound of JOHN opening up the cellar door, running outside, all around the outside of the house.)

JOHN

(Outside.)

Get out of here—you *devils!*

MAGGIE

It's boys, probably, Momma ... having fun with us. Because we're new here ...

CATHIE

(Strangely.)

It's the river ...

MAGGIE

Boys fishing in the river ... It's all right, Momma, don't be scared ...

(Silence. Then:

A knock at the front door. They're terrified.)

JOHN

(Through the door.)

It's me.

CATHIE

—Don't open it, Momma. Please.

(A moment: MARGARET looks inquiringly at her daughter.

More knocking at the front door.)

JOHN

(Outside.)

—Let me in!

(With great nervous difficulty, MARGARET opens the front door for JOHN; who stumbles inside, coatless, winded, snow on his boots up past his knees.

He sits down. MARGARET shuts the door, locks it.

JOHN speaks, bewildered:)

JOHN (cont'd.)

There's no one out there ... not even some footprints in the snow ...

(A long pause here. No one moves. They listen.

Silence. Is he gone?)

CATHIE

He's having fun with us.

(MARGARET moves—and just as she steps the floor comes alive with rapping sounds.

The rapping follows her wherever she steps. She tries to evade, as if the floor burns her feet.

The girls shriek—they're clinging to each other, their mother. The crackling raps follow them as they move. Their shrieking is almost joyful.

JOHN rushes to them—to contain them, to still them, as much as to protect them. All together, they're embracing each other now, not moving, breathing hard.

The rapping stops.

They breathe, holding onto each other.)

JOHN

I'll get help.

MARGARET

—We'll stay here.

MAGGIE

Why?

(Short pause. MARGARET looks to JOHN.)

JOHN

I'll go to the Redfield's, I saw a light on in their window, across the field—

MARGARET

Hurry up, John.

CATHIE

Yes, hurry up, Poppa. —And bring back lots of friends! The more the better it will be ...

(He exits through the front door again. A moment, then:

The rapping sounds, like footsteps walking away ...)

CATHIE (cont'd.)

He wants us to go into the bedroom.

(MARGARET takes her daughters' hands, and together they rush into the:)

6. BEDROOM.

(Continuously:

The room is messy, cramped. The parents' bed unmade, the air close.)

MARGARET

Get in bed.

(They climb into bed, all three of them. CATHIE laughs.)

MAGGIE

Don't laugh ...

CATHIE

I'm scared, that's all.

MARGARET

Hold my hands now please. Both of you.

(MARGARET lights a dim stub of candle.

They wait, huddled together in the bedclothes.

They listen.)

CATHIE

Momma, can we stay in here forever ... ?

(Their mother doesn't answer.

They sit, breathing hard. Listening.)

MAGGIE

What now?

(Silence.)

CATHIE

Mr. Splitfoot?

MAGGIE

—Don't say that.

CATHIE

Why not?

MAGGIE

What if it's true?

CATHIE

Mr. Splitfoot? Do as I do:

(CATHIE claps her hands three times.

The sound of someone rapping, as if their knuckles on wood, in response three times.

The girls cry out.)

CATHIE (cont'd.)

Ask him a question, Momma.

MARGARET

Ask him?

CATHIE

Anything you've always wanted to ask a soul ...

MARGARET

Anything?

MAGGIE

Something only a spirit would know, Momma.

CATHIE

A secret.

MARGARET

Secret?

CATHIE

Only a spirit would know ...

MARGARET

... How many children have I, Spirit?

(Slowly, we hear six knocks. The sound of MARGARET gasping.

Then: a seventh knock.)

MAGGIE

There aren't seven of us ...

(A pause. An unfamiliar sound.)

MAGGIE (cont'd.)

Momma?

(It sounds like MARGARET is crying.)

MARGARET

Oh, Spirit ... how could you know ... ?

(A long pause.)

MARGARET (cont'd.)

Is this a human being that answers my questions so rightly?

(Silence.)

MARGARET (cont'd.)

Is this a spirit? If so, make two raps.

(Silence. Then: two raps.)

MARGARET (cont'd.)

If an injured spirit, make two raps.

(Two very loud raps. The girls make terrified noises.)

MARGARET (cont'd.)

Were you injured in this house?

(Two raps.)

MARGARET (cont'd.)
How many years ago were you murdered, Spirit? Count the years for me, please.

(Five raps.)

CATHIE
—The Bells!

MARGARET
And where are you now? I mean, of course, where is your body buried?

(Knocking.)

MAGGIE
... That wasn't a yes or no question, Momma ...

(The sound continues: urgent rapping from below, the arrhythmic crackle on the floor.)

MARGARET
—Spirit?

CATHIE
He's buried downstairs, in the cellar!

(Two raps.)

MARGARET
How did you die? Were you killed by a shotgun blast?

(Nothing.)

MARGARET (cont'd.)
Were you poisoned in your food?

(No raps.)

MARGARET (cont'd.)
Were you stabbed by a butcher's knife?

(Two raps.)

MARGARET (cont'd.)
Was your throat slit by a butcher's knife like a pig while you slept as a guest in this house?

(Two raps.)

MARGARET (cont'd.)

Are you the pedlar, then? Are you indeed the traveling man of whom we've heard such tales?

(Suddenly, a draft of wind seems to blow the candle out—)

MARGARET (cont'd.)

—Oh!

(As a wind sweeps through the darkness and time passes—a few minutes or an hour, who knows?

Wind subsides as more knocking sounds break out—randomly issued, nonsensical, sounding very quickly like the sound of many people, knocking at the front door, the back door; doors opening, footsteps now in the house, voices.)

JOHN

(Off.)

... Margaret? ... girls? I've brought the Redfields, and the Redfields brought the Dueslers, and the Hydes. There's more coming! —Everyone wants to hear the sound!

END OF PART ONE

Part Two: "Come and Investigate"

7A. DARKNESS.

(A woman's voice:)

LEAH

Is the spirit desireth of conversation right now?

(Two raps.

The raps sound differently now: a new quality, if not character.)

LEAH (cont'd.)

Are you the spirit of Charles B. Rosna, murdered pedlar at Hydesville, New York?

(No raps.)

LEAH (cont'd.)

Are you someone new? some new soul?

7. BEDROOM.

(The sound of flies buzzing. Water in a stream, a crowd beyond. Lights rise on:

A spring morning. A month and a little more time has passed. Sunlight and some green budding leaves fill the dirty window pane.

The room is dim, cut with a shaft of dust-filled light ...

The women and girls only: MARGARET, *in bed, looking tired;* MAGGIE *and* CATHIE *beside her.* CATHIE, *especially, looks drained if not ill. Perhaps they have just woken up.*

LEAH, *34, strong-jawed, handsome; and* LIZZIE, *her daughter, a homely, dull-faced girl of 17; stand in the doorway together, appraising the room, each in their own way ... Their few bags lie at their feet. The room is crowded: where to stand?*

Both mother and daughter are dressed plainly in grays like Quakers. Their shoes and skirts are muddied to the shins, if not their knees in places. LIZZIE is lacking one shoe; her stocking droops with mud.

LIZZIE also suffers a light pink rash on her face, and the backs of her hands. She looks around, bored, distracted, grumpy. She scratches her face and body and hands.

LEAH holds a rolled up pamphlet; speaking with surprising humor:)

LEAH

I heard while I was playing, I was teaching my pupils, I was teaching them Bach. My pupils are amongst the brightest of the children of the most influential in the city: Grovers, Grangers, Posts. —Whom you know. Hicksites and reformers mainly, progressive philanthropists all. They respect me, despite our many—differences.

(She takes a step into the room, away from her daughter.)

LEAH (cont'd.)

And the mother of my pupils—this is Mrs. Little, I was with the Little girls—she interrupts me at my work and says, Have you read the pamphlet? And I say, What pamphlet is that, dear ... ? About Hydesville, says she. Where's that, in Canada? To which she replies, Where your family has gone to. *(Short pause.)* "Gone to" ... Can you imagine? — It's all about your family, this "pamphlet" ... Have you not heard the news? ... And of course I say I have heard, I *have* heard the news, when of course I have not. She hands me this pamphlet to read ... You may keep it, she says. Smiling at me. I do not wish to keep such trash inside my house.

And she's right, it is trash, it is poorly written trash! this writer is a very stupid man. It is vulgar, sensationalistic, hyperbolic if not outright fictitious. —It is truly unbelievable! Full of purplish prose and a quoted epigraph—from Shakespeare! no less, the title of which I shall not deign to mention ... It's fortunate she let me keep her copy though. Considering, as I have learned, in all our great, progressive city of nearly seven-aught-thousand souls ... there is not one copy left for purchase.

(No one can speak.)

LEAH (cont'd.)

Who is this, Mother? Who took your "affidavits"? He's made a fortune off you already ...

(LEAH kills a fly with the rolled up pamphlet.

LIZZIE jumps, as LEAH flicks the carcass off.)

MARGARET

(Wearily.)

He's a man ...

LEAH

Who is he?

MARGARET

A lawyer.

LEAH

Oh! —Well!

MARGARET

From Canandaigua. —He asked!

LEAH

Did you say this? Did any of you say anything *remotely* like this? —It doesn't sound like you—*or* Father.

I notice the girls have not been quoted ...

MARGARET

They're girls ...

LEAH

How can any of this possibly be true?

CATHIE

You must use your imagination, Leah ...

(Short pause. LEAH looks at CATHIE.)

LEAH

Oh no. I'm afraid I must use too much imagination, Cathie. In fact I fear I am spent.

I wasn't talking to you, by the way—

MARGARET

All of this is true, Leah. *(Short pause.)* More or less.

LEAH

In what ways less?

MARGARET

I don't know—I haven't read it all!

LEAH

How could you not?

MARGARET

—I haven't had the time!

LEAH

What have you been doing all day besides sleeping?

CATHIE

I have read it, Leah. And every bit of it happened just like it says it did in that pamphlet. —Right, Maggie?

LEAH

Yes, Maggie. You've been quiet.

(MAGGIE doesn't reply, turns her gaze away from LEAH's.)

LIZZIE

I'm hungry, Momma ...

(LEAH swats another fly with her pamphlet.

LIZZIE, startled, scratches at her rash again.)

LEAH

How can you be, you had chocolate on the boat—against my expressed wishes! She hides it in her clothes, poor thing, her sweets ... Will you just look at that face!

(LEAH swipes at LIZZIE's face now, with a tongue-moistened thumb.)

LIZZIE

—Get off me!

LEAH

(Still wiping.)

We took the packet-boat first thing this morning ... All the workingmen ... Her rash is flaring up!

Why don't you run outside and play with your cousins now, Lizzie? I'd like to speak with Nana alone.

CATHIE

We're not her cousins we're her aunts.

MARGARET

They'll have to play *inside,* Leah.

LEAH

Why?

LIZZIE

Yes, why ... ?

MARGARET

You've seen outside ... They'd be harassed, or worse.

LEAH

In what ways worse?

MARGARET

Lynched, by some.

LIZZIE

(Scratching herself.)

—"Lynched"?

CATHIE

Someone threw a brick through the window last night. That window there. Or they tried to anyway—it missed.

LEAH

What luck!

MARGARET

Some of them have called us horrid names, Lizzie ...

LIZZIE

Like what?

LEAH

Yes, like what, Mother?

MARGARET

I don't know why that is ... Some of them are our neighbors, even! yet they mean us only harm ...

CATHIE

Some of them are friends. Or they mean to be. *(Short pause.)*

It's not even eleven o'clock, on a Sunday, and already there are dozens and dozens— !

LEAH

You're famous. Congratulations.

(LEAH smiles. CATHIE watches her intently.)

LIZZIE

That's why we came to your back door ... When we came to the front we had to deny who we were. Somebody called out our names. Somebody tried to touch me ...

And then I lost my shoe in all that mud ...

(LEAH advances on the window, almost martially:)

LEAH

Why have they come?

CATHIE

Same as you ...

MARGARET

Why *have* you come here, Leah ... ?

(Short pause.)

LEAH

I'm your daughter. I'm their sister. The pamphlet says, "Come and investigate!" *(Short pause.)* So here I am.

(LIZZIE flops on the foot of the bed.)

LIZZIE

Have you *seen* the ghost, Cathie?

MAGGIE

We don't see him, Lizzie. When we let them in.

LIZZIE

—You let the lynchers *in?*

LEAH

Hello, Maggie. We thought you'd lost your tongue, we thought you'd been bewitched.

(MAGGIE meets LEAH's gaze this time, only briefly.)

MARGARET

We always let a few people in, Lizzie dear. A dozen at a time. Friends of friends.

CATHIE

That first night we had the whole town in here, practically! —A hundred or so, at least!

LEAH

Surely not a hundred ...

CATHIE

The Dueslers, and the Redfields—

LEAH

Where did they all stand?

CATHIE

—The Hydes and Jewells—

MAGGIE

More people kept coming, Lizzie.

LIZZIE

—What did the ghost say? when you let the people in?

MARGARET

Haven't you read the pamphlet, dear?

LIZZIE

She won't let me. She calls it a disgrace. She says I'll be corrupted.

LEAH

All she says is true. —Now go outside and play, Lizzie.

LIZZIE

—I haven't got a shoe!

LEAH

Whose fault is that, mine? —Stop scratching, I said! You'll only make it worse.

(With the rolled up pamphlet, LEAH swats LIZZIE's hands away from her face.)

MAGGIE

Everyone wants to know how many children they have, Lizzie. Or had. It's funny. That's always the first thing they ask! How many children have I, Spirit? And always ... he knows.

(MARGARET crosses herself. LIZZIE scratches slowly, surreptitiously.)

MARGARET

(To LIZZIE.)

It truly is a miracle, dear ...

MAGGIE

He told Mrs. Samuelson her son had died from morphine. He'd been a pharmacist: it was a suicide.

(MARGARET crosses herself again. LEAH sniffs.)

MAGGIE (cont'd.)

He told Mr. Iverson that his wife killed herself and her baby boy—with a shard of mirror glass! She'd been deranged, by winter.

LEAH

I presume Mrs. Samuelson and Mr. Iverson knew all this already ...

MARGARET

What?

CATHIE

—No one else did, Leah.

LEAH

So this ghost knows everybody's secrets?

(LEAH kills one, then two flies with her pamphlet. Where she kills them on the wall: dots of blood remain.)

LEAH (cont'd.)

Why the flies, Mother ... ?

MARGARET

(Shrugging.)

They're flies, it's spring ...

CATHIE

They sleep in the walls in winter, and they wake up in the spring.

LIZZIE

—That's filthy!

MARGARET

It's true: our house has come alive—with nature!

CATHIE

We've got fungus in our cellar ...

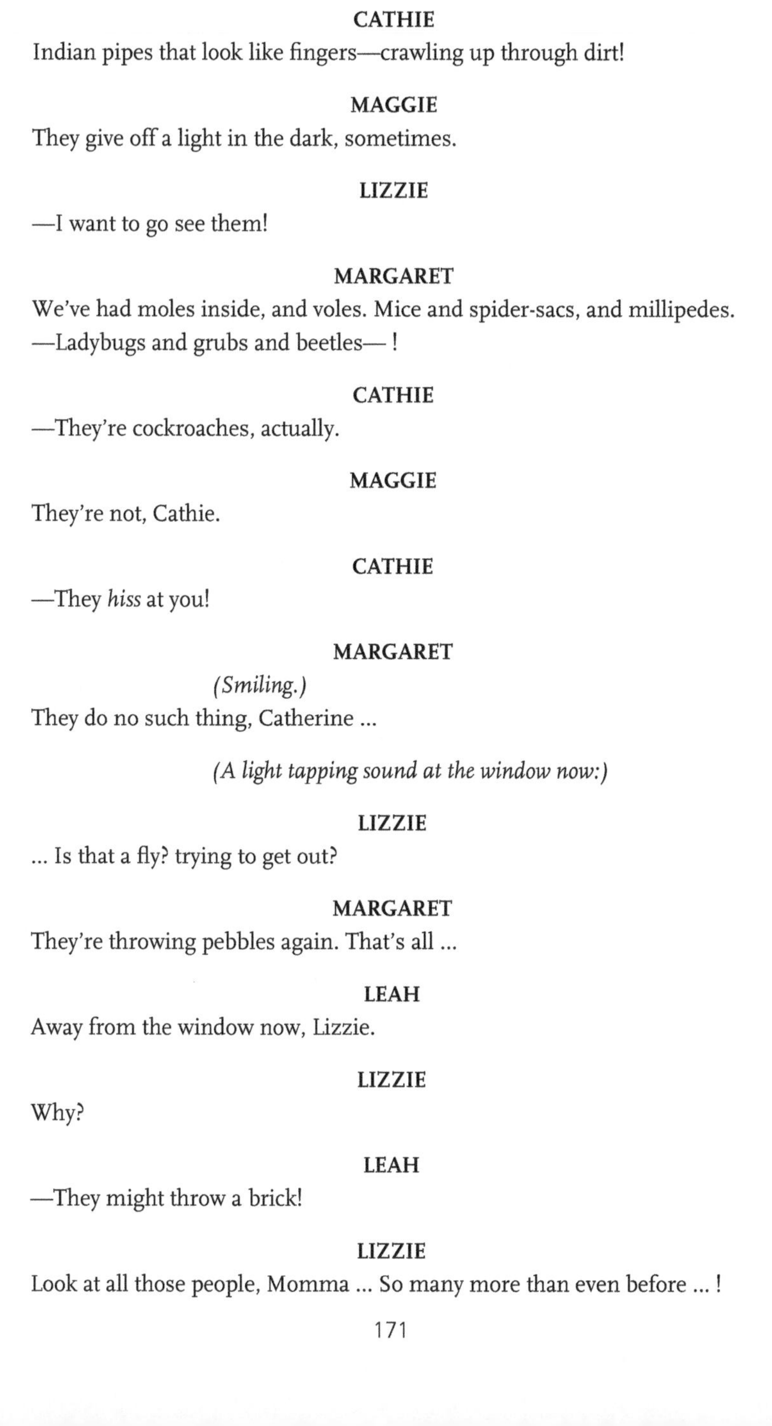

MAGGIE

Toadstools, Lizzie.

CATHIE

Indian pipes that look like fingers—crawling up through dirt!

MAGGIE

They give off a light in the dark, sometimes.

LIZZIE

—I want to go see them!

MARGARET

We've had moles inside, and voles. Mice and spider-sacs, and millipedes.
—Ladybugs and grubs and beetles— !

CATHIE

—They're cockroaches, actually.

MAGGIE

They're not, Cathie.

CATHIE

—They *hiss* at you!

MARGARET

(Smiling.)

They do no such thing, Catherine ...

(A light tapping sound at the window now:)

LIZZIE

... Is that a fly? trying to get out?

MARGARET

They're throwing pebbles again. That's all ...

LEAH

Away from the window now, Lizzie.

LIZZIE

Why?

LEAH

—They might throw a brick!

LIZZIE

Look at all those people, Momma ... So many more than even before ... !

(LEAH peers out the window now too, over her daughter's head.)

LIZZIE (cont'd.)

Sitting on the fence, in carts ... in the mud, in the field ... There's too much mud out there! my shoe got stuck in all that mud ...

LEAH

Enough about your shoe, Lizzie, we'll find it again soon—

LIZZIE

And the peppermint I smelled from miles away, on the road in from Newark ...

Some have brought their chairs from home. —They're sitting on the grass—like it's a dining room outside! —They can't stop staring at the house!

(A moment more of LIZZIE and LEAH peering out: LIZZIE with growing wonder, LEAH with increasing distaste.)

LEAH

These windows are filthy.

MARGARET

It's not dirt on that window. It's not my house. It's rented. This glass is old and warped.

LEAH

Do these windows not open?

MARGARET

They've been nailed shut. —We didn't do that neither!

LEAH

I don't know about you three, but I think one ought to be in church of a beautiful Sunday morning ...

MARGARET

Is that what you think?

LEAH

I'm a stout one for church, Momma. Even you know that.

CATHIE

A Quaker one ...

LEAH

I do not subscribe to the Quaker faith wholesale, Catherine. As you must surely know. As our Mother most assuredly *must* have told you, *all* about me, many times over the years ... I know our mother is quite fond of discussing the private lives of her children, *with* her children ...

And so you must also know that I believe there is much *good* in it: good deeds. In the Quaker faith. And good deed is the only thing to count with me, whatever your intention ...

Why are you three not in church this morning?

MAGGIE

They won't have us there.

LEAH

Why not?

MARGARET

Margaret—

CATHIE

Because we're witches.

(LIZZIE may gasp.)

MARGARET

Some have said ...

LIZZIE

... Are you?

CATHIE

"Some have said" ...

MARGARET

Others know the truth.

(LIZZIE scratches herself. LEAH pulls her daughter's hands away.)

LEAH

I won't tell you again. Where is he?

LIZZIE

—What?

MARGARET

Who?

CATHIE

Charles?

LIZZIE

—Who's Charles?

LEAH

Where's your father, I mean.

MARGARET

He's *your* father too, Leah.

MAGGIE

Up at David's.

LEAH

Why isn't he down here with you? protecting you all?

CATHIE

From what ... ?

LEAH

From the hordes, outside.

LIZZIE

(Shooing.)

—From these flies!

MARGARET

Charles needs us here. He's made that much clear to us.

LIZZIE

Who's "Charles" again, Momma?

LEAH

He's the ghost. —Stop scratching, I said!

MARGARET

They're coming down to dig. Your father went to get David's tools, that's all. You'll see them both here soon.

LIZZIE

What are they digging for ... ?

LEAH

Stop asking so many questions, Lizzie, it isn't ladylike. —David will come too?

MARGARET
In the cellar, Lizzie. For the bones of the murdered pedlar Charles. They want proof. As do we all.

LEAH
The pamphlet says you dug weeks ago—

MAGGIE
We dug down three feet and found only water then.

CATHIE
But the body's buried at ten.

LEAH
How do you know that?

CATHIE
Spirit said.

LIZZIE
Ten feet? that's deep ...

MARGARET
They found some things though. They did.

LIZZIE
Like what?

CATHIE
Like lime, red hair ... And some teeth.

(MARGARET crosses herself.

LIZZIE scratches.

LEAH swats a fly.)

LIZZIE
—That's filthy!

CATHIE
It's the truth.

LIZZIE
—*Human* teeth?

CATHIE
And a piece of jawbone.

LEAH

Why aren't you up at David's then? If you're so frightened down here. If you're in danger of lynching. If there are ghosts speaking to you out of ghost-holes—

MAGGIE

We went up there, Leah, when it all began—

LIZZIE

And then what happened, Aunt Maggie?

CATHIE

He followed us!

LIZZIE

—No!

MARGARET

Yes. He got cross with us. He did. For leaving. —He follows us wherever we go!

LEAH

Somehow I believe at least that part is true ...

LIZZIE

You believe in him now, Momma?

(LEAH takes in her daughter's stupidity.)

MARGARET

He hurt your brother David. —Tell her what happened to David, Maggie.

LIZZIE

What happened to Uncle Davey?

CATHIE

—Charles attacked him while he slept!

LIZZIE

—Poor Uncle David!

LEAH

Attacked him how?

CATHIE

Raised his bed halfway up to the ceiling! —With him inside it!

MARGARET

He did, Leah! —We were in the other room!

CATHIE

Tell them, Maggie. —Maggie.

MAGGIE

(A hesitation.)

Charles raised his bed up to the ceiling ... then it crashed back down to the floor.

Whereupon David cursed and hurled himself back down on his bed, like a thin little boy, averring he would never have "nothing to do with those fiendish spirits again"—his words: "This is the work of the Devil and his imps!"

LEAH

How often have you used the verb "to aver," Margaretta? *(Short pause.)*

On my word you should write novels.

MARGARET

Are you calling us liars?

(MARGARET brushes a fly from her face.)

MARGARET (cont'd.)

You may call us deranged, if you like. If you must. I'd expect as much from you ... But you have not heard the sound!

And if there's one thing we are, your father and I, it is honest. You know this. —*Especially* your father: he is honest to a fault. *(Pause.)* You *know* this.

(LEAH addresses her sisters:)

LEAH

Does your spirit have a surname?

CATHIE

Rosna.

(She pronounces it "Rose-na.")

MARGARET

His full name is "Charles B. Rosna." To be precise.

LEAH

That *is* a precise name.

LIZZIE

It is a pretty name.

LEAH

It's an *odd* last name ...

LIZZIE

—His first name's almost regal!

LEAH

Almost.

LIZZIE

What's the B stand for?

LEAH

Bull shit.

LIZZIE

(Thrilled.)

—Momma!

MARGARET

That's not a very Quaker thing to say, Leah ...

LEAH

I'm not a Quaker: I'm friends with Quakers.

CATHIE

Friends with Friends.

LEAH

You're clever! You're the clever one, aren't you?

MARGARET

That's right: were you a proper Quaker you might believe in God.

LEAH

I believe in God! What an hilarious thing to say! I believe in people more.
I believe that God is too busy with the clockwork of the universe to fix an evil for us. Else he'd have dropped brimstone on Charleston by now.

(MARGARET turns her eyes to the ceiling. LEAH swats another fly.)

LIZZIE

How does he speak to you? Do you hear his voice, Maggie?

MAGGIE

Mr. Duesler found out, if you speak the alphabet to him—*for* him, one word at a time—

CATHIE

One letter—

MAGGIE

Charles raps his knuckles on the letter that he wants.

MARGARET

It is a laboriously long process ...

LEAH

What's he want, then?

(LEAH stands, if she's not standing already.)

LEAH (cont'd.)

To be buried somewhere else? in consecrated ground? That's how it often is, in cases such as this, murderèd, as he was, late at night. Of a Tuesday, I believe, memory serves—

(LIZZIE giggles.)

MARGARET

This is not a joke, Leah. This is not an entertainment for you both— !

LEAH

He wants his sack of missing gold! He wants his missing limbs back! —You'd have to find his body first—

CATHIE

We will!

LEAH

When?

MARGARET

When the ground dries out.

MAGGIE

It's been a wet spring, Leah ... All this snow to melt ...

LEAH

He wants nothing more then, this spirit? just to get his bones dug up?

CATHIE

—He doesn't care if he gets himself dug up or not! That's for people with no faith—like you!

LEAH

All he wants then is to chat?

MARGARET

What *should* he want, Leah?

LEAH

—*Revenge!*

LIZZIE

(Scratching up under her skirt.)

Momma!

LEAH

—Stop scratching yourself, I said!

MARGARET

That's you, Leah! You want revenge, all the time, though no one knows what for ...

CATHIE

He says Mr. Bell will pay in the next life.

LIZZIE

Who's Mr. Bell?

LEAH

The "murderer," dear.

CATHIE

He lives in Lyons now.

LEAH

That's a strong thing to say about someone you don't know.

CATHIE

We didn't say it—about the Bells: Charles did.

LEAH

Mr. Bell could well be outside ... With a rifle. You're right to stay locked away inside ...

LIZZIE

Will he be hanged do you think, Momma?

LEAH

Who? Mr. Bell? Of course not, dear.

MARGARET

They'd need more evidence for that, Lizzie.

CATHIE

They'll find it.

LEAH

But you don't need evidence for slander? *(Short pause.)*

Where are these teeth, by the way? I'd like to see them. I'd like to hold them in my hands.

CATHIE

We lost them.

(LEAH can not help but smile at this.)

LEAH

Of course you did. No ...

What I mean to say is: I should think, if some person were to come back to us, from the past, from beyond the grave, so to speak: he would have something worthwhile to teach us. Some wisdom to impart. About this life. —*How to live.*

What's his opinion, for example, on the morality of keeping human souls in bondage?

MAGGIE

You mean slaves ...

LEAH

I was thinking about wives. And children, but all right.

MARGARET

You're ridiculing us now ... I know what's going on here ...

(A long, tense pause. LEAH paces the room a bit.

She swats another fly.)

MARGARET (cont'd.)

Let them be, you'll only bloody the walls.

LEAH

We'll clean them then ... Flies spread filth, Momma. Disease.

CATHIE

Ella's sick again, you know.

LEAH

Are you smiling at that ... ?

CATHIE

She's always sick. She's a sickly girl. She's small, like me. Poppa said.
Ella is David's daughter, you know.

LEAH

I know who Ella is. Thank you, Catherine.

CATHIE

You've never met her. Have you?

LEAH

I have not yet met David's infant daughter Ella. I am much anticipating the introduction, however. I thank thee.

MARGARET

(Quietly.)

"Thee"! how grand ...

(Pause.)

LEAH

Where's Charles now, I'd like to speak with him.

CATHIE

You can't.

LEAH

Why not? —You don't speak *for* him, do you?
Mr. Rosna? have you a moment? He's probably busy sleeping, poor thing—he has such busy nights!

MAGGIE

It's daylight, Leah. It must be dark—

LEAH

Now why is that, do you suppose? Why should he prefer things to be dark?

LIZZIE

He's a ghost, Momma.

LEAH

—Must you always be so stupid?

(LIZZIE shrinks back, as LEAH knocks on the wall.)

LEAH (cont'd.)

... Charles? ... Charlie?

MARGARET

You mustn't test him, Leah ...

LEAH

What's he going to do, lift me up to the ceiling?

CATHIE

And then drop you.

LEAH

I'm waiting ... My feet are firmly on the ground ...

(A longer pause.)

LEAH (cont'd.)

I'd expect much more from you, Maggie ... Cathie's always been strange.

CATHIE

I'm not feeling well, Momma ...

(MARGARET pulls back from CATHIE.)

MARGARET

Are you well? If you're sick then you must lie down.

CATHIE

I'm lying down now—

MARGARET

In your own bed. In the pantry.

—With Lizzie here tonight you'll have to sleep in the pantry. All three of you together. Will you be afraid?

CATHIE

I'm tired, that's all ...

MARGARET

Lie over there then, against your sister ...

(Reluctantly, CATHIE leans back against her sister.)

MARGARET (cont'd.)

Lay your head back ... Try for sleep ...

(CATHIE lays her head back against MAGGIE, who covers her with blankets so that only her pale face shows.

MAGGIE strokes her sister's arm.

After a very long pause:)

MARGARET (cont'd.)

... You don't know how awful it's been, Leah ... What an awful responsibility we've had! ... How we've suffered!

(MARGARET sighs, strangely as if contentedly, closing her eyes.)

MARGARET (cont'd.)

Have pity on us, please ... for once in your life ...

(Long pause here. LEAH seems almost chastened. MARGARET soon appears to doze. CATHIE too has closed her eyes ...

LEAH sits back in her chair. Begins to hum, quietly. A sad, almost pretty tune.

MAGGIE remains sitting up in bed, stroking CATHIE absently, watching LEAH furtively. LEAH watches her mother and sisters with outright suspicion, softly humming her tune ...

Nobody watches LIZZIE, who scratches herself all the time.)

LIZZIE

I'm hungry, Momma ...

LEAH

Get an apple from the kitchen then. —Stop. Scratching.

(LIZZIE goes.

LEAH keeps humming, very low, her melody.

She crushes an insect, with her pamphlet, quietly this time: we hear the insect crack.)

LEAH (cont'd.)

A "beetle" ...

(LEAH continues to hum.)

MAGGIE

... What are you singing?

LEAH

A song.

MAGGIE

What kind?

LEAH

A hymn. Of emancipation.

(She hums some more.

Only LEAH and MAGGIE seem to be fully awake.

MAGGIE speaks softly now:)

MAGGIE

... How did you learn the piano, Leah?

LEAH

My husband taught me. Bowman Fish. You never met him.

He used always to say to me: "How strange a Fox has married a Fish. I'm afraid you'll eat me up one day ... " *(She smiles.)*

He recognized in me a great—facility. For art.

(She watches MAGGIE some more.)

LEAH (cont'd.)

You and I are very much alike ...

MAGGIE

Do you like teaching?

LEAH

Not at all. Why?

MAGGIE

I'd like to—teach. One day. —I'd like to play music, *and* teach.

LEAH

Don't you want a husband?

MAGGIE

Of course I do. Why?

LEAH

It can be dangerous ... Music excites the passions ... Your own and others'.

(LEAH studies MAGGIE's face.

MAGGIE looks elsewhere.)

LEAH (cont'd.)

Why have we never talked like this before, Maggie?

MAGGIE

You ought to be nicer to Mother, you know.

LEAH

Why?

(MAGGIE doesn't respond.)

LEAH (cont'd.)

I want to thank you for that letter you sent me, months ago ...
But you're wrong, you know. About forgiveness.

(LIZZIE returns, biting her apple.)

LIZZIE

This apple's mealy.

LEAH

Spit it out then.

LIZZIE

Where?

LEAH

On the floor. No one will notice, it's such a pigsty in here ...

(LIZZIE keeps eating, she's so hungry. LEAH swats a fly and misses.)

LEAH (cont'd.)

Damn.

LIZZIE

... I heard him in the kitchen, by the way.

LEAH

Whom, dear?

LIZZIE

Your ghost.

MAGGIE

He's not *my* ghost—

LEAH

Don't play games with us. You're much too old for games now.

LIZZIE

I heard him! —Why won't you ever *believe* me—about anything? I heard a knock. I felt the floorboards jar, in a tremulous motion—

LEAH

"Tremulous"?

MAGGIE

—That's him.

LEAH

Are you trying to impress us with such language? Remember: Clean soul speaks plainly.

LIZZIE

You don't.

(LEAH fixes her daughter in a withering stare.

Now: a knocking sound, as if from the cellar. LIZZIE *stops chewing her apple.)*

LIZZIE (cont'd.)

... You see?

MAGGIE

Where's it coming from?

LIZZIE

Down below— !

LEAH

Shh. Listen.

(More sounds: indistinct knockings, a shuffling sound.)

MAGGIE

... Some nights we hear the sounds of his burial ... in the cellar. We hear the coffin being made, the planes and saws and hammers ... We hear the sound of the pickaxe, and the spade ...

(MARGARET rouses; then CATHIE.)

CATHIE

... Is he here?

MARGARET

He never comes in the morning ...

MAGGIE

He's here now.

LIZZIE

—I heard him first!

CATHIE

I don't feel well, Momma ...

(CATHIE rushes out of the room, as if to vomit.

After a moment:)

LIZZIE

... Maybe she has what Ella has?

(MAGGIE rushes after her sister.

The others remain; listening.)

MARGARET

... Is that you, Spirit?

(After a moment: JOHN's voice, up from the cellar.)

JOHN

Margaret?

LEAH

You see?

MARGARET

—John!

LEAH

It was him all along ...

(MARGARET's voice when addressing JOHN has taken on something new: shrill and nervous still, but almost youthful, giddy—almost as if flirtatious.)

MARGARET

Is David with you?

JOHN

He's up at the house! With the doctor! —Ella's worse!

MARGARET

Leah's here, John!

(A telling pause. Then:)

JOHN

Do you hear him now?

MARGARET

Do you?

JOHN

On the wall! —By the stairs!

MARGARET

Spirit! If you hear me! When John stands over your burial hole, please knock for us! Loudly! Three times! So that we might better know where you've been hidden ... !

Move slowly, John, all over!

(Silence. The sound of shuffling feet.)

MARGARET (cont'd.)

Are you moving!

JOHN

—I am!

MARGARET

Do you hear him!

JOHN

I do! He's rapping! gently! On the floor over my head! —Three times!

MARGARET

Dig there, John! Dig!

(The sound of the pickaxe and the spade.)

LIZZIE

I want to see ... !

(LIZZIE moves quickly to exit—LEAH grabs her arm, a bit roughly: the apple core tumbles.)

LEAH

You'll stay clear of him. Understand? On the stairs.

(LIZZIE goes. LEAH picks up the half-eaten apple.)

JOHN

... Was that a rap, Margaret?

MARGARET

An apple, John! Falling!

(LEAH and MARGARET alone.

MARGARET is concentrating mightily on listening, apparently.

LEAH watches MARGARET a long time, but MARGARET won't acknowledge her daughter's gaze.

The sound of the pickaxe and the spade.

After a long moment, with almost childlike yearning:)

LEAH

... Why didn't you tell me what was happening, Momma ... ?

(Pause.)

LEAH (cont'd.)

Momma? If you told me I would have come home ...

(MARGARET doesn't answer her daughter.

The digging has stopped.)

JOHN

—It's nothing!

(A long, dispiriting pause.)

JOHN (cont'd.)

There's nothing down here but water and mud again ...

(MARGARET exhales, disappointedly. She starts in surprise at:

DAVID standing in the doorway to the bedroom, suddenly, silently; pale, voiceless.

MARGARET rises from the bed: a presentiment of sorts.

LEAH is startled too, at first. She speaks formally:)

LEAH

Hello, David.

(MARGARET looks into her son's face, can not stifle a wail:)

MARGARET

—Oh!

(Blackness. The sound of the pickaxe and the spade.)

8. OUTSIDE.

(A setting sun. The crowd noises. More water in the stream.

Beside the back door, outside the kitchen: CATHIE, MAGGIE and LIZZIE sit out on rock, log, step; surrounded everywhere by mud ... They cling to the house, hiding from the pilgrims in the road.

CATHIE looks out over the river to the fields and hills beyond, a vacant stare. MAGGIE watches her sister closely.

LIZZIE watches them both. She doesn't scratch herself yet.)

LIZZIE

I saw you on the stairs.

MAGGIE

Who are you talking to, Lizzie?

LIZZIE

Both of you.

When you went out here to be sick, Cathie: you weren't. You went down to the cellar, on the stairs. Maggie went with you. I saw you, both ... I stood in the pantry and looked down on you. You didn't see me, you were hiding from your father while he digged.

MAGGIE

"Dug," Lizzie.

LIZZIE

Who cares?

CATHIE

We wanted to see. Like you did.

MAGGIE

You think we're lying?

LIZZIE

I *saw* you.

CATHIE

... Is this the time to talk like this?

(Short pause.)

LIZZIE

What time is it ... ?

(CATHIE continues to look out over the river, to the fields, up a hill, perhaps to the spot where Ella's been buried.

LIZZIE follows her gaze.)

LIZZIE (cont'd.)

She's a baby. She was. It's sad. That's life! Babies die all the time, especially out here ...

CATHIE

Where poor people live ...

LIZZIE

We're poor people too, you know. We're poorer than you are, probably! I'll bet you did not know that ...

MAGGIE

You have friends.

LIZZIE

Momma does ...

She's started taking in wash. Of friends ... I bet you did not know that. In secrecy ... Underthings, and things.

(Suddenly CATHIE begins to cry. MAGGIE tries to soothe her.)

LIZZIE (cont'd.)

Why are you so sad? 'cause of Ella?

If Charles Rosna's taught you anything it's that nobody ever really dies ... Not anymore, not really ...

CATHIE

You believe in him now?

(LIZZIE hesitates to answer.)

CATHIE (cont'd.)

How do we do it then? if you think we're fooling ...

LIZZIE

If you're fooling: I do not know how.

MAGGIE

—Why would we fool them, Lizzie? For what reason?

LIZZIE

I think you like it.

CATHIE

Wouldn't you?

MAGGIE

Cathie ...

LIZZIE

I know I'd like it.

CATHIE

You'd like to scare your mother.

LIZZIE

Why ... ?

CATHIE

Because she says you're slow, and ugly.

MAGGIE

Cathie. You mustn't say such things.

CATHIE

Why not? if it's the truth ...

LIZZIE

—I can't help it!

CATHIE

She says your brain is like a beast's is. You scratch like one.

LIZZIE

—She does not say that!

CATHIE

We heard her, last summer. It's the truth. When we went to live with you. We heard. Right, Maggie?

MAGGIE

(Quietly.)

No ...

CATHIE

Don't be afraid, Lizzie ...

LIZZIE

—It's an illness!

CATHIE

Don't scratch yourself. Watch. *(Pause.)* Don't scratch yourself, Lizzie. *(Pause.)* Don't scratch—

(LIZZIE scratches her face.)

CATHIE (cont'd.)

See?

LIZZIE

—I can't stop it!

CATHIE

She's put a spell on you! That's why you'll never marry.

LIZZIE

How do you know I'll never ... ?

CATHIE

How old are you now, seventeen? That's what your mother's been saying. Last summer, when that boy you knew stopped coming ...

It's only the truth, Lizzie. Don't be sad.

(Now it looks like LIZZIE might cry. She's scratching herself a lot, her face and hands and neck.

She's fighting back tears.)

LIZZIE

She says I must get used to it ...

MAGGIE

(With tenderness.)

... To what, Lizzie?

LIZZIE

Living, like her ...

CATHIE

Alone?

LIZZIE

—But she's a teacher!
I want to be a nurse one day ...

MAGGIE

Why won't you be ... ?

LIZZIE

She won't let me. —She wants me with her all the time!

CATHIE

Would you like to know how we do it, Lizzie? The sounds?

MAGGIE

Cathie—

CATHIE

You've got to be barefoot first—

MAGGIE

Stop it!

CATHIE

You're halfway there already ... Both feet now, that's good ...
Now your stockings too ...

LIZZIE

It's squishy!

CATHIE

Close your eyes ...

LIZZIE

All right. —Don't you play games with me!

CATHIE

We won't.

Now crouch down low, Lizzie ...

LIZZIE

Crouch ... ?

CATHIE

Like a dog would ...

(LIZZIE crouches, scratching herself.)

CATHIE (cont'd.)

Now howl. *(Pause.)* Like a wolf does.

LIZZIE

A wolf?

CATHIE

A she-wolf. —You're angry. You need to be, for this spell to work. It's a spell.

(LIZZIE hesitates.)

CATHIE (cont'd.)

Don't you believe in invisible things ... ?

LIZZIE

I know I do!

(Then: LIZZIE howls, unconvincingly.)

CATHIE

Now be a cat. Because all girls are really cats ...

(LIZZIE bashfully meows. She giggles, eyes closed.)

CATHIE (cont'd.)

A bug now.

LIZZIE

What?

CATHIE

Living, in the dirt.

LIZZIE

—I don't want to be like an insect living in the dirt!

CATHIE

A cockroach. Put your face down in the mud. You'll have to eat some.

LIZZIE

It's mud!

CATHIE

This is *very* special mud, Lizzie. Right, Maggie?

LIZZIE

What?

CATHIE

Maggie? ... This land is sacred Indian land. This mud is made of bones. *(Short pause.)* Maggie knows.

LIZZIE

What about the worms ... ?

CATHIE

Don't eat the worms if you don't want to, I'll pick them out for you ...

(LIZZIE lowers her face down, close to the mud.)

CATHIE (cont'd.)

Keep your eyes closed, Lizzie. Open up your mouth.

(LIZZIE still won't open her mouth; eyes still closed.)

CATHIE (cont'd.)

This is how it was for us. This is how it happens.

(LIZZIE presses her face into the mud, opening her mouth to it, for an instant—she comes up spitting, retching. Her nose and mouth and chin are daubed with mud.)

MAGGIE

—Run away, Lizzie!—don't you spy on us again!

LIZZIE

You *devils!*

MAGGIE

—Stupid crow!

LIZZIE

I hate you both!

MAGGIE

You're just jealous of us! —Get away from here, Lizzie! Go!

LIZZIE

I'm going to tell my mother that you're fakers! *Liars*— !

(LIZZIE runs out towards the fields; thinks better of it when she sees the crowds. She turns tail, sliding on mud—)

LIZZIE (cont'd.)

—Oh!

(—and into the house: back door slams.

MAGGIE watches CATHIE for a while.)

MAGGIE

... That was *too* cruel, Cathie ...

CATHIE

Why? ... If she'd done it it might have worked ...

(CATHIE slips her hand into the mud, pulls out LIZZIE's lost shoe.

She hands it to MAGGIE, who is amazed ...

They each hold one of Lizzie's shoes now.

As CATHIE stares off into the distance again; as if watching someone moving in the fields.)

CATHIE (cont'd.)

(Pointing.)

There she is.

MAGGIE

Where?

CATHIE

She looks like a woman again. Like I saw her that day, in the field. In snow ... She's standing in the river now ... Water's rushing past her knees ...

Poor Ella. She doesn't yet know where she is.

(Pause.)

CATHIE (cont'd.)

Can't you see ... ?

(MAGGIE can not. Sun is setting.)

9. KITCHEN.

(Night. The teakettle shrieks. LEAH lifts it from the stove.

JOHN is standing in the doorway from the sitting room, spectacles on, his Bible in hand. Mud up and down his trousers, arms, shirt; some on his face. His large hands are clean though, raw.

He looks at LEAH for a moment; not meaningfully. His eyes are hidden behind mud-specked glasses. He may be smiling mildly, strangely.

He walks over to his wife's chair and sits.

He doesn't rock, just sits there; looking strangely calm ...

He watches LEAH for a while, straight on, staring at the back of her head. She notices but won't return his gaze.)

LEAH

I bet you're thirsty.

(He doesn't answer. She turns to face him.)

LEAH (cont'd.)

Don't you bet? you're thirsty?

(He doesn't answer.)

LEAH (cont'd.)

I'm just now finishing up some tea, for myself ... Would you like some? Tea?

(She finishes, brings her cup of tea to him, in the chipped cup, on the chipped saucer. She plunks it down beside him.

JOHN stares past the cup.)

JOHN

There's a fly on it.

LEAH

Whisk it off then.

(He doesn't.)

JOHN

It's hot.

LEAH

Let it sit.

(She moves to exit, to the sitting room.)

JOHN

No tea? *(Pause.)* No tea for you, Leah?

LEAH

I'm not thirsty anymore.

(Suddenly JOHN slams his hand down on the table.)

JOHN

A beetle ...

(He wipes his hand on his pants; he rubs and rubs ...)

JOHN (cont'd.)

Keep me company ... won't you? Don't you want to speak to your father, whom you've not seen in so long ... ?

LEAH

You should wash yourself. You should change out of your clothes. Is that from outside or downstairs?

(He laughs strangely.)

JOHN

I began the day digging in the cellar ... I end the day digging outside ...

(LEAH moves to exit the room.)

JOHN (cont'd.)

How are things in Rochester?

LEAH

Fine.

JOHN

You don't seem fine to me.

LEAH

I am well.

JOHN

You don't seem well.

LEAH

I am.

JOHN

You don't look it.

(Pause.)

LEAH

I don't think I like how you're speaking to me—

JOHN

I'm telling the truth. Asking for it. You don't have a problem with truth-telling, do you?

(He begins rocking slightly in his wife's chair.)

JOHN (cont'd.)

Because you look really just terrible ...

LEAH

—*I* look terrible?

JOHN

What are we going to do about this ... ?

You look absolutely—something must be wrong with you! ... The way you look now ...

LEAH

How do I look?

JOHN

Like a Quaker.

(He rocks.)

LEAH

I thank thee.

JOHN

—Not even a real one: a Hicksite. A *sect*. You dress like one—

LEAH

This is how I dress.

JOHN

An agitator for fornicators—

LEAH

It's called equal rights. For women—

JOHN

And a lover of negroes ... You look like one—a Hicksite, not a negress ...
What makes you love negroes so much?

(He rocks some more. LEAH's almost speechless now.)

JOHN (cont'd.)

And your hair—

LEAH

—What's wrong with my hair?

JOHN

What happened to your face? You're old now. You've grown so old, and stout ...

(A short pause. He's rocking.)

JOHN (cont'd.)

Now, Lizzie looks worse than you—

LEAH

She's beautiful— !

JOHN

She's like you are now—every way! Around here she'd be called a harlot ... *(He rocks.)* ... the way she *looks* ...
Agitators for fornicators ...
What's wrong with you both? Something must be terribly wrong, the way you both look now ...

(He rocks. LEAH is stunned, straining for words:)

LEAH

—Well—you look like a—*Methodist!*

JOHN

Your mother says you've been rude to her. About the sounds. Is that so?

LEAH

Have I?

JOHN

She says you've been calling her a liar. Speaking to her like she's a fool.

LEAH

Is that what she says?

JOHN

Are you calling her a liar?

LEAH

What happened to the house you're building, Father?

JOHN

It's not finished. It's winter.

LEAH

Not anymore, it's May.

Does she know you'll never finish? Does she know you've not begun?

JOHN

—Who's "she"?

LEAH

What?

JOHN

Who's this she of which you speak?

LEAH

Your wife. Does she know you're drinking still? Does she know you're drunk right now?

(JOHN stands suddenly, flings his cup of tea against the floor or wall where it shatters.

LEAH flinches, against her will.)

JOHN

Come outside with me—

LEAH

—No—

JOHN

We're going for a walk.

LEAH

No, we're not—

JOHN

There are things you do not know— !

LEAH

—Then tell me!

JOHN

—There are things you *do not know!*

(LEAH stands still, in the middle of the kitchen; watching him intently.

Will he strike her?)

LEAH

I went down to the cellar. I found them. Quite easily. Anyone can find them, if they're looking. —The children could find them without looking ...

(He sits again, suddenly. Confused, searching.)

JOHN

... Don't you believe in him?

LEAH

Whom?

JOHN

In Charles.

LEAH

I was speaking of the other kind of spirits ...

JOHN

Don't you think he's real ... ?
I thought I'd find proof ...

LEAH

That's not in the nature of faith, is it Father?

JOHN

(Exploding; desperately.)

—Do you know your Bible?

(He holds his Bible out to her; voice quavering:)

JOHN (cont'd.)

Spirits are in the Bible! There are angels, and devils—who speak to men!

(His hands are shaking, delicately, the Bible is too heavy: he lays it back in his lap.)

LEAH

I'll go get Mother ...

JOHN

(Overlapping.)

A bone, a boot ... no let her sleep.

LEAH

She's not sleeping. Can't you hear?

JOHN

—Let her weep then!

LEAH

You found hair, they said. Quicklime. Some teeth.

(JOHN seems to laugh a little.)

JOHN

I know what we found ... I think it had been a badger ...

(He rocks, and laughs feebly.)

JOHN (cont'd.)

... I don't know what's so *wrong* with you, Leah ... I honestly do not know ...

LEAH

Has it never occurred to you ... ?

(Short pause.)

LEAH (cont'd.)

They deceive you. With art.

(She smiles.)

LEAH (cont'd.)

... You're so much easier to fool now than when I was a girl. *(Pause.)* You can not tell me you've not thought of this before ...

JOHN

Why would they ... ?

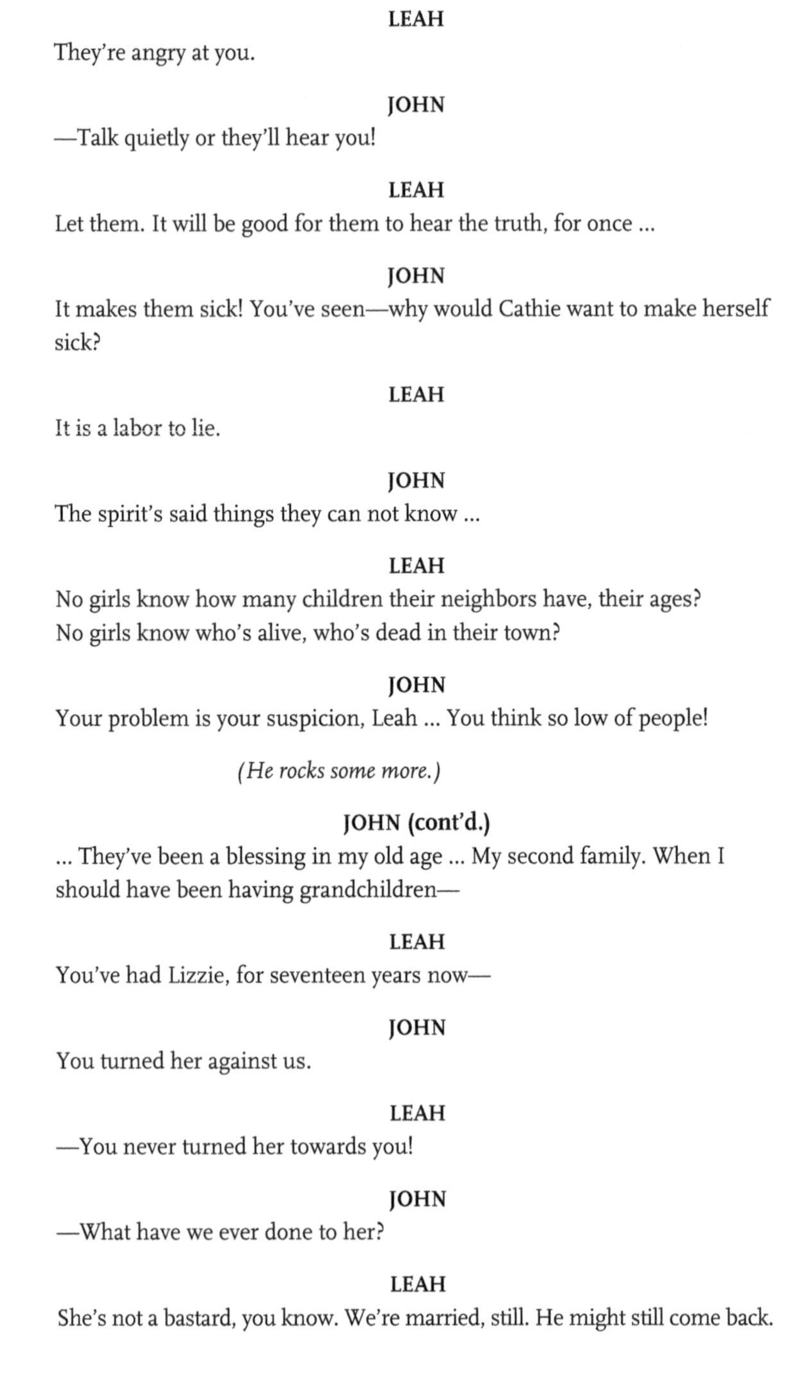

LEAH

They're angry at you.

JOHN

—Talk quietly or they'll hear you!

LEAH

Let them. It will be good for them to hear the truth, for once ...

JOHN

It makes them sick! You've seen—why would Cathie want to make herself sick?

LEAH

It is a labor to lie.

JOHN

The spirit's said things they can not know ...

LEAH

No girls know how many children their neighbors have, their ages? No girls know who's alive, who's dead in their town?

JOHN

Your problem is your suspicion, Leah ... You think so low of people!

(He rocks some more.)

JOHN (cont'd.)

... They've been a blessing in my old age ... My second family. When I should have been having grandchildren—

LEAH

You've had Lizzie, for seventeen years now—

JOHN

You turned her against us.

LEAH

—You never turned her towards you!

JOHN

—What have we ever done to her?

LEAH

She's not a bastard, you know. We're married, still. He might still come back.

JOHN

He's been gone and married fifteen years now. To a widow in Illinois!

LEAH

That's a story.

JOHN

He's not coming back! You act so smart because really you're so stupid ...

LEAH

He might still come back. You of all people should have sympathy for that.

JOHN

—So much anger, Leah!

LEAH

—*I* do?

JOHN

So angry! —Full of hate!

LEAH

—And don't I have cause?

JOHN

Arrogance! —Don't you come here and persecute me! —Don't you crucify me!

(LEAH speaks plainly now:)

LEAH

You were guests in my home ...

JOHN

—Petty! —You're *nothing!*

LEAH

And you spoke with contempt. All summer long. For my friends, my daughter—

JOHN

You *liar*— !

LEAH

How I raise her—

JOHN

Without God!

LEAH

—You don't know who God is!

JOHN

That's why your man ran off, years ago—you're like a man. —You crush everything!

LEAH

And when I could no longer stand to be around you, I found somewhere else for you. Didn't I? Some friends I knew would take you in, like they took me in, years ago. When I had no one—*they took me* ... Like they took you, last summer ... Because you're poor now. Because you're nothing. You've wasted everything.

What did you do? You disgraced yourself, even there—

JOHN

Those people think they're better than us.

LEAH

They are. *(Pause.)* How much money did you steal from them?

JOHN

Why do you hate us so much ... ?

(JOHN rocks again, smiling.)

JOHN (cont'd.)

Your own family ... I don't know why that is ... You have only one family in life. Only one life. Don't you? Why won't you *love* us ... ? *(He smiles.)* You've always been that way, Leah, came out of the womb that way. Stinking of it.

LEAH

Why did you leave, like a coward, when I was eight?

(JOHN hesitates to speak.)

JOHN

Go to bed.

LEAH

You ran off. There must have been a reason ...

JOHN

I came back. Unlike that husband of yours.

LEAH

Where were you? Where did you go?

JOHN

I came back. I'm here now. Aren't I?

LEAH

He may come back still ...

JOHN

—After so many years? and still you can't find another?

LEAH

Are you rotten inside? Is that all?

(Pause.)

JOHN

It's the truth.

LEAH

I see ...

JOHN

It's simply the truth I'm speaking here. —You're worse than any man!

LEAH

I am glad of it.

(JOHN rocks in his chair.)

JOHN

Get out of my house.

LEAH

What's wrong here? Something must be terribly wrong, for all of this to happen.

(Pause.)

LEAH (cont'd.)

Now I see it. I remember.

JOHN

No more talking now, Leah.

LEAH

You can not stop me—

(He stands up, finger pointing in her face.)

JOHN

Not another word! —You get out of my house!

LEAH

It's not your house, it's rented. This house is yours but only for a time. Your Bible should have taught you that.

(She takes the spectacles from his face, gently, almost as if a loving gesture ...

She holds them in her hands, grips them tightly, suddenly as if she might twist and break them ...

Slowly she folds them, places them on the table just out of her father's reach.)

LEAH (cont'd.)

Go up to David's house tonight, to sleep. Don't come back till we're gone.

(He sits again, a tremor in his arms and face, the Bible in his lap.

She leaves the room.

A moment. Then he stands again, puts on his coat and hat and gloves ... He slips out the back door, into the night. He's left his Bible behind.)

10. KITCHEN.

(Quiet.

Late that same night. The kitchen is dark. But in the darkness we see:

LEAH, standing still, still dressed, listening to the house ... for a moment. Something of a tableau: she thinks she hears something.

A shriek comes from the pantry:)

LIZZIE

—Momma!

LEAH

(Reflexively.)

It's all right, it's a dream—

(LIZZIE enters through the pantry door; meets LEAH who's rushing towards her.)

LIZZIE

—He touched me!

LEAH

Who touched you, dear?

MARGARET

Where did he touch you, Lizzie?

(MARGARET has entered with an unlit candle; from her bedroom.)

LIZZIE

On my face!—and all down my back! —It was so cold!

MARGARET

Maybe it was a beetle, dear, while you slept?

LIZZIE

—Oh!

LEAH

It's a dream then, darling, shh ...

(LEAH has sat her daughter down in the rocking chair, by the cold stove; kneeling beside her. Touching her now.)

LIZZIE

I felt it, on my skin and—all down my back. —It *was* a hand!

(MARGARET succeeds in striking a match, lighting her candle.)

MARGARET

Where's your father gone to ... ?

LEAH

Up at David's.

MARGARET

Why?

CATHIE

We saw him too, Momma.

(MAGGIE and CATHIE have appeared in the doorway from the pantry, shyly, barefoot.)

MARGARET

You saw Charles ... ?

LIZZIE

I didn't see him, I *felt* him—

MARGARET

What's he look like?

CATHIE

He was lying on our bed, at our feet. —*On* our feet. We could scarcely move!

He was breathing, with the sheets all wrapped around his neck ... He was trying to stop bleeding. He was coughing up so much black blood!

LIZZIE

I didn't see any of that, Momma ...

LEAH

Did you, Maggie?

CATHIE

It was Charles. We saw him.

LEAH

Maggie?

MARGARET

Why would he want to hurt you, Lizzie?

MAGGIE

He was cross with her, Momma.

MARGARET

Why?

MAGGIE

She's been saying things about us—

LIZZIE

—That's not true! They're liars!

(LIZZIE is now scratching herself vigorously.)

MAGGIE

She says we've been lying, all the time. About Charles.

CATHIE

—She says *you're* lying too, Momma!

LIZZIE

That's not true! I didn't say anything like that— !

MARGARET

Why would I— ?

LIZZIE

Not all of you, not you—just these two—*witches!*

CATHIE

—Crow! Quaker! Negro-lover!

LEAH

Cathie! —Quiet!

(Pause. LEAH has silenced CATHIE, for the moment.)

LIZZIE

(Trying for calm.)

When I went down to the cellar today ... to see Grandpa dig ... the girls were supposed to be outside, throwing up—

CATHIE

We were *in*side—

MAGGIE

We wanted to *see* things, Lizzie ...

LIZZIE

—Why do you both *lie* so much?

LEAH

Put your hands down, dear, there's a good girl.

LIZZIE

I'm burning up!

LEAH

You're not, be still—

LIZZIE

(Quietly.)

It's a spell, Momma. Maybe they've conjured one on me ... ?

(CATHIE's eyes go wide: she gasps.)

MARGARET

What is it, dear?

CATHIE

He's here. In the room now. Can't you see him?

(CATHIE points.)

MARGARET

Is he watching us? Charles?

CATHIE

—Can't you see him?

MAGGIE

—I see him now too!

LIZZIE

They're lying! They're both lying—it's so obvious!

(A rapping is heard, along the floor beneath the girls, like footsteps.)

CATHIE

He's coming at me!

MARGARET

Why?

LIZZIE

—They made me eat mud, Momma!

CATHIE

His neck and mouth is black ... *So* black—with blood!

(CATHIE gags.)

MARGARET

Oh Lord she's sick—

CATHIE

Don't touch me!

MARGARET

I won't, Cathie! —Oh I won't!

CATHIE

—*He* is!

MARGARET

Charles— ?

CATHIE

—"Help me!"

(A rasping sound in CATHIE's throat. The voice is somehow masculine, pained.)

MARGARET

(Quietly.)

Whose voice is that ... ?

CATHIE

"Help me!"

LIZZIE

She sounds like a man now, Momma ...

MARGARET

You're not Catherine ... Who are you?

CATHIE

"Nobody."

LEAH

—*You're* doing this to us!

(LEAH has seized CATHIE, as if she might strike her— but something stops her cold.

She lets go of CATHIE's body now, a stunned look on her face.

CATHIE stands in place, swaying, as if in a daze.

She stares ahead at nothing, shivering. Her body twitching, sometimes jerking ... The rapping sound continues: slow, as if stalking steps, all around them.

LIZZIE's crying again softly.)

CATHIE

"To be with Christ is better far ... "

LIZZIE

... Is this all a dream, Momma? ... Are we dreaming this together?

(LEAH is moving to the cupboard, withdrawing two mismatched glass tumblers.)

MARGARET

What are you doing— ?

(LEAH crouches and places the two glasses on the floor at CATHIE's feet.

She returns to the cupboard, withdraws two more tumblers. Places them in front of MAGGIE now.

CATHIE continues to sway, jerking slightly, shivering. The rapping continues.)

LEAH

Stand on them please.

MAGGIE

We'll break them, Leah—

(MAGGIE doesn't move.)

LEAH

Stand or I will make you.

(Slowly MAGGIE steps up onto the glass tumblers; balancing there barefoot ...

The rapping continues, but less so, quieter. As if there are fewer footsteps in the room, as if Charles has grown smaller. As if he is farther away.)

LEAH (cont'd.)

Help your sister now ...

(MAGGIE helps CATHIE to stand on the tumblers too.

CATHIE balances there, precariously, shivering, twitching. Eyes wide. MAGGIE reaches out with one hand to steady her.

They stand together, side by side, on their glasses, a hand held between them.

Rapping's stopped.)

MARGARET

Where's he gone ... ? Catherine?

(CATHIE stands there, beside her sister; breathing, twitching. As if in a trance.)

LIZZIE

She's faking, Momma—she *has* to be— !

LEAH

Take her to bed.

LIZZIE

Me?

LEAH

Your grandmother will help you ...
I want to speak with Maggie, alone.

(MAGGIE looks to her mother, as if for help.

An uncanny pause; MARGARET speaks, after her usual manic fashion:)

MARGARET

Oh yes. That's a grand idea. Let's get her into bed. She needs her rest, that's all. That's true! She's overwrought. She's fine! ... You two stay here, talk, you and Leah, and if you can make some sense of this—Lord knows I can't! It's a mystery to me. And Lizzie and I will put your sister to bed. — We'll sing to her maybe!

(MARGARET, with LIZZIE's help, has guided CATHIE off the tumblers, towards the pantry now ...)

LIZZIE

Momma ... ?

(LEAH doesn't answer; simply watches MAGGIE closely.

MARGARET, CATHIE, and LIZZIE exit for the pantry ...

A long silence follows.

LEAH continues to watch MAGGIE.

A moment; then MAGGIE sits down at the table. Picks up that last apple in the bowl.)

MAGGIE

We did it with an apple first. —*She* did.

(LEAH sits across from her sister.)

MAGGIE (cont'd.)

She threw it against the house, from the outside, that day we first moved in ... They were inside. It made a thumping sound.

Mother talked about it all night long ... Like it *meant* something.

Then she started fooling *me*, Cathie did, with a different apple: she tied it to a string and hung it down, behind her back, by her fingertips. It dangled to the floor ... All she had to do was hold it, see, like this? out of sight. And the apple jumped ... thump, thump. *(She smiles, in spite of herself.)*

I saw her do it once. I didn't tell her. I didn't know she knew I knew.

(Another pause.)

MAGGIE (cont'd.)

It's so easy to frighten people, Leah! Especially Momma ...

LEAH

She never looked?

MAGGIE

At first she did ... But all Cathie ever did was pull it up, on the string, and hide it in our bedclothes ...

LEAH

You haven't done it all with apples though.

(LEAH watches her.)

MAGGIE

We keep finding new ways to fool them ... There's always new ways. Especially in the dark, or near-dark.

Especially when you say that doubters ruin everything.

Or when you point out what's already happening, all around them, in nature.

LEAH

You must have talent. And conviction. You're an artist.

(Now MAGGIE watches LEAH, almost boldly.)

MAGGIE

How did you know to make us stand up on those tumblers ... ?
You saw the muscles in my feet. My feet were bare—

LEAH

I touched her. When I went to strike her. I felt her bones.

(Pause.)

MAGGIE

It's our big toes, mainly. That's what makes the loudest sound, on wood. This house is like a sounding board! it's so empty ... When we pop it back in place:

(We hear a rapping sound, soft and unimpressive.)

MAGGIE (cont'd.)

You can hardly see the bones ... Can you?
... Cathie does it with her ankles and knees too. We use our knuckles when we want a lighter sound, but that's recognizable sometimes ... Cathie pops her jaw. It's easier for her.

LEAH

It must hurt sometimes.

MAGGIE

Of course it does. *(She smiles.)* Can I teach you?

(LEAH doesn't answer. Watches MAGGIE.

Who lowers her head.)

LEAH

... You expect me to believe you've fooled everyone, all the people who've come here ... with just apples and knees and toes?

(Short pause.)

MAGGIE

... You think I'm lying about a lie?

LEAH

You're scared. You're protecting her. You think: If I confess it then it will all just go away. That *I* will go away.

MAGGIE

I don't want you to go.

(Another pause.)

LEAH

I believe you fake it sometimes. I believe it started out that way ...
But I believe there's something in it now.

(She touches MAGGIE, on the arm, very gently.)

LEAH (cont'd.)

Sometimes, Maggie, what begins as a lie can become a kind of truth.

MAGGIE

I do wonder ...

It upsets people. They cry. They seem overjoyed by it, somehow. Even though we say such terrible things sometimes ...

And—the less I think about what Spirit will say to me, the more I *listen* and let the words come to me, as if *through* me ... the more people seem to believe that all I say is true.

And—I'm faking it always, like you said. But sometimes I forget, and I know what I don't know. —I say what I can't *possibly* be thinking!

The truth is it feels good sometimes: it doesn't feel like me.

LEAH

What does Cathie do?

MAGGIE

She does it without thinking, her bones ... She hears and sees things all the time now ...

Maybe we let something in, Leah ... ? Mr. Splitfoot ... ?

(A pause.)

LEAH

What if I said I could take you with me, to the city?

MAGGIE

Cathie too?

LEAH

Cathie too.

(Pause. MAGGIE smiles wide.

LEAH calls off to her mother:)

LEAH (cont'd.)

—Momma?

(MARGARET appears immediately in the doorway from the pantry. Has she been eavesdropping?)

MARGARET

She's sleeping now, poor girl. It's all right. I think she's only overwrought. It has been a terrible day. Has it not? —Just terrible!

Because some people grieve well and others do not—

LEAH

—Momma! I'm sorry I did not believe!

(LEAH rushes to her mother, embracing her.)

MARGARET

—Oh!

(MARGARET pulls out of the embrace quickly—as if astonished, if not affronted.

MAGGIE exits quickly to the pantry.

Lights shift into a continuous split-scene of sorts:

LEAH and MARGARET in the kitchen; MAGGIE and LIZZIE in the pantry with CATHIE, who lies in bed with her eyes closed, sick-looking.

MAGGIE sits down on the bed next to CATHIE, stroking her arm; LIZZIE is lying in the bed also, her face to the wall, awake or asleep, who can tell?

MARGARET sits at the kitchen table; still reeling:)

MARGARET (cont'd.)

(Quietly.)

... Now you believe?

LEAH

There's no mystery: you saw me. I stood here. I heard it with my own ears. I heard the spirits.

MARGARET

There's only ever been *one* spirit here ...

LEAH

That's not true. There are many. —They fill up all of nature!

MARGARET

Now you sound like Cathie does—so grand!

LEAH

Cathie knows. She's seen them.

MARGARET

Have you?

(Short pause.)

LEAH

No. I'm not as sensitive as they are ... *(She joins her mother at the table:)* But I think all of us are gifted ...

You're gifted too. I know it.

(Another pause. MARGARET speaks quietly, as if in confidence:)

MARGARET

... Have you heard them when you're alone?

LEAH

I have.

MARGARET

—As have I!

(MARGARET reaches out and touches LEAH's hand, briefly—as if overjoyed.)

MARGARET (cont'd.)

This morning I heard them on my collar. Fluttering. Like moths! When I turned—there wasn't anybody there!

I've smelled their perfume, when there's no one in the room—

LEAH

I've heard a voice, too.

MARGARET

—What's he saying to you?

LEAH

"Go forth and speak the truth."

MARGARET

Go where ... ?

(MAGGIE whispers in the pantry:)

MAGGIE

Cathie ... Wake up ...

(CATHIE doesn't respond.

LIZZIE lies motionless in bed beside them, her face still turned to the wall.)

MAGGIE (cont'd.)

I told her ... I had to. She felt your bones ...

LEAH

We've been *chosen*, Momma ...

MARGARET

That's what I think. —But I've been afraid to say so.

LEAH

They're speaking to us for a reason. —*Through* us.

MARGARET

—What reason could they have?

LEAH

My friends will find great value in this.

MARGARET

Friends? —You mean Hicksites? —What for?

LEAH

They want proof. Guidance.

MARGARET

From you?

LEAH

From the spirits.

MAGGIE

(Whispering.)

She wants us to come with her, to Rochester. To live.

She said she wasn't angry ... She said a lie can become a kind of truth, sometimes ...

LEAH

Think of all the people who come here, Momma. They don't need to hear anything—they *imagine* they do!

MARGARET

—Some of these people want to kill us, Leah!

LEAH

Some love us. Some will worship us.

MARGARET

(Crossing herself.)

Don't blaspheme, they're girls ...

LEAH

They'll pay us too.

MARGARET

You want to make money off them—like a circus?

LEAH

Like a church.

(Short pause.)

LEAH (cont'd.)

Think of that house you want ... There's no money left ... There's no house. He's lied to you, as ever.

Or you know everything I'm telling you already.

(Short pause.)

LEAH (cont'd.)

He's a drunk. He gambles. —God knows what else he's done ...

(MARGARET says nothing.)

LEAH (cont'd.)

I know you hear me, Momma. I know you know it's best for them to go.

(MARGARET begins to rock slowly in her chair.)

MARGARET

... You want to take them from me ... ?

LEAH

Unless you want to come too.

MARGARET

Do you want me to?

(LEAH hesitates.)

MARGARET (cont'd.)

No ...

We're a family. Aren't we? No ... A loving—*aren't* we? Why would I want them— ? What kind of mother would I be then? And who should I let them go with— ? *You?* An agitator for fornicators ... A woman who can't keep her man—no, no ...

(MARGARET continues to rock in her chair.)

MARGARET (cont'd.)

Because some people can get over things, others can not ...

Some people have forgiveness in their hearts. Others—*I* forgave my father! *And* my mother! What they did to me ... I will not say! He locked me in a room, all day one day, and when I came out he said, Remember who has made you. Oh, no no no ...

Because some people are cruel, their hearts are locked like stone. And never will we forgive. —Why is that, Leah? Why is that? do you know? It's a mystery to me ...

(She rocks for a long time in silence.

In the pantry, CATHIE moans feverishly, frightening MAGGIE.

LIZZIE turns as if fitfully in her sleep beside them.)

MAGGIE

—Oh no don't die, Cathie. If you die I'll die too. —I promised you ...

Open your eyes, Cathie. Please.

(Silence. MARGARET still rocking in the kitchen, staring ahead into nothing ...

Then: a low sound, a rapping, in the kitchen, it would seem.

LEAH blows out her candle; moonlight from the windows.

In the pantry, CATHIE rouses.

More rapping, as if from the kitchen. MARGARET rises from her chair:)

MARGARET

—Girls?

MAGGIE

It's happening now—without us.

(MAGGIE leads CATHIE uneasily into the kitchen. LIZZIE hangs back, in the pantry.

The rapping is heard from all points, as if by many hands, as if the girls have brought more spirit-hands with them.)

MARGARET

What's he want with us now, do you think?

LEAH

He wants you to let them go—with me. To the city.

MARGARET

How do you know that? —You *can't* know that!

MAGGIE

—I hear him now too, Momma. His voice.

(The rapping sound continues, resurges.)

LEAH

Kneel down with us, girls. We'll pray.

MARGARET

—To Charles?

(All four of them kneel. They hold hands.)

MAGGIE

Take my hand, Cathie ...

LEAH

Close your eyes, Momma—everyone.

(LIZZIE has appeared in the doorway from the pantry, shivering in the cold. Barefoot. She watches, unseen, in the shadows.)

MARGARET

What do we say, Leah ... ?

(LEAH prays.)

LEAH

Spirit, forgive us our blindness. We are only but poor women, who see only with women's eyes. Who see only the Devil's world, the world of decay and deceit. —You must show us the truth, you must *teach* us! —What do you want from us? Play us, your instruments. —Play your song in us!

(The others' eyes are still closed ... but LEAH's opened hers; she's withdrawn a hair pin from her mother's hair:)

MARGARET

—My hair!

LEAH

Keep your eyes closed, Momma.

MARGARET

My pin!

LEAH

—It's floating in the air above you!

MARGARET

It's fluttering my collar! —Like a butterfly!

(LEAH flutters MARGARET's collar with the pin.

Then pricks MARGARET's neck with it.)

MARGARET (cont'd.)

—Oh!

(CATHIE, still dazed, feverish, stares ahead into nothing.)

LEAH

—They're pricking you with pins now, Momma!

MARGARET

Who is? They are? —Stop that!

(LEAH drops the pin.)

MAGGIE

—It's dropped, Momma!

(Now it's MAGGIE's turn: she lifts her mother's sleeping cap off her head.)

MAGGIE (cont'd.)

Your cap is floating off your head— !

MARGARET

Where's it going?

LEAH

—Keep your eyes shut— !

(MAGGIE drops the cap, just as MARGARET opens her eyes for a peek.)

MARGARET

It's on my head again! Oh! —It's fallen!

(Now both MAGGIE and LEAH are poking their mother, when their mother's not looking, lightly slapping her arms, squeezing, pinching.)

LEAH

—They're touching you!

MAGGIE

—They're poking!

LEAH

—They're pinching you!

MARGARET

—Pray to God, girls! Pray to God to save us from them! —Who are they?

CATHIE

"I can't pray now I feel like cursing."

MARGARET

What's Cathie saying ... ?

LEAH

Keep your eyes closed, Momma—

(MAGGIE and LEAH have been crouching and standing over their kneeling mother, poking her, making rapping sounds on floor and furniture with their fists and feet and joints, the noise ever increasing ...

For all the sounds they make, we should feel as if there is always more noise, more agents of that noise, in the room.

Perhaps CATHIE *is popping her joints, though who can tell? She appears entranced, still, feverish and dazed. She rises to her feet.*

MARGARET *speaks as if enraptured:)*

MARGARET

They're angry at me! Why do they hate me? Why must they torment me? Why do they *abuse* me? Why do they want me dead? What have I ever done to *them?*

(Suddenly CATHIE *flings a chair over, behind her mother's back.*

LEAH *and* MAGGIE *are surprised—then as if inspired, by* CATHIE*'s escalation of aggression.*

LEAH *shoves the table, throws some cups and plates, when her mother's not looking.* MAGGIE *joins in, breaking plates, cups, saucers, tumblers. Forks and knives are thrown. All four of them are screaming, crying: a hysteria, or dance.*

Once or twice it looks like someone might do some real violence to their mother; but always the violent blow is displaced.

MARGARET *has stood up now too, or is trying to stand, opening her eyes: just as she looks in one direction, something breaks somewhere else. She is being played expertly; a virtuoso performance.*

Long pause here.

Everyone is speechless, breathless. Dumbstruck.

Then CATHIE *breaks a window pane with her hand.* MARGARET *screams; then crying ...*

MAGGIE *has rushed to her sister, wraps her nightgown around* CATHIE*'s cut hand.*

MARGARET *collapses into her rocking chair. After a moment:*

LEAH *sees* LIZZIE, *in the doorway from the pantry. She has watched it all.*

She holds her hand out to her daughter:)

LEAH

Elizabeth.

(LIZZIE turns her back on her mother, disappears into the dark pantry.)

11A. DARKNESS.

LEAH

Are there those here tonight who do not believe that death has been destroyed? That life is everlasting, and always has been?

(Silence.)

LEAH (cont'd.)

And what is the purpose of this life then, oh Spirit? if not to learn?

(Two raps.)

LEAH (cont'd.)

What does this life mean to teach us? Namely: that we are the authors of our lives.

Only we can save ourselves. Because life is not for forgiveness ... Life is not for sacrifice, and suffering ...

Life is for loving life. And respect. And knowledge ... *Progress.*

(Silence.)

LEAH (cont'd.)

Are you listening, Spirit? And don't you agree ... ?

(Strongly: two raps.)

11. KITCHEN

(Next day. Morning. MARGARET has not moved.

Dawn light in the windows; the house is still dark, though growing brighter. Birdsong. The window pane is broken, a hole to the outside. The room is cold, the stove cold.

MARGARET sits in her rocking chair still, amidst the debris, as if calm, a smile on her face. She sits alone for a while, no blankets on her, not rocking. She must be very cold. She stares ahead into nothing.

LEAH appears in the doorway from the pantry, with LIZZIE behind her, dressed smartly for travel, bags packed. LEAH is holding LIZZIE's hand quite tight.)

LEAH

We'll up to Newark then.

MARGARET

Your father's coming. Let him drive you. He likes to drive.

LEAH

We'll get the packet-boat first thing. We'll be home before dinner.

MARGARET

Don't you worry because your grandfather's coming, Lizzie ...

(Short pause. MARGARET begins to rock in her chair.)

LIZZIE

Will you be all right, Nana?

(LIZZIE tries to step closer to her grandmother, but LEAH holds fast to her hand.)

MARGARET

Why wouldn't I ... ?

The flies are gone. Have you seen? how quiet ... I'll have to get that window patched ...

LIZZIE

You can visit us. In the city. We'll let you visit.

MARGARET

(As if baffled.)

Why would I ... ?

(During the following MARGARET will get up and begin straightening the room, slowly at first, as best she can; in ever increasing manic fashion:)

MARGARET (cont'd.)

Because by that time we'll have our own house ...

Won't we ... ?

... In Hydesville. Oh yes. —Won't we? Up the hill, beside David's ... A big house, bigger than this one. Brighter! and cleaner. Full of light! You'll see. You'll see. You can all come and visit us then ... We'll have rooms for every one. Elizabeth, in Consecon, in Canada. And Marie, who lives nearby though we never see her ...

LEAH

We're leaving now, Momma.

MARGARET

You'll wait for your father. You should. Shall we? He's coming, he'll be so glad to see you to the boat—

(MAGGIE and CATHIE have appeared in the doorway from the pantry.

CATHIE looks better, as if her fever's gone, or at least lessened; her hand is tied with a rag. There's something wasted in her eyes.

MAGGIE looks troubled, pale—but there's relief in her face also.

LEAH holds her hands out to her sisters; they come to her.)

MAGGIE

We can't take everything—

LEAH

We'll borrow whatever you need.

MARGARET

We'll send your things to you. —You'll see!

MAGGIE

There's too much to take with us, Momma—

LEAH

You'll leave it here then, for now. My friends will lend us things.

MARGARET

We'll send money. Your father will.

LEAH

Say goodbye to your grandmother, Lizzie.

LIZZIE

Goodbye, Nana.

(LIZZIE goes to her, hugs MARGARET who doesn't hug back—just allows herself to be embraced, limply. LIZZIE seems close to tears again.)

LEAH

Momma. Goodbye.

(MARGARET doesn't answer. She won't look at her daughter.)

LEAH (cont'd.)

You'll send the extra bags along. All right? We'll send money—

LIZZIE

You can bring them, Nana, when you come.

CATHIE

Will you come to see us again, Momma, before you die?

(Pause.)

MARGARET

Will I die so soon?

(CATHIE doesn't answer. MARGARET knocks on wood, crosses herself.)

MARGARET (cont'd.)

What an unkind thing to say— ! *(She laughs.)* What a cruel— !

(A knock on the back door.

CATHIE unlocks it; and DAVID enters. He's filthy with dirt and mud, arms and legs especially.

He speaks only to CATHIE.)

MAGGIE

What's wrong, David ... ?

DAVID

Where is she? I've been looking for her ...

LEAH

Whom, David.

LIZZIE

... What's wrong, Uncle David?

DAVID

I saw her, last night ... She woke me up, she knocked on the bedstead ... She was like a woman, like Cathie saw her once ... Her dress was wet ... She tried to say something.

But she couldn't—her mouth was full of dirt—

LEAH

What did you do, David?

DAVID

I went up the hill with a spade—

MARGARET

(Rocking.)

No no no no no ...

DAVID

I broke it open—it wasn't her inside. —It *was* her, but—where is she? Have you seen her, Cathie?

(CATHIE moves to him. Takes his hand. She's about to say something—)

LEAH

Spirit? Are you listening? —Charles? Are you here with us now?

(No answer.)

LEAH (cont'd.)

Can we speak to someone new? Or is it only Charles we can speak to? —May we converse with another discarnate soul ... ?

(A pause. Then, two raps.)

LEAH (cont'd.)

May we speak to the spirit of the infant Ella Fox, recently deceased?

(Another pause. Then: two small delicate raps, almost taps.

DAVID cries, his sister CATHIE's hand still on him, as lights slowly fade.)

12A. DARKNESS.

(LEAH sings to the melody she hummed in scene seven:)

LEAH

Tune, tune your harps, your harps, ye saints in glory—
All is well, all is well!
I will rehearse, rehearse the pleasing story—
All is well, all is well!
Bright angels are from glory come,
They're round my bed, they're in my room,
They wait to waft my Spirit home,
All is well, all is well!

(Silence.)

LEAH (cont'd.)

That was a lovely hymn we've sung. You've taught it to us all, spirits. What an enlightened colloquy we've held here tonight ... We thank thee!

There are so many here with us, right this moment, in my house in Rochester, on Sophia Street. Are there not? a multitude of friends?

(Two raps.)

LEAH (cont'd.)

So many spirits, for every man and every woman at this table, holding hands ...

(Silence.)

LEAH (cont'd.)

... Is Benjamin here, the child of the Quaker reformers Amy and Isaac Post?

(Two raps.)

LEAH (cont'd.)

... The daughter of Lyman Granger, poisoned by her husband?

(Two raps.)

LEAH (cont'd.)

... The sister of Frederick Douglas, the great Negro man.

(Two raps.)

LEAH (cont'd.)

All say life is precious! The slave is not merchandise; the wife is not merchandise—

(A cascade of hand-bells.)

LEAH (cont'd.)

In our house in New York City tonight: the sister of James Fenimore Cooper, thrown from a horse to her death at such an early age?

(A hand-bell rings.)

LEAH (cont'd.)

... Pickie, son of Horace Greeley, dead of typhus, age five?

(A hand-bell rings.)

LEAH (cont'd.)

The table lifts! Feel it, gentlemen! ladies! Feel it—lift!

(Lights have slowly grown. Hand-bells are ringing. A year has passed.

What had been the sitting room of the house in Hydesville has become the sitting room of Leah's townhouse in New York City: opulent, a bit gaudy, theatrically spooky. The sounds of the city outside—crowds, horses' hooves, trolley cars.

Gas lights flicker low.

The table does indeed appear to levitate, at a tilt.

Seated round it we can just make out: MAGGIE and CATHIE, heads bowed, veils over their heads and faces; with LEAH between her sisters.

The others are in shadow, or with their back to us: strangers, alternating men and women, played by the actors who played MARGARET, JOHN, LIZZIE and DAVID.

There are seven at this table, all holding hands.)

LEAH (cont'd.)

How wondrous! What miracle! What great new age! —Who else is here with us now? Who else is waiting their turn to speak? Speak, Spirit, speak to us! Speak, Spirit! —Speak!

END OF PLAY

THE CHERRY SISTERS REVISITED

Characters

EFFIE	The youngest, the smartest.
ADDIE	The next youngest, the funniest.
LIZZIE	The middle one, the prettiest.
ELLA	The next-to-eldest. Slow, prophetic.
JESSIE	The eldest.
POPS	Their father; and also their agent.

Time

1892 – 1935, and the present.

Place

Various. The stage is fluid but in its foundation looks like the husk of an old, decrepit barn in Iowa, a wintry landscape outside.

Notes

1) While many scenes are meant to take place somewhere specific, usually marked in the script by a scene title, much of the play takes place in a kind of limbo outside time and space: at once the theater itself, and the memory of a ghost inside an old, decrepit barn, heartless plains wind howling through the boards.

2) Regarding the ages of the various Cherry Sisters: ideally all of the actors will be in their 20s and 30s or thereabouts, playing a little younger and then older as the play progresses. As the play is meant to be a vaudeville and a fable, and happens in the theatrical present tense, the age of the actors doesn't really matter so much as the dynamic between them.

3) Concerning the "true story" of the Cherry Sisters, I am indebted to Avery Hale's 1944 article for Coronet, "So Bad They Were Good," as well as Anthony Slide's *Selected Vaudeville Criticism* (Rowman & Littlefield, 1988).

The Cherry Sisters Revisited was supported in part by a residency at Yaddo, the Hodder Fellowship at Princeton University, and the Tennessee Williams Fellowship at The University of the South (Sewanee).

The Cherry Sisters Revisited was developed at The Perry-Mansfield New Works Festival and premiered at the Humana Festival of New American Plays at Actors' Theatre of Louisville, Marc Masterson, Artistic Director, in 2010, with original music by Michael Friedman and directed by Andrew Leynse.

EFFIE CHERRY	Renata Friedman
ADDIE CHERRY	Katie Kreisler
LIZZIE CHERRY	Kate Gersten
ELLA CHERRY	Cassie Beck
JESSIE CHERRY	Donna Lynne Champlin
POPS	John Hickok

Creative Team

Music Director / Pianist	Stephen Malone
Scenic Designer	Scott Bradley
Costume Designer	Lorraine Venberg
Lighting Designer	Brian J. Lilienthal
Sound Designer	Matt Callahan
Properties Designer	Mark Waltson
Wig / Makeup Designer	Heather Fleming
Movement Director	Delilah Smyth
Production Stage Manager	Paul Mills Holmes
Dialect Coach	Rocco Dal Vera
Production Assistant	Cadi Thomas
Dramaturg	Julie Felise Dubiner
Casting	Stephanie Klapper
Directing Asistant	Jay Briggs
Scenic Design Assistant	Ryan Wineinger
Lighting Design Assistants	John Burkland Andrew Cissna
Stage Management Intern	Nick Busset
Assistant Dramaturg	Emily Feldman

The mouths of their rancid features opened like caverns,
and sounds like the wailing of damned souls issued therefrom . . .

—W.E. "Billy" Hamilton in the *Odebolt Chronicle*
February 17, 1898

Act One

EFFIE

Do you believe in ghosts?

You, in the audience. Think about that. *(Pause.)* 'Cause you're looking at one.

(She points a finger:)

EFFIE (cont'd.)

—You did this to us.

(Iris-light widens on the sisters in the world ...)

1: CEDAR RAPIDS, IOWA. OUTSIDE THE THEATER.

EFFIE

Let's see it again.

JESSIE

You say that every time we see it, Effie ...

EFFIE

And every time it's beautiful. —A miracle!

ADDIE

I'll go back inside the theater with you, Effie. If you want.

(ADDIE takes EFFIE's hand.)

JESSIE

Lizzie, stop looking at yourself in that mirror, it's vain!

LIZZIE

It's not a mirror, it's a shop window, that dress is pretty—where's Pops?

(They all look for him.)

JESSIE

I'm beginning to get worried ... He should've been here by now ...

(ELLA points. The others look to where she's pointing.

JESSIE takes her hand in hers.)

JESSIE (cont'd.)

That's not Pops, dear, that's a pile of dead leaves.

EFFIE

Let's see the show again! Can we? Please? —Just one more time—

LIZZIE

You can't spend all day inside a theater, Effie.

ELLA

Effie can.

(They're all a bit startled, but only a bit, by what ELLA's said.)

EFFIE

Thank you, Ella.

ELLA

Don't mention it.

EFFIE

I only like it in there because it's not like at home. It's the opposite of home. It's profound! in there ...

LIZZIE

"Profound," Effie?

ADDIE

It means very much.

LIZZIE

I know what profound means. I'm not stupid, like Ella is ...

JESSIE

It's too crowded in there. It's raucous, and it smells like sin.

You mark my words: in the Twentieth Century, there will be no such thing as the vaudeville!

EFFIE

You say that every week, Jessie. And every week we come back.

JESSIE

We have to—someone has to make sure Pops gets home ...

(ELLA points to the pile of dead leaves again. JESSIE takes her hand once more.)

JESSIE (cont'd.)

Stop pointing at nothing, dear, that's rude.

EFFIE

We've never seen some of them before. Some of them were famous—

ADDIE

They're on jump-break from New York City—

JESSIE

You don't even know what "jump-break" means.

ADDIE

Do you?

(LIZZIE starts singing to herself, absentmindedly beneath the ensuing dialogue:)

LIZZIE

(Wistfully.)

I'm so lonely for Old Broadway,
I'm so bored by these cornfields and hay ...

EFFIE

Then came the Spanish gypsies! Remember? That daring young girl in her pink underwear—

JESSIE

Pull your skirts down now, Effie—

EFFIE

—holding onto that long, thick rope with just her long, strong teeth.
She clenched herself, spinning there, like a great, pink, blurred abstraction ...
She can't be much older than we are!

JESSIE

Get down off that post, Effie Cherry—you're going to fall down— !

EFFIE

Then she falls! like an angel on a pin, upon a prancing pony's jouncing spine—

JESSIE

Oh, Effie, stop! Please! —People are *looking* at us!

EFFIE

That's the point!

—Then on one leg she poses *(she poses)*, the daintiest ballerina—better than that, because she's balanced on a gosh darned moving horse!

ADDIE

Hurrah! Huzzah! "Gosh darn"!

JESSIE

Such language— !

(JESSIE covers ELLA's ears.)

EFFIE

She *leaps!*

(EFFIE leaps, and lands—or falls, rather, ungracefully, possibly painfully.

The others look on, concernedly ...

JESSIE runs to her, kneels, gathers EFFIE into her prodigious bosoms.)

JESSIE

Oh Effie dear, are you all right ... ?

(EFFIE stands, a bit shaken: she's fine.

She smiles at her sister JESSIE. A moment.)

ADDIE

Then her sister bounds onstage—

(ADDIE bounds in the dirt and dust.)

JESSIE

Oh no, I'm not playing—

ADDIE

I'm talking about myself.

LIZZIE

That's funny, that misunderstanding.

ADDIE

In her pink underwear also—

JESSIE

Pull your skirts down, girls! Now you both look like whores!

ADDIE

—Jessie!

JESSIE

What?

ADDIE

"Such language"!

JESSIE

"Whores" is in the Bible, my dear Addison—all the time.

EFFIE

—They defy gravity! They shimmy upside down! They shift from palm to palm as graceful as any two Orientals do!

(ADDIE and EFFIE attempt some approximation of the above, failing badly at it but who cares?

LIZZIE giggles, JESSIE disapproves; ELLA might smile, then yawn, or drool.)

LIZZIE

Then a handsome young man *erupts* on the scene—like a gazelle—

(She prances herself—a gazelle, but a clumsy one.)

EFFIE

A gazelle?

ADDIE

"Erupts"?

EFFIE

There were others—Ella, come here.

JESSIE

Don't you involve her in this—

ELLA

(To JESSIE.)

I want to—let me go!

(JESSIE does let her go.

The four sisters have formed a kind of human pyramid around JESSIE, as if their older sister is in on the act.)

EFFIE

An entire family of Spanish gypsies balanced there, one beside—

ADDIE

—on top of!

EFFIE

—the other! A structure of un-heretofore-dreamt-of perfection ... !

(The five of them: a very imperfect pyramid.

Another pause.)

EFFIE (cont'd.)

I want to go into show business.

(They all come tumbling down.)

JESSIE

Don't joke like that.

EFFIE

I want to write acts. And perform them. I want to make costumes. And wear them. I want to rehearse in our own little barn, during long winter months, while the snow piles four fathoms deep on the prairie outside. I want to travel out ahead of ourselves in time and space on the steam of our own imaginative locomotion—leave Pops behind, leave Iowa behind, and journey—to New York City!

(As before, LIZZIE sings to herself while EFFIE goes on talking.)

LIZZIE

I'm so homesick for Broadway's crowds,
I'm so sick of these donkeys and plows.
The something, something, something else ...

EFFIE

New York City, which might as well be Rome for all I care, for New York's so far away and full of fast-talking wisenheimers, immigrants and sons-of-immigrants who'll swindle you within a dime of your life—oh, New York City! *(she swoons, a little)*, where the banks are like churches, and the people all live in coffins so close to one another you can reach out your hand, out your window, and boil your tea right off your neighbor's stove. And all the streets are numbered because nobody knows how to read—who's got the time? and time's money, in New York City. And the only livestock to be found are pigeons, and roaches, and rats ... Oh, the manifold lovelinesses of New York!

We'll tour, the old world, to Europe—and Spain! Somewhere brown and papery—I love paper—where it never snows, and corn is an alien commodity ... A land full of gypsy girls, just like us, who wear kerchiefs round their heads to keep the robust lice in, and squat round fires on their wide, mannish haunches, singing and joking their rough gay lives away ...

And men too!—of course there'll be men there ... Brown gypsy-types with wavy black hair and dark eyes set in a face of tan wrinkles, like the lines in a leather-bound book ...

(She gasps, an epiphany of some kind.

The others look at her as if they're looking in a mirror—and liking what they see.

Except JESSIE, who looks disturbed.

A long pause here. They wait to see what JESSIE will say.)

JESSIE

What about Pops?

(A long, long pause here.)

ADDIE

What about him ... ?

JESSIE

He needs us ... He'll fall apart without us.

ADDIE

Good.

LIZZIE

Oh, Addie ...

JESSIE

Remember that time we found him in the barn, with a rope in his hand, standing on a chair ... ?

(Pause.)

LIZZIE

He said he was about to hang something.

ADDIE

He was.

(Another pause.)

EFFIE

Well we'll have to leave him one day ... won't we?

JESSIE

We will. When we get married.

LIZZIE

Someone has to ask us first.

(Another pause. They look each other up and down.)

EFFIE

Jessie's right: we can't leave him, ever. Poor Pops ... where do you think he's gone?

(Slowly, again, ELLA points to the pile of dead leaves downstage.

A cold wind blows.

This time no one scolds her.

Pause.

EFFIE moves downstage first.

She pulls away the blanket of leaves to reveal:

POPS Cherry.

Curled up like a fetus.

Hugging whiskey bottles to his chest. A stub of wet cigar bit tightly in his teeth ...

His face is deathly pale.

He looks dead.

He is.

After a short beat of horror, and then a mysterious, long exhalation of something like relief ... EFFIE speaks to us.)

EFFIE (cont'd.)

You saw it coming, didn't you.

You're used to such surprises, in "the theatre."

As my slow sister Ella had discovered, I know not wherefrom—from the ether, perhaps?—our father died that day. While we were inside at the show ...

How—providential, you might say ...

Because our father, Pops Cherry—"Pops" is just a nickname, by the way, and he's only a Cherry by way of corruption from the Irish—O'Chernussy, probably, originally, though who can be sure of anything he's ever told us?

Our father had not been well since the death of our mother, now many, many years ago. Nineteen years ago, in fact. My age, to the day. And since that day he'd been drunk. Sometimes worse.

(POPS jumps to his feet, his whiskey bottles stuck to him. As if he's wearing a suit made of whiskey bottles.)

POPS

You always were unlucky!

EFFIE

I love you, Pops. I miss you.

POPS

Ech?

EFFIE

I said I—

POPS

Everything you touch turns to pewter!

EFFIE

"Pewter"?

POPS

I ought to say manure, but this is a family crowd.

EFFIE

(Looking out.)

It is?

POPS

—Like your mother was, bedad!

EFFIE

(Excited.)
In what ways am I like Momma, Pops?

POPS

You're too smart for your own good, that's what. Look at that great big horse's head of yours. Like a great big horse's skull! all long in front and fat in back. It's what killed your mother before the start of it all, that great big horse's nut of yours ...

(EFFIE touches her head, with fear and wonder.)

POPS (cont'd.)

You took what it was your mother had.

EFFIE

What did she have, Pops?

POPS

Babies. One Cherry right after the other—pop, pop, pop, pop, pop. And heaving one last long sigh she took a great big soaring lep' out of that writhing birdlike body of hers up into the basin of sky and out of the throes of trying to bring you and that monstrously fat head of yours out into the world of men. *(He inhales extravagantly, staggers.)*
Poor girl, poor wife, poor me.

(He tries to rip one of the bottles off his clothes. But they're empty now anyway.)

POPS (cont'd.)

Damn it all to Hell! *(He tries to smoke his cigar. He asks the audience.)* D'you got a match?

EFFIE

We're going into showbiz, Pops.

POPS

—*Shoe*-biz? what for? Do you know what that's like, handling feet all day ... ?

EFFIE

Show biz, Pops, the vaudeville.

POPS

Oh. Och no.

EFFIE

What's wrong?

POPS

You're not whores now, are you?

EFFIE

Not all prostitutes are actresses, Pops.

POPS

Name one. —And you can't do nothing, neither!

EFFIE

Like what?

POPS

—Like talent!

EFFIE

How do you know that? You don't know that yet—we're good! You'll see!

POPS

Will I? I don't think I will ...

EFFIE

Why not?

POPS

You see, because I've died ...

EFFIE

Oh, I forgot ...

POPS

And so have you, died, too ... You're a ghost now too, you know.

EFFIE

Am I?

POPS

Don't forget that now.

EFFIE

I always do ...

POPS

Don't we all?

EFFIE

Where am I then?

POPS

In the ether.

EFFIE

Where's that?

POPS

In the theater.

EFFIE

Which theater?

POPS

In the barn, back in Iowa. In a way. In the future. Or no-time at all ...
You're haunted, me girl. Ghosts can be haunted too, you know.

(Pause. She pushes him offstage.)

EFFIE

Get offstage now, Pops. —Go!

POPS

If you're ever famous, remember—you got your talent from me!

(He sings, as he goes:)

POPS (cont'd.)

Me bodice, neat an' modest, O, is slippin', sir
—Be careful, sir, be careful, please!
The silken thread that holds it up is rippin', sir
—O, do be careful! —O, do be careful!
There now, it's down about me waist,
Me pearly goods are all uncased,
I hope they're temper'd to your taste
—St. Patrick's Day in the morning!

(He disappears, singing, bottles tinkling into the wings.)

POPS (cont'd.)

Fiddle-dee-dee, fiddle-dee-die ...

(Emphasis on the "die" ...

EFFIE doesn't want to cry.

Wind and snow.)

2: THE BARN IN MARION. REHEARSAL. WINTER.

(ELLA's not here.

LIZZIE's wiping the dirt on her skirt ...)

LIZZIE

He looked so sad in that pinewood box, as they lowered him into the ground ...

ADDIE

You couldn't see his face. The lid was screwed on.

(JESSIE eats some cheese, and sighs:)

JESSIE

Sad ...

EFFIE

Here's what I envision:

Numerous acts, some funny, some sad. Some songs, Lizzie, you'll sing a few pretty ditties. Something sentimental of the euphemistic school. You know the score. I have the titles, you can fill in the rest.

One: *I Ain't Never Been Kissed.* Two: *Let's Canoodle in the Doodle-ee-doo.* And three—*Corn Juice!* Exclamation point. Naturally.

Let me write this all down:

(She does, in a little brown book that seems to appear in the ether.)

ADDIE

Where'd you find that?

EFFIE

In the ether.

JESSIE

(Eating cheese.)

You're nuts, Effie Cherry ...

EFFIE

What's nuts? to dream? —Perchance to dream, Jessie!

LIZZIE

Who said that?

ADDIE

Walt Whitman.

LIZZIE

Who's he?

ADDIE

Some nurse.

LIZZIE

How's this sound?

(LIZZIE sings, with her ukelele:)

LIZZIE (cont'd.)

Let's canoodle in the doodle-ee-doo
And foodle with the poodle-ee-pee.
I'll piddle your diddle
If you fiddle my middle,
Canoodling in the doodle-ee-doodle-ee-doodle-ee-
Dum-m-m!

EFFIE

Keep working on that one.
We'll need some playlets—

LIZZIE

What's a "playlet"?

ADDIE

Like a play, but suckling.

LIZZIE

—That's a good one, Addie!

ADDIE

Is it? I don't know about that one yet ...

EFFIE

And some comic monologuing. Addie, that's your forte, make it fresh, make it funny.

JESSIE

—What about me?

EFFIE

What about you, Jessie.

JESSIE

What do I do?

EFFIE

Well, so far. I've got you down for the ... "heavy lifting." Jessie.

(Pause.)

JESSIE

Lifting what?

EFFIE

Props and scenery, mostly.

LIZZIE

You're the most athletic, Jessie. Everyone knows that ...

JESSIE

What about Addie?—she's got man-hands!

(ADDIE examines her hands.)

LIZZIE

It's true ...

JESSIE

I'm heavy ... if that's what you mean ... I don't eat much. Lord knows we don't *ever* eat much, any of us, except maybe cheese, on a good day ... Corn ... It's a mystery to me.

I'm just naturally matronly ...

(JESSIE eats some more cheese.)

JESSIE (cont'd.)

—But I can't lift much! My heart's not strong. Like Momma's wasn't ...

(A deep pause, surprisingly felt.

They all glance at, or away from, or just think about EFFIE and her very large head ...

EFFIE touches said head, without noticing what she's doing ...

ADDIE changes the subject:)

ADDIE

So I'm reading this book:

(Shows the cover.)

LIZZIE

So You Want to Live in Vaudeville? (Pause.)
Well do you?

ADDIE

It's a rhetorical question. It's got killer Brooklynese.

EFFIE

Definitions?

ADDIE

You betcha.

EFFIE

Phonetic?

ADDIE

No, English.

LIZZIE

Where is Phoenicia, anyway?

EFFIE

Let me hear some please:

ADDIE

"Take my seat, young goil! I'm only goin' so far as Yahnkers!"

(Pause. EFFIE savors:)

EFFIE

That's beautiful.

ADDIE

Isn't it?

LIZZIE

Where is Yonkers anyway?

ADDIE

Brooklyn, I guess.

JESSIE

That's crude. I think such speech is vulgar.

LIZZIE

What about a Negro song? some kind of sassy soft-shoeing? some black face maybe? Addie would make a very convincing coon, I think.

JESSIE

That is also in poor taste.

LIZZIE

Whose taste? I find their music stirring.

JESSIE

In the Twentieth Century no one will laugh at Negroes.

LIZZIE

Why not? Where will they have all gone?

ADDIE

The Twentieth Century is eight years from now, Jessie ...

JESSIE

I know that. —This is *America*, Addie!

EFFIE

And when our act is strong and tight we'll do a show, at home, at the Marion Grange Hall. We'll hone our craft on friendly turf, then raise enough in capital to take our show all the way to Cedar Rapids—

(LIZZIE gasps.)

EFFIE (cont'd.)

Don't gasp, it's true—it's within our reach, our grasp. Every day, a great actress dries up onstage, like a prune, and every day another one *blooms!*

JESSIE

But what if we're not good enough ... ?

(A sudden, long pause ensues ... JESSIE eats some more cheese, morosely.

EFFIE's about to touch her head again, but ADDIE takes her hand and holds it.)

LIZZIE

He looked so sad in that coffin, the earth was frozen six feet down ...

(JESSIE eats more cheese.)

EFFIE

We'll need a name.

ADDIE

We have one already, don't we?

LIZZIE

Do we? Which one?

JESSIE

The name God gave us.

ADDIE

You mean Pops gave us ...

LIZZIE

"The Cherries."

(It just sits there in the barn.)

ADDIE

We'll be popular with the men.

LIZZIE

Why?

JESSIE

Yes, why, Addie?

ADDIE

Where's Ella with our lunch?

LIZZIE

I'm hungry now too ...

JESSIE

Have my cheese.

(She offers LIZZIE some.)

LIZZIE

I've got to watch my figure. *(Pause.)* We all do.

JESSIE

(Eating more cheese.)

We all do what?

EFFIE

What's wrong with our figures, Lizzie?

LIZZIE

Well. With the possible exception of you, Effie, who's already bone-thin, like a thin old swayback mule—

EFFIE

Like a what?

LIZZIE

—the rest of us are far too ... matronly. *(Pause.)* Like Jessie said.

EFFIE

How can we be matronly? we're not even married—

LIZZIE

That's my point exactly.

It hardly matters much for you, Addie—you're the funny one, all that matters is your wits. If you get fat you'll be *more* funny, probably, because fat people are mostly jolly, except when they're mean, and then they're positively evil ...

And as for Effie it's her brains inside that great big head of hers ... And Jessie here is for the heavy lifting, as we've discussed, despite the danger to her heart.

No: I'm the one who must stay pretty, Pops would always say.

ADDIE

Where's Ella with our gosh darned lunch!

JESSIE

—Such language!

EFFIE

She's inside sewing our new leotards.

JESSIE

Are you sure that's such a good idea?

ADDIE

Some of history's best seamstresses have been mentally impaired.

LIZZIE

Really?

ADDIE

No, I was just trying out a joke—does it work?

JESSIE

I don't think she should be let loose out there, what with all this wind and driving snow ...

EFFIE

She's not a cat.

ADDIE

It *is* snowing fiercely out there, Effie ...

EFFIE

It's always snowing here.

LIZZIE

I know. Why *is* that?

EFFIE

—We need to focus, girls! —Focus! We've got so much more work to do!

LIZZIE

I think I see her coming now ...

JESSIE

That's her outside in the wind and driving snow—keep walking, Ella! You can make it!

LIZZIE

Are you sure that's Ella out there in the wind and ... ?

JESSIE

Driving snow.

LIZZIE

Driving snow?

JESSIE

Who else could she be?

LIZZIE

I don't know, a ghost maybe?

ADDIE

Whose ghost?

LIZZIE

She looks a lot like Momma did ...

JESSIE

Do you remember when Momma would take the washing from the line, in the snow? The temperature would drop, and the snow would sweep in ... The sheets would be frozen, they'd crack like boards when she folded them in front of the fire.

EFFIE

—What about: "The Beautiful Cherry Sisters"?

(They look each other up and down.)

EFFIE (cont'd.)

No.

ADDIE

That won't work.

LIZZIE

—*I'm* not ugly!

ADDIE

That's mostly true.

EFFIE

"The Four Cherry Sisters" simply?

LIZZIE

"The Four Cherry Sisters Simply" is far too modest.

JESSIE

Five. With Ella.

(Another pause.)

JESSIE (cont'd.)

Well we have to, don't we?

We can't leave her alone out here, surely ...

ADDIE

Can she sing and dance?

JESSIE

She's one of us, Addie, she's a Cherry!

ADDIE

She's an idiot, Jessie. *(Short pause.)* I mean that in the clinical sense.

JESSIE

So?

EFFIE

People are going to laugh at her ...

LIZZIE

But that's the point, isn't it?

JESSIE

—Come on, Ella! You can make it!

LIZZIE

She's teetering in the wind!

JESSIE

She's wandered off the trail!

LIZZIE

She's carrying our new leotards—they're pretty! They're bunched before her face!

JESSIE

Look—one's flown away!

LIZZIE

Like a flamingo!

JESSIE

Do you remember how silent mother was? how graceful and composed ... ?

LIZZIE

Like Ella, though not as dumb ...

JESSIE

I remember her standing at the stove, with baby Addie in her arms, rocking her to sleep and singing ... She had such a pretty voice, like you do, Lizzie ... with her breast in Addie's mouth ...

ADDIE

I wish I could remember that.

EFFIE

—You were too young when she died, Addie.

ADDIE

What do you know—you weren't even fully born yet!

(ADDIE immediately regrets what she's said.)

JESSIE

—Keep walking, Ella, you're almost here!

LIZZIE

Oh look—she's fallen in a drift—

ADDIE

Oh now she's up again! Here she comes!

EFFIE

—"The Musical Cherries"?

LIZZIE

Redundant.

EFFIE

"Cherries A-Poppin'!"

JESSIE

Been done before.

EFFIE

"The Five Ripe Cherries"?

ADDIE

That sounds like we smell bad.

LIZZIE

Or taste good.

ADDIE

That's filthy!

JESSIE

—It doesn't matter what we're called, girls! No one's going to care! No one's going to believe us, when they see us up there on that stage at the Marion Grange Hall. They'll say, Who do these girls think they are? We knew their poor mother, we knew Pops—we know what *he* was like ...

No, they won't believe us for a minute.

EFFIE

Then we'll have to believe it first. *(Pause.)* If we believe it, then they will.

JESSIE

Is that how it works ... ?

EFFIE

What do you say, girls? Can you believe it?

(No one answers.

The answer would seem to be "maybe?")

EFFIE (cont'd.)

That's it: "The Unbelievable Cherry Sisters!" *(Pause.)* Exclamation point!

JESSIE

Well it's accurate, anyway ...

(Enter ELLA, all covered in snow.

She carries a great big bass drum, strapped vertically to her chest.

She bangs the drum slowly, loudly, with a dirty wooden spoon ...

She stops drumming. Turns slowly to reveal that one side of the drum reads:

"The Unbelievable Cherry Sisters!")

ELLA

I believe in *you*, Effie.

(All look to EFFIE.)

EFFIE

How did you know that, Ella? were you listening outside ... ?

3: MARION GRANGE HALL. NIGHT.

(ELLA continues to beat her drum occasionally, throughout the following:)

ADDIE

Good evening, ladies and Germans! *(Silence.)* That was supposed to be—just a bit of bidness. *(Pause.)* Because there's a lot of folks here of German extraction, in Marion, Iowa, you see. Immigrants, via Ellis Island, etcetera. Well—*(to herself)* "don't explain your jokes," Chapter Twelve ...

Welcome, everyone, to *le premier* performance of what everyone's just dying to pop inside their mouths: The Cherries! *(Silence.)* That's right, "The Unbelievable Cherry Sisters!" Exclamation! Point!

(Much more silence. JESSIE steps forward.)

JESSIE

You can clap, you know. It's considered polite.

(A few hands applaud.

The sisters sing the following song together, to the tune of "Ta-ra-ra boom-dee-ay."

ELLA is beating the rhythm out on her giant bass drum. She is not very rhythmical.)

ALL

Cherries ripe, boom-dee-ay!
Cherries red, boom-dee-ay!
The Cherry Sisters
Are here today!

Cherries sweet, boom-dee-ay!
Cherries wet, boom-dee-ay!
The Cherry Sisters
Came all this way!

Cherries fat, boom-dee-ay!
Cherries tart, boom-dee-ay!
The Cherry Sisters
—*Won't go away!*

(Big finish, big drumming: no clapping.)

ADDIE

So what is it about these Iowa winters? I mean, come on—we get it already!

(Silence. ELLA bangs the drum: a rimshot, of sorts.)

ADDIE (cont'd.)

Have you heard the one about why the cow jumped over the moon? The farmer's hands were cold! *(Pause.)* On her udders. *(Pause.)* Because udders are kind of like nipples ... on a cow.

(ELLA's rimshot.)

ADDIE (cont'd.)

What do you call a very clean Norwegian? —German!

(ELLA's rimshot. Silence.)

ADDIE (cont'd.)

Tough crowd ...

(ELLA's rimshot.)

ADDIE (cont'd.)

That's not a joke, Ella.

And now for a pretty little ditty from our pretty little Lizzie ... !

(LIZZIE takes the fore, singing:)

LIZZIE

I ain't never been kissed,
I ain't never been kissed.
I ain't talking cheeks, I'm talking hot lips!
No matter how hard I swing these hips,
I ain't never had no lover's kiss.

I ain't never been a dish,
I ain't never been a dish
For a boy, a goy or an Amish.
No matter how many frogs I kiss,
Not *one* becomes my prince!

What do you think, fellas?
What do you say, dames?
Ain't I got the goods?
Ain't I got good gams— ?

(Awkward finish. This question hangs lewdly in the air.)

EFFIE

(To us.)

It was a magical moment ...

Everything could have changed. They could clap, or they could not ...
They is you now: what will *you* do?

(Pause.)

EFFIE (cont'd.)

Then it happened—a smattering, a spattering of applause.

We went on, holding them, or so we thought, enthralled, through the comic bits, played by Addie, and then Addie and me together. More songs from Lizzie, including her newest, *The Spaniard That Marked My Wife.*

LIZZIE

(Correcting.)

My Life!

EFFIE

My life, my life ...

And Jessie providing a cautionary tale of lost virtue entitled,

JESSIE

"My First Cigar"!

EFFIE

And then we rounded out the evening with the five of us in leotards in what was fast becoming our signature spectacle: all the way from the banks of the River Denial ... the Human Pyramid!

(They've shucked their calico dresses. They're in their pyramid now, in leotards that look homemade, more like long underwear, dyed imperfectly pink, threadbare and puckered at the knees and elbows.)

EFFIE

If only Pops could see us now.

(He appears.)

POPS

You look like fat whores, bedad.

EFFIE

Pops—

(She tumbles down out of the pyramid.)

POPS

The five of yous wailing and shrieking, squealing and wailing, leaping about in just your undert'ings like a horde of sex-starved banshees—

EFFIE

Pops!

POPS

There's nothing special about you! —The five of yous are nothing—you're *nothing!*

EFFIE

The audience is clapping, Pops, they're loving us—

POPS

That's not love ...

EFFIE

They're clapping for us—what do you think that means?

POPS

—They know who you are!

(Pause.)

POPS (cont'd.)

It's a very small town, bedad ... This is the Midwest, me girl: they're clapping because they're *trying to be nice!*

(EFFIE is shaken.

POPS tries to detach a whiskey bottle from his clothing: it's stuck. And it's empty anyway.)

POPS (cont'd.)

Damn it all to Hell! *(He tries to smoke his cigar, calls offstage:)* I need a match—

(He's gone.)

EFFIE

Our hands were laced together ... as we bowed our heads ...

And for a moment, for no reason I could figure ... I imagined that this little stage we stood upon had become a kind of gallows.

(ELLA begins beating her drum again.)

ADDIE

Who are you talking to, Effie?

EFFIE

We're a hit. *(Pause.)* Aren't we?

(Backstage:)

ADDIE

What did you expect?

LIZZIE

A boy just asked me for my autograph. He said, "You girls really *are* unbelievable!"

JESSIE

Did you hear that applause? So well-mannered.

EFFIE

—Ella, stop beating that drum!

(ELLA stops for a minute. Then starts again, a little more quietly.

EFFIE is counting the money.)

EFFIE (cont'd.)

(Astounded.)

One hundred dollars ...

LIZZIE

That's more than Mr. Vlanck makes all year!

JESSIE

—So generous of them!

LIZZIE

Mr. Vlank asked me in the wings, he said, "Ven are you goink to Cedar Vapids?"

ADDIE

That's good, Lizzie—"Cedar Vapids"!

JESSIE

Why do you know so much about Mr. Vlanck, Lizzie?

LIZZIE

He said we should just hurry up and get to Cedar Vapids right away:
"Do not vaste anozher day—get out of zees town. Please!"

EFFIE

We're not ready.

LIZZIE

That's what he said, Effie, and he's a teacher. And German. And Germans never lie!

EFFIE

Cedar Rapids is the city, Lizzie.

LIZZIE

So? I know that ...

EFFIE

They're cosmopolitan there, they're savvy. They're used to the best entertainment the corn-belt has to offer. These people out there tonight, they're just—rubes.

JESSIE

Effie!

(Pause. Even ELLA pauses.)

JESSIE (cont'd.)

We're rubes too ...

EFFIE

They *had* to be nice, that's all I mean to say ... They know who we are. How do we know they're not lying when they clap?

JESSIE

Oh, Effie ... That's the saddest thing you've ever said.

EFFIE

—Ella! Stop beating that drum!

(ELLA stops.)

ELLA

What's the matter, Effie? Don't you love us too?

(Pause.)

EFFIE

... How do we get to Cedar Rapids, girls?

LIZZIE

By boat?

EFFIE

No, we practice.

LIZZIE

Practice what? swimming?

EFFIE

(To us.)

We went home and polished our routines. Pyramids grew taller, arms and thighs grew lither beneath pink underthings ...

And the songs—the songs needed no work at all. A beautiful little ballad entitled *Why Speak of Love When the Rent Is So High?* promised to bring Cedar Vapids to its knees.

LIZZIE

Why speak of love when the rent is so high?
Why talk of spring when winter is nigh?
Why give a darn about nothin' at all
If I can't have you?

Why speak of lunch when your stomach's upset— ?

EFFIE

Thank you, Lizzie.

ADDIE

Thank you, Lizzie.

LIZZIE

There's more.

EFFIE

No, there's not.

LIZZIE

It's a much longer song—

EFFIE

We've heard it already. Several times.

ADDIE

Today.

(Pause.)

LIZZIE

—Where's Ella with our gosh darned lunch!

JESSIE

Such language!

LIZZIE

Darn my language all to heck I'm wasting away to nothing!

EFFIE

(To us.)

And the jokes were flying fast, especially in Brooklynese, which came out thick and spicy these days:

ADDIE

(As a man.)

"Take my seat, young goil! I'm only goin' so far as Yahnkers!"

EFFIE

"Oh no! I can't take your seat, sir!"

ADDIE

"Yes you can. And I'll take yours!"

("He" pinches her.)

EFFIE

"Ooo!" —That's too hard, Addie, don't pinch me so hard.

ADDIE

That's how men are ...

EFFIE

How would you know?

ADDIE

(Prompting.)

"My dear sir—"

EFFIE

"My dear sir, I think you're fresh!"

ADDIE

"I think *you're* fresh! Like a summer rain!"

EFFIE

"And you're like a winter drizzle."

ADDIE

"I can't help it! You make me feel damp!" —Damp?

EFFIE

"Fresh!"

(EFFIE slaps ADDIE.)

ADDIE

Ow, Effie. That hurt.

EFFIE

That's how women are. You have to pay attention.
—Say your rhyming couplet now, Addie: not to me but to them.

ADDIE

"A woman is a fragile beast! She needs a man to give her peace!"
That's not funny at all.

EFFIE

I know. It's cow shit. *(To us:)*
We were ready for Cedar Vapids!

4: CEDAR RAPIDS. NIGHT.

EFFIE

The stage there was so immense ... like the surface of some enormous grand piano ...
And midway through our first comic sketch, the rehearsal of which you were just a party to ... what should happen but a horn should toot?

(A horn toots.

ELLA enters, covered in snow again.

More importantly, perhaps, she clenches a cardboard horn tight in her teeth.

She toots again and again, etc.)

EFFIE

And another. And another ...
And soon that entire theater in Cedar Rapids was clogged with such a cacophony of cardboard horns, like a flock of captive geese—no, like the Israelites at the walls of Jericho—no, as if we'd found ourselves suddenly at the center of some hive of demonically possessed bees—*shut up, Ella, please!*

(ELLA toots her horn.

They're smiling at the audience, terrified.)

LIZZIE

What's going on out there ... ?

ADDIE

They're blowing horns at us ...

LIZZIE

I can hear that—

JESSIE

How rude!

EFFIE

What's going on out there ... ?

LIZZIE

They're blowing horns at us!

EFFIE

I know but what does it all *mean?*

ADDIE

—Let me see that horn.

(ADDIE takes the horn from ELLA, examines it.)

ADDIE (cont'd.)

There was a rally here last night. See? Political. That's what it says on the horn: "Up With Greevey!" Exclamation point.

JESSIE

Who's "Greevey"?

LIZZIE

What's going up him?

EFFIE

(To us.)

It *was* strange. Not a boo, not applause ... neither cheers nor jeers nor silence ... A horn.

But if applause can be a lie ... then maybe a horn might mean applause?

(Pause.)

ADDIE

Effie, are you listening to us?

EFFIE

They're so grateful for our performance here tonight, girls ... that mere clapping will not do.

(Pause. She tries again:)

EFFIE (cont'd.)

In Cedar Rapids, if you love an act so much and mere clapping will not suffice—you blow! Your horn!

JESSIE

It's a theory ...

(ELLA takes her horn back from ADDIE, starts tooting again.)

LIZZIE

What should we do now?

EFFIE

—Give them more, girls! More!

ADDIE

"You say you're going downtown, doll, well I've been there before!"

EFFIE

(To us.)

We finished our euphemistic comic interlude, and sang a song or two. Jessie came out alone and spun her speech on—

JESSIE

"Marriage and the Advantages of Male Chastity in the Twentieth Century!"

EFFIE

Exclamation point, naturally. —She was so obsessed with this coming century!

ADDIE

What did the corn cob say to the corn stalk? You leaf around here?

(ELLA's rimshot.)

ADDIE (cont'd.)

Two cows in a field: one cow says moo. The other says, You readin' my mind?

(Rimshot.)

ADDIE (cont'd.)

What do you call a lonely bull in a pasture all alone? —Beef stroganoff!

(A very long, confused rimshot.)

LIZZIE

What does that one even mean, Addie?

ADDIE

I don't know but Pops used to say it ...

EFFIE

(To us.)

And gradually, horn by horn, the tooting died away.

Silence returned. No laughter, no applause. Nothing. Just one long, unbroken hush ...

We can't see a thing, with the lights in our eyes. We know you're out there. Breathing. Watching. Listening ... as if concentrating, mightily ... trying to figure something out ...

What are you trying to figure out?

(Silence.)

EFFIE (cont'd.)

Then something even stranger occurred:

ALL

We are all five yerrow queens.
Some are fat and some are rean.
Prease to take a rook at us
Whire we dance our fine loutine!

(They're all dancing, in a line:

ELLA looks Chinese, in a "coolie" hat; LIZZIE is dressed like a Japanese geisha; EFFIE has a Hindu dot on her forehead, and a sari; and ADDIE wears Eskimo furs and brandishes a spear with a fish on it.

JESSIE, the Hawaiian Queen, wears a grass skirt and lei:)

JESSIE

I am Queen Lili'uokalani,
I am queen of all Hawai'i.
From O'ahu to green Maui
I enjoy the mahi-mahi.

At every royal luau
I will eat my Pig Kalua.
Then some mangos and papaya,
And then something called hapia.

Mai Tai cocktails, lomi salmon,
Coconut sure cures your famine!
And don't forget the Pupu platter—
Avoid the poi or you'll grow fatter.

Some have said that I too heavy
But I think they simply jeal-y.
Watch my sister's ukulele
While I dance my hula-hula.
Wiki! wiki! wiki! wiki! wiki!

EFFIE

(Whispering.)

Jessie!

JESSIE

What?

EFFIE

Move over that way—

JESSIE

There's a foot light over there—

ADDIE

Move your feet!

LIZZIE

—Keep smiling, girls! Move those hips like you mean it!

JESSIE

Don't you push me please missie— !

ADDIE

Jessie—

JESSIE

What—

EFFIE

Jessie!

LIZZIE

—You're going to catch on fire!

(And LIZZIE screams, as:

JESSIE catches fire.

Or, rather, JESSIE's skirt goes up in flames. Or up in smoke, as the case may be. Now JESSIE screams.

The others scream now too. Pandemonium, Pan-Asian style.

They try to put it out, blowing, screaming, waving their hands, swatting her skirt with their skirts.

But ELLA, somehow, has been quickest. Here she comes running back onstage with a fire extinguisher.

She sprays it all up and down JESSIE's front. She sprays her sister's face too, a lot, just to be safe.

JESSIE's skirts smolder, her face drips: a tableau vivant, with a touch of presentiment, perhaps ...

Pause.

A seismic eruption of laughter in the audience now, rolling on beneath the following:)

EFFIE

They could not stop laughing ...

(More laughter. The girls are in ecstasy, bewildered.)

EFFIE (cont'd.)

Is this what love feels like?

POPS

(Appearing.)

Hear that?

EFFIE

—Do *you* hear that?

POPS

They're laughing at you, Effie ...

EFFIE

They're laughing *with* me, Pops. With us. We made them laugh, it's beautiful— !

POPS

You made them laugh because you caught yourselves on fire! *(Pause.)* Jessie did. At least she's got *some* talent ... They wish you'd all catch fire, that way they'd be sure to get their money's worth.

EFFIE

—Liar!

POPS

When have I ever?

EFFIE

What you've seen tonight is the mark of true genius. We encounter accident and we subsume—we spin it into gold!

POPS

You're mixing up your metaphors now, me girl.

EFFIE

Why don't you just go back to Hell—that's not a metaphor, that's where you *live!*

POPS

Your sister went up in flames. Does that mean nothing to you at all?

(Pause.)

POPS (cont'd.)

I need a match ...

(He walks over to JESSIE's still smoldering skirts, lights his brand new cigar off it.)

EFFIE

Where'd you get that?

POPS

Me stogie?

EFFIE

Where are your bottles?

POPS

Me drink?

EFFIE

Your whiskey. You've always got them, hanging off your person like cowbells so I can hear you coming ...

Why are you wearing that suit? You've changed, you're changing now ...

POPS

Listen, sweetheart—

EFFIE

Your brogue—

POPS

This is where we say goodbye for now.

EFFIE

Your hair's not even white anymore ... That mustache—

POPS

You're getting ahead of me now, Effie. Watch it.

(POPS finishes wiping the death-pallor from his face with his handkerchief. He affixes a mustache.

He pushes her out of the way.)

EFFIE

—Pops!

5: BACKSTAGE, CEDAR RAPIDS, MOMENTS AFTER THE SHOW.

POPS

Pops is my name, talent agentry's my game.

(He doffs his hat. EFFIE is suddenly quite shy. ADDIE is folding her arms.)

ADDIE

We knew a Pops once ...

POPS

It's a popular name these days, Pops, in the voe-dee-veal at least, 'specially 'mongst us men. Managers and agents mostly—"of course," you say!—whose job it is to fan the flames of the artist's soul into a more mature, that is, profit-making, conflagration. A veritable forest fire of profit, if you will. Smell that smoke? *(He inhales his cigar.)*

I've got a real name, of course, one my mother gave, but I'm not about to give that to you ...

(He laughs. A pause, then to LIZZIE:)

POPS (cont'd.)

Except you, maybe you, you I might tell one day.

(He touches LIZZIE on the chin: she swoons.)

LIZZIE

—Oh!

JESSIE

May we help you with something, "Pops"?

POPS

Who's this, your spinster aunt, visiting from England?

JESSIE

—Oh!

POPS

Please, do not become affronted. I mean merely to be familiar with you girls. A real confidante.

ADDIE

We've already got confidantes, Pops: each other.

LIZZIE

We can always use more confidence, Pops—we're *so* insecure!

POPS

You girls really are something, you know that?

I was out there tonight, watching the show, as is my wont, whenever I'm on jump-break from Chicago—

LIZZIE

"Jump-break"!

JESSIE

"Wont"?

ADDIE

You don't sound Chicago, you sound Brooklynese.

POPS

—I always make a point of slowing myself down here, in Cedar Rapids, of all places, to peruse the local talent.

LIZZIE

You think we've got talent? —*I* do.

POPS

Who cares what I think? The audience loved you! You killed them! You slaughtered them! They're decimated! Massacred! —It's beautiful!

ADDIE

(To JESSIE.)

He's spitting on you—

POPS

Only in America ... I mean, I'm a patriot. And only in this country, in this day and age, could five motherless girls from Wherever-The-Fuck-You're-From-Iowa—

JESSIE

Oh-h!

(JESSIE almost faints—at the language.)

POPS

—find stardom on the voe-dee-veal stage!

ADDIE

Why do you keep saying it like that, the "voe-dee-veal"?

POPS

It's French. Don't you girls know any French?

LIZZIE

You mean like kissing?

EFFIE

How do you know we're motherless?

POPS

Well that's obvious, isn't it?

(Pause. Is that compassion in his eyes?

Then, to ELLA:)

POPS (cont'd.)

Fatherless too?

(ELLA shakes her head, "No."

She points at him.)

POPS (cont'd.)

What's wrong with her, she dumb?

ADDIE

She's an idiot.

POPS

I can see that.

JESSIE

She means that in the clinical sense, Pops.

LIZZIE

She got kicked in the head by a mule when she was five. It wasn't all her fault.

(ELLA smiles, and nods, and holds up four fingers.)

POPS

Testy beast, the mule. It's because they're so sterile.

No, I mean is she dumb in the sense of speechlessness? can she talk?

JESSIE

She can talk if she wants to. Say something, Ella.

ELLA

You're the very bad man.

(Pause.)

POPS

She's perfect, don't ever change.

Who's in charge here?

LIZZIE

Jessie's the eldest.

JESSIE

I'm only twenty-nine. —And I've never even *been* to England!

POPS

No no, who's the brains, the *artiste*. Who's got the vision here?

(Another pause.

EFFIE shyly replies:)

EFFIE

That would be me. The *artiste* ... Effie Cherry.

(He sizes her up and down. She lowers her gaze some more.)

POPS

Beauty and brains. It just isn't fair.

EFFIE

(Blushes crimson.)

Lizzie's the pretty one.

POPS

Oh no, you're pretty also. 'Cause you got prettiness ... in here.

(He taps her big fat head. She smiles widely, though she's trying not to.)

POPS (cont'd.)

Want my opinion though?

EFFIE

Of course!

POPS

You're gonna be stars.

(He re-lights his cigar.)

LIZZIE

We are?

POPS

Aren't we?

ADDIE

Who's we?

LIZZIE

Even Ella is?

POPS

Especially Ella! Audiences love retarded gals—

JESSIE

We prefer "idiot," if you don't mind.

POPS

—so long as you keep their noses clean.

(He gives ELLA a handkerchief: she uses it, a lot.)

POPS (cont'd.)

Keep it.

I'm gonna take you fours to Chicago. What do you think of that idea?

JESSIE

Five.

LIZZIE

What's in Chicago, Pops?

POPS

The Chicago World's Fair's in Chicago next year, that's what.

EFFIE

You want to take us to the World's Fair?

POPS

That's the next step in this story of ours, the story of your lives, and you are writing it, I'm just proof-reading and there ain't no type-o's I can see:

Chicago World's Fair, 1893. It's your destiny!

EFFIE

He's a philosopher ...

POPS

I don't like books much, they make me suspicious of my fellow man.
—But trust me: you four girls are one of a kind—

JESSIE

Five.

POPS

—and I'm not the only one who's gonna think so!

(He takes out another handkerchief to mop his brow.)

JESSIE

He's sweating so much ...

LIZZIE

He can't help it. He's Latin.

ADDIE

I don't trust him at all ...

EFFIE

What's not to trust?

JESSIE

The slicked back hair ...

LIZZIE

(She sighs.)

His slicked back hair ...

ADDIE

The olive skin ...

EFFIE

Such olive skin!

JESSIE

His waxed-up mustache.

LIZZIE

—Let me stroke your waxed-up mustache!

(Pause.)

POPS

I'm sorry, doll. You say something?

LIZZIE

Did I?

EFFIE

Are you originally from Spain?

POPS

What's that?

EFFIE

A country near France. —Don't you have some Spanish blood in you somewhere?

POPS

As a matter of fact, I do ... Let me see here, I'm part Spanish-Dutch-Welsh-French-Slovakian-Sioux. If you go back a generation or—ten. How'd you know all that?

LIZZIE

It's your mustache.

POPS

You're observant. You both are.

EFFIE

And your skin—like a leather-bound book ...

(Pause. Both LIZZIE and EFFIE are batting their eyes, blushing fiercely.)

POPS

You girls sure know how to flatter a man.

But listen: there's one thing you gotta do if you want to go all the way with me.

(JESSIE gasps, maybe gags a little.)

EFFIE & LIZZIE

—What?

POPS

Write ... a one-act play!

LIZZIE

Ew. Why?

POPS

You're darling because you're so dim.

(He touches LIZZIE on the chin, again. She swoons—again.)

POPS (cont'd.)

Everyone knows that every multilayered, multifaceted vaudeville show needs a stirring one-act play—a "short dramatic thunderbolt!" as they say, within the machinery of variety—a diamond, if you will, set upon the ring of the revue ...

EFFIE

He's poetic, too ...

LIZZIE

I love diamond rings!

POPS

And, as a short, dramatic thunderwork, it must contain some deep human truth.

LIZZIE

What's a human truth?

POPS

You're the ingénue: thinking gives you wrinkles. *(Her chin, again: swoons.)*

It's good business sense, girls: if you want to reach the top of your profession you'll have to write a short, sharp one-act play with deep, human truth.

EFFIE

I've been working on that.

(Pause.)

ADDIE

No you haven't, Effie—ow.

POPS

Oh yeah?

EFFIE

"Yeah."

POPS

Well you work on it some more, doll. And you work hard. Till your hand cramps. Then longer.

And when you're done working you send it on to me, via U.S. parcel post. On my dime.

(POPS gives EFFIE a shiny, sparkling dime.)

POPS (cont'd.)

There's plenty more where that came from ...

And if your one-act play is any good, I promise you girls we'll go all the way together ... to the Chicago World's Fair! —In Chicago!

(He reaches into his pants pocket again, pulls out a chocolate bar, offers to LIZZIE.)

LIZZIE

What's that.

POPS

Milk chocolate.

LIZZIE

I can't, I'm matronly.

POPS

Who ever told you such a thing? You're as skinny as an aborigine! As your agent, I am telling you, in the next few months you must *all* gain at least thirty to forty pounds per female person. *(To EFFIE:)* Maybe more, in your case.

LIZZIE

—Oh!

(LIZZIE takes the chocolate bar, begins eating ravenously.)

POPS

Here's my card.

(POPS reaches into his pants pocket again, pulls out his business card.)

LIZZIE

—There's so much in your pocket!

POPS

What's your name again?

EFFIE

Effie. It's short for Iphigenia.

ADDIE

No it's not, Effie—stop touching me!

POPS

No, I'm talking about your show.

LIZZIE

(Mouth full.)

"Unbelievable Cherry Sisters"!

POPS

That's the name of your act. You're going to have many more shows, I promise you, for years to come ... Let's name your first show ... something special ...

EFFIE

(Thinking.)

Let me think—

POPS

How's about: "The Unbelievable Cherry Sisters in: Seeing Is Believing!"

(He gives EFFIE his card.

She takes it.)

POPS (cont'd.)

Because you girls need to be seen to be believed.

6: THE BARN. WINTER AGAIN. IS IT EVER NOT WINTER?

(EFFIE's alone this time.

She speaks to us.)

EFFIE

I know what you're thinking ...

But I'd never known men could be beautiful before.

I didn't even know you could use that word, "beauty," with men ...

And I don't think he's handsome in the conventional sense. He is a touch ... mature.

—But he said I was an artist.

He touched my big fat head.

He told me to write a one-act play—for him ... with deep, human truth ...

ELLA

(Appearing.)

How can a face be like a book?

EFFIE

—Ella! you scared me.

(ELLA's carrying a basket of supplies. She has some snow on her hair and shoulders.)

ELLA

Can a face be like a book ... ?

EFFIE

Is that a riddle, Ella?

ELLA

Do you want to have a wedding one day?

EFFIE

Of course. Don't you?

ELLA

I won't have a wedding ... I'm too slow ... I'll never catch a man.

EFFIE

Maybe he'll catch you.

ELLA

Will it be beautiful?

EFFIE

My wedding? I hope so. One day.

ELLA

What will you wear?

(Before EFFIE can answer:)

ELLA (cont'd.)

I see you in a white dress, like snow ...
A veil over your face ... of snow ...
Your wedding will take place out of doors, at night.

EFFIE

(To us.)

Like Tiresias in the plays of William Shakespeare, Ella had the gift of second sight. Or future sight. As the Scots say. As you may have guessed already ...
It could be unnerving sometimes.

ELLA

Let me stay and watch you write.

EFFIE

Okay. *(Time passes.)* It's boring. *(Time passes.)* Do you see anything happening yet ... ?

(ELLA shakes her head "no.")

ELLA

I'll be making your waxed-up mustache ...

(She pulls out some tarpaper, a scissors, a bottle of glue.)

EFFIE

(To us.)

How did she know I'd need a mustache for Addie ... ?

And why did she say I'd be married out of doors at night, with a veil of snow?

ELLA

(Dreamily, quietly.)

How can a face be like a book?

EFFIE

(To herself, as much as to us.)

How old am I now? I must be twenty-one, twenty-two ... *(Time passes.)* What on earth should I be writing about? *(Another pause.)*

If I close my eyes, weeks later, I can still hear his voice ...

(An idea. She writes:)

LIZZIE

"Enter an innocent young gypsy girl."

(LIZZIE enters, dressed innocently enough: something white, diaphanous; though dirty and ratty still, her nightgown maybe.

She has a few pages of script in her hand. She shakes off some snow.)

EFFIE

What are you doing?

LIZZIE

I'm freezing!

(LIZZIE grabs a "gypsy" shawl.)

EFFIE

That's my part, I'm the innocent young gypsy girl.

LIZZIE

No you're not—you're writing.

EFFIE

I can both write and act.

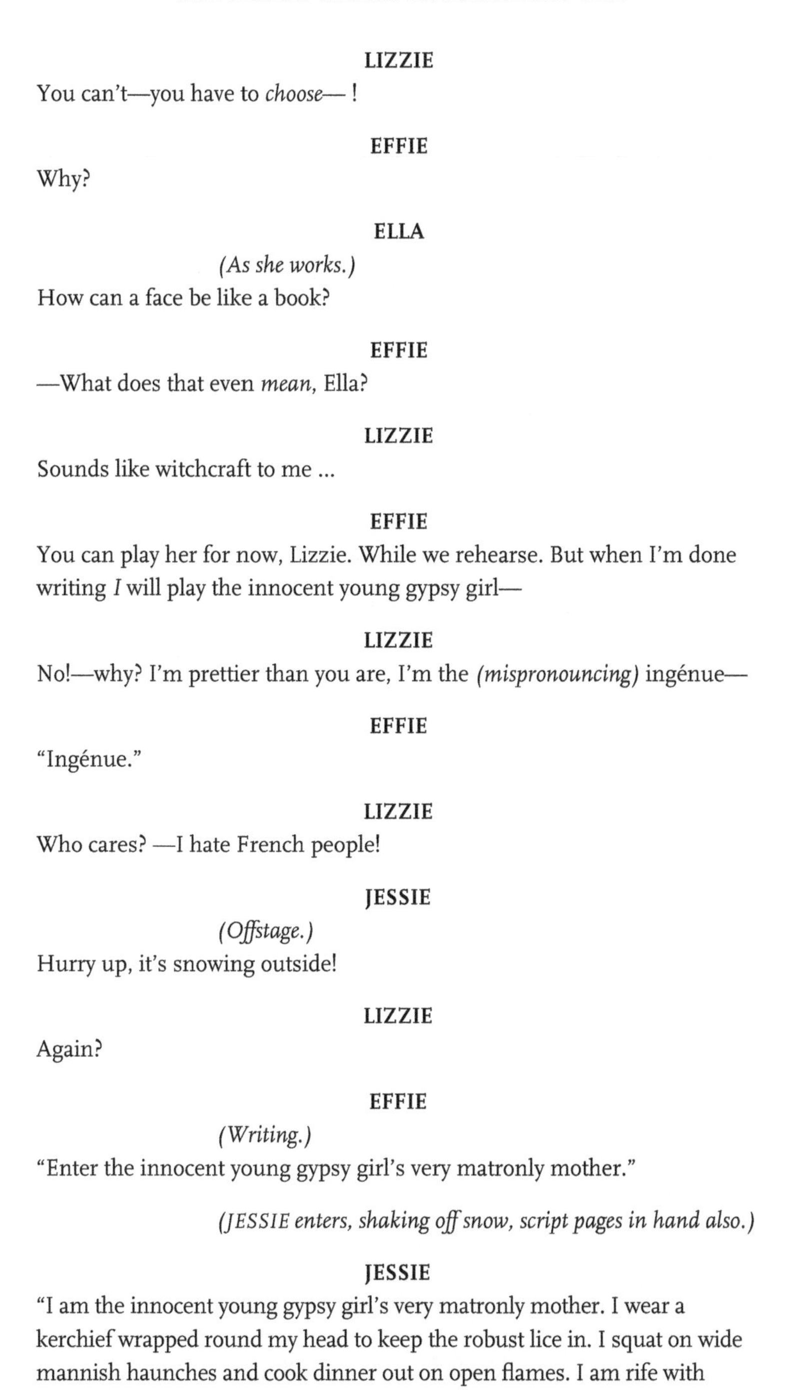

LIZZIE

You can't—you have to *choose*— !

EFFIE

Why?

ELLA

(As she works.)

How can a face be like a book?

EFFIE

—What does that even *mean*, Ella?

LIZZIE

Sounds like witchcraft to me ...

EFFIE

You can play her for now, Lizzie. While we rehearse. But when I'm done writing *I* will play the innocent young gypsy girl—

LIZZIE

No!—why? I'm prettier than you are, I'm the *(mispronouncing)* ingénue—

EFFIE

"Ingénue."

LIZZIE

Who cares? —I hate French people!

JESSIE

(Offstage.)

Hurry up, it's snowing outside!

LIZZIE

Again?

EFFIE

(Writing.)

"Enter the innocent young gypsy girl's very matronly mother."

(JESSIE enters, shaking off snow, script pages in hand also.)

JESSIE

"I am the innocent young gypsy girl's very matronly mother. I wear a kerchief wrapped round my head to keep the robust lice in. I squat on wide mannish haunches and cook dinner out on open flames. I am rife with superstition. I fear no man, only Fate. Yes, Fate, and—the Spanish Cavalier!"

(Enter ADDIE, with gusto, script pages too. In leather chaps.)

ADDIE

"I am the Spanish Cavalier! A-ho! Hallo!"

(ADDIE's "Spanish Cavalier" strongly resembles Pops the agent.)

EFFIE

(Murmuring, writing.)

"Spanish Cavalier, with olive skin, swaggered thighs ... chest cocked out and mustache ... "

ADDIE

Mustache.

LIZZIE

Mustache?

EFFIE

—Waxed-up mustache! —Ella!

(ELLA has just finished crafting the tarpaper mustache.

She moves to ADDIE, daubs glue on her sister's lip, sticks the mustache in place.)

ADDIE

"A-ha! A-ho!" —A-choo. This itches, Ella.

EFFIE

(Prompting.)

You are the Spanish Cavalier.

ADDIE

—I know who I am!

LIZZIE

Why can't you be the cavalier, Effie? if you have to act. Why does Addie always have to play the man?

ADDIE

"I am the Spanish Cavalier! Hallo! As I have already made mention! And my way is to be cavalier—with women!

("He" does a little dance. Castanets.)

ADDIE

List to me while I tell you
How much I enjoy your young women!
In some very naughty ways
I have been known to have my way
With them!

Because you see I am guapo,
Muy guapo,
Muy muy muy muy muy muy
Muy guapo,
And I nunca take nay for an answer!

LIZZIE

"Hello. I am the innocent young gypsy girl."

ADDIE

"You're squatting."

LIZZIE

"Yes. Do you like it?"

ADDIE

"Yes. —But also, you are squatting on my land."

LIZZIE

"I don't pretend to understand what it is you think you're saying, Señor Cavalier! We gypsies are like the Red Indian that way, like the mighty Sioux, or the wily—*(a la the French:)—Iroquois,* in that we know this land to be no man's land. It is God's land, and we are all but gypsies wandering God's frontier."

JESSIE

That's good, Effie. That's patriotic.

ADDIE

It's too wordy. As usual.

EFFIE

Don't make me self-conscious—it's flowing through me!

ADDIE

"Impertinent gypsy tramp! How dare you speak to me in such bald romantic platitudes. This is my land, not God's! *('He' spits. Dances.)* I will punish you now, striking you once, no twice, firmly, upon your delicate soft bustle with my stiff riding crop—and yet, I won't. Why? Because I see something in you."

LIZZIE

"You see something ... ?"

ADDIE

"In you."

LIZZIE

"In me? Already?"

ADDIE

"Something ... I've never seen before. Something quite like—"

LIZZIE

"What. Tell me. Oh do not be afraid, Monsieur Cavalier, to tell me what-all you are seeing inside of me already!"

(A pause. The "Spanish Cavalier" turns away.)

ADDIE

"I must go. *('He' turns back.)*

"But tonight: meet me here again, young buxom gypsy wench. And we shall wed. You and me. By the light of the full, full ... full moon."

(ADDIE exits the scene—but not the barn—singing:)

ADDIE (cont'd.)

Muy muy muy muy muy muy
Muy muy muy muy muy ...

(ELLA moves to ADDIE, gives her mustache a touch-up of glue.)

EFFIE

(To us.)

A wedding! Out of doors! at night! How do I come up with these things?

ELLA

How can a face be like a— ?

EFFIE

Okay, we get it already, Ella.

(JESSIE shuffles on.)

EFFIE (cont'd.)

Come on, Jessie, be quicker than that ...

JESSIE

I'm old.

EFFIE

Then start sooner.

JESSIE

—My *character* is old!

LIZZIE

—"Mother!"

JESSIE

"There, there, my child. There, there. There. Now, rest your head, here, upon my pendulous breasts. These breasts are large with mother-feeling. As if bursting with the sweet milk of mother-love. Rest your head ... and unburden your heart's woe to me."

LIZZIE

(Smothered in JESSIE's breasts.)

"I met a man!"

JESSIE

... Hmn?

(LIZZIE breaks free:)

LIZZIE

—I said "I met a man!"

JESSIE

"O dear Lord! Undone!"

LIZZIE

"In the woods—"

JESSIE

"How often have I told you not to wander these woods alone? You may be nothing but an impertinent gypsy tramp, but you are virginal and therefore tasty as a cherry tart, and men will snap you up if they can."

LIZZIE

"He is a Spanish Cavalier—"

JESSIE

"O Lord! O Lord! Undone! Undone!"

LIZZIE

"His hair is dark, and his face is brown—like a book."

JESSIE

"A book?"

ELLA

A book.

LIZZIE

"And his mustache—"

ELLA

Is made of paper.

EFFIE

Ella! Be quiet!

LIZZIE

"He said I should meet him, in the woods again tonight. By moonlight we shall wed. In a wedding dress like snow. A veil of snow, also. And then ... well, then—I know not what will become of me!"

(She swoons. Falls down.

JESSIE, as the Gypsy Mother, seems to think long and hard about something.)

JESSIE

"Here is what I think: I have thought long and hard about this ...

"If you meet him tonight in the woods, he will only pretend to wed. One can not wed by moonlight without a priest. I learned that the hard way. Have you never wondered who your father is? Never mind. Because he won't bring a priest, your Spanish Cavalier. He hates God, and all that God stands for. *(She spits.)* It will be a *façade*. A *charade*. A *canard*. And he will fool you just to have his way!"

LIZZIE

(Standing up.)

"His way with what?"

JESSIE

"Why—with whatever it is men do with women."

LIZZIE

"Which is what, exactly?"

JESSIE

"Which is what?"

LIZZIE

"Exactly."

JESSIE

"What do they *do?*"

LIZZIE

"Yes, tell me please, Mother, I've never understood!"

JESSIE

"Why—they *love* them!"

LIZZIE

"O!"

JESSIE

"Yes, over and over again—and not always in very nice ways."

LIZZIE

"O! O!"

JESSIE

"List to me while I tell you, young innocent gypsy girl tramp daughter: if you meet this Spanish Cavalier in the woods again by moonlight: you are lost! Forever! —Do not go, my girl, do not go!"

EFFIE

(To us.)

She goes.

Just as we go, to the World's Fair, in Chicago, 1893 ...

It really is the World's Fair: the whole world's there ... *(She sings softly, to herself:)*

I'm so lonely for Old Broadway ...

It's not New York ... but we're getting closer ...

In a dark room at the Palace of Fine Arts, Edison exhibits a moving picture machine. It will kill the vaudeville, someone whispers by my side ... But when I turn to see who's speaking: I see Pops with his mouth next to *Lizzie's* ear ...

(In tableau, in shadow, POPS is whispering to LIZZIE, who giggles ...

The sound of an audience laughing.)

EFFIE (cont'd.)

I let her keep her role, for the time being ... She's right: you can't both write and act.

(On stage now, ADDIE and LIZZIE are off-book, more costumed: a cape and gleaming sword for ADDIE.)

ADDIE

(Swaggering.)

"You've come! My innocent young cherry tart-like gypsy wench!"

LIZZIE

"Of course I've come—you *rake!*"

("She" slaps "him.")

ADDIE

"You love me!"

LIZZIE

"Of course I do! How could I *not* do? —But I know you not! I know not love. How could we two *but* love? You are a mystery to me, a buzzing hive of bees. You are the dark, sea-salty depths—"

ADDIE

"Take off your clothes."

LIZZIE

"Yes, right away."

(LIZZIE takes off her clothes, down to her pink leotard.)

LIZZIE (cont'd.)

"What ho! Where is the priest?"

ADDIE

"Don't be so naïve. A 'padre'? *('He' spits.)* Do you see this sword that hangs from my belt? This is all the padre I need!"

LIZZIE

"I don't even understand the comparison!"

ADDIE

—"Take off *all* your clothes!"

('He' draws his sword.

LIZZIE screams, a long drawn out contralto scream ...

Lights out. Lights up again.)

7: BACKSTAGE, WORLD'S FAIR.

LIZZIE

I feel so different ...

(LIZZIE sits. Her hands go to her stomach.

JESSIE is reading a newspaper.)

JESSIE

It makes no sense at all ... It's like they saw some other show, someone else, not us. Some *imposters* ...

ADDIE

Read it out loud to everyone.

JESSIE

"The Unbelievable Cherry Sisters in: Seeing is Believing!"—exclamation point—"wowed the audiences last night"—

LIZZIE

That's not bad.

JESSIE

—"with their awesome dearth of saving graces,"

(Pause.)

ADDIE

That's bad.

LIZZIE

What's "dearth" mean? a little or a lot?

JESSIE

"with their alternately mewling and booming howls disguised as music,"

LIZZIE

I do not howl!

JESSIE

"their leotards like madhouse uniforms,"

ADDIE

Sorry, Ella.

(ELLA seems quite hurt by this.)

JESSIE

"their disgraceful bovine leaping,"

LIZZIE

What's "bovine"?

ADDIE

Worse than matronly. But only just a little.

JESSIE

"and their one-act melodramatic play, *The Gypsy's Warning!*"—exclamation point—"which betrays an all-too-obvious spinsterish anxiety."

(A long pause. JESSIE puts the paper down.)

LIZZIE

What's "spinsterish anxiety" mean?

(EFFIE sits down heavily.)

EFFIE

It means I wrote it.

(LIZZIE is wearing the white dress.)

LIZZIE

... Where's Pops?

JESSIE

He's dead, Lizzie. He's been dead these last few years ...

ADDIE

She's talking about the other one, Jessie.

LIZZIE

Am I?

JESSIE

Oh.

ELLA

I'm going to be going away ...

(She raises her hand and points spookily at:

POPS, who's entered the scene, unseen. His new suit's newer, his slick hair's slicker. He's smoking a thicker, longer cigar.

But he's sweating a lot more.)

POPS

How's it feel to be famous?

ADDIE

—Infamous, more like it.

JESSIE

Have you read these reviews?

POPS

Who reads reviews? Sure, I read them ...

JESSIE

The New York Times sent someone—

POPS

What's that, a weekly?

JESSIE

—and the headline reads simply: "Five Freaks From Iowa."

(Pause.)

POPS

That depends on your interpretation.

ADDIE

Of Iowa?

POPS

We're sold out all week long, girls. Now tell me: would that happen if we were a flop?

LIZZIE

Maybe ...

POPS

Lizzie! ... I'm surprised at you.

(He goes to chuck her under the chin—she turns away this time.)

LIZZIE

Sometimes I get the feeling ...

POPS

What feeling?

LIZZIE

—I'm going to throw up.

(She exits to throw up. POPS takes out his handkerchief to mop his face. His handkerchief is getting bigger and bigger ...)

POPS

What's the matter with you gals? Didn't they laugh?

ADDIE

In all the wrong places.

POPS

Ipso facto, that's a contradiction in terms— !

JESSIE

What about Lizzie's songs? They laughed at the sweet ones, and they laughed most impertinently, I must say, at the comic ...

POPS

Do not doubt, my girls! Do not give in! Remember what Lincoln said.

ADDIE

What did he say?

POPS

"Don't worry about it!"

Look, you're green. It's sweet. I see this every day. You don't yet know how hard this business can be ... But this is how they love you on stage!

Love is a mysterious thing, onstage ...

It does not always come when you want it to. It does not always come from whom you would like it to come from. Sometimes people love people they're not supposed to love. Or they love you in a way you really wish they wouldn't—that's a crime, in certain states.

But love is love, like money's money, so please, girls—don't be so picky!

(The sisters look unconvinced.)

ADDIE

You sure are sweating a lot, Pops ...

POPS

Am I? I think I got a touch of whatever Lizzie's got ...

(LIZZIE has returned, looking peaked.

POPS reaches into his pants pocket.)

POPS (cont'd.)

Guess what I have for you here, girls ...

LIZZIE

Please don't say chocolate.

(He pulls out a telegram.)

POPS

It's a wire—

LIZZIE

That's a piece of yellow paper.

POPS

From Hammerstein.

JESSIE

Who's Hammerstein?

ADDIE

A kind of cow.

POPS

You're kidding me, right? Only the biggest producer on Broadway ...
And here it says, in regulation English, that you four gals have been invited to New York City ... to play the Olympia Theatre on Broadway!

JESSIE

What do you mean four?

(Pause.)

LIZZIE

You mean five of us, right Pops?

ELLA

I'm going to be going away ...

POPS

Try to understand things, girls. Hammerstein runs a family establishment. He's cleaned up the vaudeville. He values, as do I, as does everyone who's ever seen your show, your ... fidelity to one another.

But he knows you'll get more laughs without her.

And I have to say I agree. I was wrong about Ella. In a melodrama, she'd be fine. Drama's kind to imbeciles. But no one wants to laugh at a girl like this ... it's *too* cruel.

(Pause.)

POPS (cont'd.)

Here's your advance: five hundred dollars. One for each of you—even Ella.

(He holds out a hundred dollar bill to ELLA.)

POPS (cont'd.)

What do you say, Ella? You don't mind going home, do you girl? There's a good girl ... I'll bet you miss it there, all that snow.

(ELLA takes the bill. Puts a corner in her mouth, tastes it.)

POPS (cont'd.)

... So what's it gonna be, Effie? New York City, yes or no?

(He's holding out the remaining cash to EFFIE.

A quick beat; then EFFIE takes the money, gives a hundred dollars to ADDIE, then to LIZZIE.)

JESSIE

How could you ... ?

ADDIE

We'll send her more money, Jessie ...

LIZZIE

She'll be happier at home—

JESSIE

Alone? —Have you all lost your minds?

ADDIE

It's for her own good, Jessie.

LIZZIE

She's ridiculed, I hear them sometimes.

JESSIE

—So are we!

EFFIE

We'll never get where we need to go if we keep her with us. She's holding us back.

JESSIE

She's our sister.

EFFIE

You can go home with her, if you want. We're going to New York City.

(ELLA smiles mysteriously.

EFFIE holds the remaining hundred-dollar bill out to JESSIE.)

EFFIE (cont'd.)

... What's it gonna be, Jessie? Are you coming with us? Yes or no.

(JESSIE looks away from ELLA. She looks away from all her sisters.

After a pause, she takes the remaining hundred-dollar bill from EFFIE.)

EFFIE (cont'd.)

(To POPS.)

Wire Hammerstein we're coming.

(Lights out. Or down to that sharp iris-light again, on:

EFFIE, to us:)

EFFIE (cont'd.)

And that's how we got to the top of our profession.

(Iris-light shrinks to black.

Intermission.)

Act Two

8: NEW YORK, OSCAR HAMMERSTEIN'S OLYMPIA THEATRE ON BROADWAY.

(All the sisters onstage, except ELLA.

JESSIE's banging the bass drum now, still with that old wooden spoon.

Bright lights, big show, big finish:)

ALL

Cherries ripe, boom-dee-ay!
Cherries red, boom-dee-ay!
The Cherry Sisters
—*Are on Broadway!*

EFFIE

—Oh!

(A small dense head of cabbage has come flying out of the darkened house and pegged EFFIE in the back, or the front, or the side of her very large head.

She's down.

The other sisters rush to her aid, help her to stand, etc.)

JESSIE

(To the audience, with fury.)

Who did that? *(No response.)*

Who threw that head of cabbage at my sister's head? You? fat man, fourth row, mustache, very sad-looking wife ... Did you throw that cabbage at my sister? *(No response. Some titters. To another:)*

You—you look like the sort of man who'd throw a vegetable at a girl ... What do you have against women? You came from a woman, if I'm not mistaken, from her *womb*—

(Someone throws a rotten tomato at JESSIE—it explodes off the wall.)

EFFIE

Let's move on, Jessie.

JESSIE

Yes, let's.

Let's move on to the homily then, shall we? —Does everyone know what a "homily" is? Probably not. I'll let you in on a little secret here: a homily is "a tedious moral lecture," according to Dr. Webster. And let me *also* tell you, my homily's going to be *very* moral tonight, and exceedingly tedious! I can assure you ... There's no reason why the theater can not be both tedious *and* educative, is there?

(EFFIE whispers in her ear.)

JESSIE (cont'd.)

(To the audience.)

Not tedious. —Not tedious at all! Or tedious to you, perhaps, who have no moral compass ...

VOICE

(In the audience.)

Why don't you go back to Idaho!

JESSIE

"Idaho"? No, sir, I am no lowly spud-grubber ... I am one proud Iowonian woman, of the golden-tasseled corn state. Though I doubt very much you'd be able to find either Iowa or Idaho on a color-coded map of the Union—with labels. —Can you even read?

No, I shall remain here on stage. Because my sisters and I have been engaged by one Mr. Oscar S. Hammerstein—the S. is for savings!—to perform for you all here tonight. And we are at the top of that bill—for a reason: "The Cherry Sisters in: Something Good, Something Sad!" Exclamation point!

(Some lettuce lands limply onstage.)

JESSIE (cont'd.)

That's it. That's good. Get it out of your system. Any more fruit and veg'? Cough it up:

(Several more tomatoes hit the back of the stage; a sack of potatoes; some overripe melons; a chicken carcass.

Silence.

JESSIE steps into a special light:)

JESSIE (cont'd.)

Tonight's homily is entitled, "Manners in The Twentieth Century!" Exclamation point, naturally.

(Silence, as JESSIE arranges herself for oration.

The other three sisters stand patiently upstage, listening, or pretending to listen. EFFIE is still rubbing her sore head.

JESSIE speaks with the overblown gestures and rhetorical flourishes of a temperance crusader, or some other zealot.)

JESSIE (cont'd.)

"There are many things one must do, and many more things one must *never* do! These are the customs of a people ...

"From sun-spangled Borneo, to the snow-swept Aleutians. From stone-strewn Tierra del Fuego, to the fish-friendly coasts of Nova Scotia. *(Pause.)* From Mohamed-loving Istanbul—"

VOICE

To your fat white ass!

JESSIE

(Trying to ignore.)

"—every people have evolved their own especial manners, for good and for ill. Sometimes manners differ, from a people to a people, in their particular. But all good manners have one thing in common:"

VOICE

Shut your cake hole!

JESSIE

"*—kindness!*

"For what are good manners 'good' for? Well, as Dr. Darwin has suggested none too recently, nothing exists for no good reason at all—"

(Someone throws a cat on stage—ADDIE quickly hurls it off.)

JESSIE (cont'd.)

(Flustered, heroic.)

"—Well. I don't know about you, but I believe that in the coming century Man's manners will have evolved to such dizzying heights of decency that wars shall have become uncouth. Gauche, if you will."

(Some offal, internal organs. A cascade of dubious condoms.)

JESSIE (cont'd.)

"—*Famine!* What well-bred man will withdraw his crust of bread from within the mouth of one starveling Swahili?

"Nay, as I have proved, and as Dr. Darwin has none too recently divulged, as I mentioned, we learn, and we learn. And then we learn some more. And as we learn we become much nicer mammals. —Ah! For we are mammals, are we not? Argue me that! What man amongst us here will argue with me that we are not mammals!"

(A kitchen sink.)

JESSIE (cont'd.)

"And so I believe, in the very core of my being, nay, in the white hot wet molten core of my most feminine parts *(she beats her chest)*, that one hundred years from now we shall live together, every last one of us—even you, Mustache!—in a state of Edenic good manners.

"For who amongst us desires pain and cruelty before kindness and love? Who confounds the rose for the knife, the slap for the tickle, the— ?"

(A watermelon is heaved out of the front row and hits her in the gut.

She catches it, staggering back.)

JESSIE (cont'd.)

Oh dear God—

(An enormous wave of laughter.)

EFFIE

(Stepping forward, to us.)

There it is again. There you go ...

I heard it this time, maybe for the first time ...

I'm thinking ... is this what laughter is?

LIZZIE

(Gamely; jauntily.)

Corn juice!
I'm so thirsty for corn juice!
It's been so long
Since I sang this song
O, for corn juice!

I've had the juice of *naranjas*,
I've slurped the juice of the grape,

I've sucked the nectar of the gods,
But Iowa's juice is great!

EFFIE

I'm thinking of Jessie's Dr. Darwin. I'm thinking: you're an audience of baboons, of chimpanzees and apes in your tuxes and your gowns, or whatever it is you're wearing these days, sitting up on your hind legs, baring your yellow fangs ... as you howl and shriek and gibber and drool ...

I could've said something. I could've shut you up. I could have shut my sisters up. We could always just leave the stage. Can't we?

Why can't we— ?

LIZZIE

O, corn juice!
I'm addicted to corn juice!
I've got the shakes
And my stomach aches
For some of your corn juice!

I've sniffed the cocaine powder,
I've smoked the marijuana leaf,
I've jacked the morphine in my veins,
But Iowa's juice is so cheap!

EFFIE

The fruit and veg' rained down ...

(The fruit and veg' rains down.

A dumb-show of dodging:

Every time a Cherry sister's hit, the audience erupts in an orgy of laughter and applause.

LIZZIE begins to cry. Despite the assault, she finishes her song, tears and refuse staining her face.)

LIZZIE

O corn juice!
I'll do anything for corn juice!
Just name your price
And I'll treat you nice
For some of your corn juice!

(Lights move in on LIZZIE, a grotesque mask, then out.

POPS is waiting in the dressing room.)

9: BACKSTAGE, HAMMERSTEIN'S OLYMPIA THEATRE ON BROADWAY.

POPS

Don't be so naïve. This is what happens in New York when they love you: they feed you!

It's like the zoo, girls. Consider it a compliment.

(LIZZIE's still crying. JESSIE tries to comfort her.

POPS is drenched in sweat. He mops his face with a handkerchief throughout. This handkerchief is now really a towel.)

ADDIE

Those weren't compliments they were throwing out there ...

LIZZIE

Do they hate us? —They don't even *know* us!

POPS

They're jealous, I'm telling you.

JESSIE

Jealous of what?

ADDIE

Yes, what exactly are they jealous of, Pops?

POPS

Not the audience, girls. The stars!

LIZZIE

Stars get jealous?

JESSIE

Which ones?

LIZZIE

You mean like astrology?

POPS

The brightest in the firmament today: Dixey, Dockstader. That slut Lottie Collins. Sheldman's Educated Dogs. —They're all so jealous of you and your red-hot ascendancy. Face it, girls: you're hot. And what happens in New York City when you're hot is they hire some young gallery gods to pelt you with defunct fruit and veg'. And other things. Rubbers. —It's time-honored Gothamist tradition!

ADDIE

Are *you* hot, Pops?

POPS

Just a little.

ADDIE

It's November.

POPS

Maybe I got T.B., I don't know.

LIZZIE

I don't find T.B. funny anymore ...

POPS

I'm excited is all! It's obvious we got something going here, girls. Your talent, I dare say your genius, and of course your very popularity right now, are all so enormously immense that you're gonna have to expect fruit and veg' at every show!

LIZZIE

I had no idea that stars could be so cruel.

POPS

Believe it, doll, they're heartless.

(POPS touches LIZZIE on the chin: she turns away.)

ADDIE

Should we do it back to them, then?

POPS

Do what, Butch.

ADDIE

Go to their shows and throw garbage at the stars.

POPS

No no no—

ADDIE

Why not?

JESSIE

Yes, why not, Pops?

POPS

We're better off being stoic. Like what's his name, Jesus. Or Joan of Arc—in your case.

There's only one thing Americans love more than success and that's failure.

(EFFIE sits down, looking dejected and confused.

ADDIE takes her hand.)

POPS (cont'd.)

(To EFFIE, re. her head.)

You should ice that thing.

And now, ladies. For your own protection—

(A net rises up, or descends, between the audience and the actors.

EFFIE talks to us through it:)

EFFIE

We made the stars jealous, every time we stepped on stage ...

(EFFIE starts to slowly undress, throughout the following:)

LIZZIE

Did you see how much garbage I got during *Corn Juice* tonight? A steady barrage, a constant volley, a deluge of rotten envy!

ADDIE

I got sprayed during my comic monologue: some joker threw diced carrots through the net.

JESSIE

That fellow with the melons was back again tonight. Thank goodness for our protective netting!

EFFIE

(To us.)

I read the papers to myself instead. I don't know why I did it.

LIZZIE

Someone threw a bottle at me tonight!

EFFIE

"The most talentless act to hit Broadway since Poodles Malloy in '84" ...

ADDIE

Someone threw their chair!

EFFIE

"Miss Lizzie Cherry narrowly escapes being pretty, but her sisters were never in any such danger" ...

JESSIE

(Pulling a gun out.)

Someone threw this gun at me during my homily—

(ADDIE and LIZZIE duck for cover.)

JESSIE (cont'd.)

It's not loaded ... but it's the thought that counts, right?

EFFIE

(Reading, in her underwear.)

"Their long, skinny arms, equipped with talons at the extremities, swung mechanically, and anon were waved frantically at the suffering audience. The mouths of their rancid features opened like caverns, and sounds like the wailing of damned souls issued therefrom."

(EFFIE puts the newspapers down. Looks out at us:)

EFFIE (cont'd.)

And every night: we sold out.

ADDIE

They hate us ...

LIZZIE

They loathe us!

JESSIE

They absolutely despise us.

(EFFIE joins in:)

ALL

—We're the best act in New York City!

ADDIE

What's the matter, Effie. Aren't you coming with us?

(JESSIE and LIZZIE and ADDIE disappear, leaving EFFIE alone, backstage, late at night, in her underwear.

Her underwear is rather ornate, frilly, almost a bit tarty.)

POPS

(Appearing.)

Baby doll.

EFFIE

You scared me.

POPS

Who'd you think I was?
You decent? I'll turn around.

EFFIE

No, I'm fine.

POPS

No you're not: you're in your underthings.

EFFIE

Am I? *(Coquettishly:)*
I'm sure it's nothing *you've* seen before, Pops ...

POPS

You mean it's nothing I've *never* seen before.

EFFIE

That's a double negative.

POPS

I know. Ergo I have seen women in their underwear before, Effie. All the time.

EFFIE

Have you? that's fresh ... *(She flirts strenuously:)*
I don't think you should be talking to me like this, Pops ...

POPS

Abramowicz. Myron Abramowicz.

(He sits down beside her.)

POPS (cont'd.)

That's my name ... I ever tell you that?

EFFIE

Are you Jewish?

POPS

Is my fly open? Just kidding. I'm Episcopalian. You got a problem with the Jews?

EFFIE

No.

POPS

Good. 'Cause my father was Hasidic.

EFFIE

Is that near Spain?

POPS

Not in a very long time ...

Where is everyone? You know, I thought you were Lizzie from behind.

EFFIE

—Oh!

(She moves in for a coquettish slap.)

POPS

What are you doing?

EFFIE

I wasn't going to do it hard ...

POPS

Well don't do it at all, okay? —Where is she?

EFFIE

Home. At the boarding house ... She's not feeling well, as usual.

POPS

What about you?

EFFIE

I feel—

POPS

Desperate? just kidding.

What do you think of New York City, Effie? Is it everything you ever dreamed it would be?

EFFIE

I don't know yet ...

POPS

Well you should find out. Fast. You should go out sometime, on the town. Find a man. An accountant, maybe. Somebody with very poor eyesight. You like men, don't you?

EFFIE

Like them how?

POPS

You're not like that sister of yours, are you?

EFFIE

I get lonely sometimes ... if that's what you mean ... After the show.

POPS

Tell me about it ...

(He lays his head lightly on her shoulder.)

EFFIE

You smell like my father.

POPS

That's probably just 'cause I'm drunk.

(Pause.)

POPS (cont'd.)

—And shvitzing! Jesus! all the time ... I keep sweating around you girls ... It's disgusting—*I'm* disgusting, aren't I? *(Pause.)*
It's so hard, Effie ...

EFFIE

What's hard? —It is?

POPS

Performing, all the time. You know? Isn't it?

EFFIE

You're not performing.

POPS

I am! All the time! So are you ...

Sometimes I get so, so tired ...

(He leans his head against her shoulder again.

He closes his eyes.)

POPS (cont'd.)

You're the smart one ... You're so much smarter than the other girls ... Why are they all so dumb?

Are they dumb? or do they just pretend? Maybe I'm the stupid one here. I mean, *you* knew what was going on the whole time, right? ... you've always known what was *really* going on ...

(With his eyes closed, slowly, his hand has begun moving up her body, to her breasts.

He gropes her for a bit. She's frozen.

After a beat: EFFIE tries to kiss him.

POPS stands up.)

POPS (cont'd.)

Sorry, you're not my type.

EFFIE

But—

POPS

It's not personal—

EFFIE

You said my head was beautiful— !

POPS

Listen, Effie, I'm marrying your sister.

EFFIE

—Which one?

POPS

Which one? Are you crazy? We're doing it Monday morning. City Hall. Hot shit.

EFFIE

Why?

POPS

Monday? it's our day off.

EFFIE

Why are you getting married at all?

—Because she's pretty? She's not that pretty, she's prettier than me, but—

POPS

Effie—

EFFIE

Did you knock her up? You seduced her, right? —You forced yourself on her probably, backstage, in Chicago, I saw you whispering—

POPS

This isn't one of your one-act plays! ... I love her. Simply put. In my way. More or less.

EFFIE

What about the show?

POPS

Show's over. Don't cry—New York City, at least. That's what I came back here to tell you girls. That's why I've been out celebrating ... Hammerstein's cancelled our gig. Something about a joke getting old.

EFFIE

What about the money?

POPS

I'm keeping most of it. You'll understand ... for Lizzie, the kids ... It's the right thing to do.

You'll tell the other girls, okay? I can't face them all tonight ...

(Pause.)

POPS (cont'd.)

Hey, don't look so sad ... We had some fun, didn't we? —We were popular! Most people are *never* popular, even with their own families ...

And remember, love's like money: every bit counts.

You'll get home okay?

(She doesn't answer. He turns the lights out on EFFIE as he goes.)

POPS (cont'd.)

(From off.)

So long!

LIZZIE

So long, everybody! Good bye!

(LIZZIE appears in a wedding dress, bouquet in hand.

Crowds, train whistles, shoes clacking on marble ...)

JESSIE

Congratulations, Lizzie!

ADDIE

Congratulations, Lizzie ...

(JESSIE is crying.)

LIZZIE

I only wish Ella could've come! What a hurry it's all been!

EFFIE

What do you expect from a shotgun wedding?

LIZZIE

What did you say, Effie ... ? I can't hear you so well anymore, what with all the crowds of Grand Central Station, and the whistles of the trains, and the sounds of shoes clacking on marble—

EFFIE

I said you got knocked up!

(A train whistle shrieks.)

POPS

(Offstage.)

—Come on, Lizzie, train's leaving!

(LIZZIE begins to cry now too.)

LIZZIE

I'll write you from Saratoga Springs. We're going there for the horses, and the baths. And the horses. Everybody knows the only thing Pops loves more than a good horse race is taking a bath! *(She cries a lot.)* It'll be so lovely, you'll see.

And by the time I'm home again ... I promise you all I'll be pregnant!

JESSIE

Where's home, Lizzie?

LIZZIE

What, Jessie?

JESSIE

Where are you going to live from now on?

LIZZIE

Flushing! —Isn't that the most beautiful name? So clean!

(LIZZIE cries, a lot.)

EFFIE

—Did you know his name is Myron?

LIZZIE

Of course, Effie! He told me that months ago ...

What's wrong with you ... ? You look like you've seen a ghost.

POPS

(Off.)

Lizzie! Train's leaving!

EFFIE

Goodbye, Lizzie.

LIZZIE

What did you say? I can't hear you ... I can't hear you so well anymore ... !

(LIZZIE goes.

But before going:

She turns and throws her bouquet up over her shoulder, into the air.

She's gone.

The bouquet lands onstage and breaks into many small pieces.)

EFFIE

(To us.)

Five months later she died in childbirth. *(Pause.)* Unlike me, this baby died too.

We never heard from Pops again ...

(ADDIE and EFFIE slowly pick up the pieces of Lizzie's bouquet while they quietly sing:)

ADDIE

I ain't never been kissed ...

EFFIE

(To us.)

After Lizzie died, Addie and I sang her songs as duets. *(She sings:)*

I ain't talking cheeks, I'm talking hot lips.

ADDIE

No matter how hard I swing these hips ...

EFFIE & ADDIE

I ain't never had no lover's kiss.

(Music continues, becomes a new song:)

EFFIE (cont'd.)

I wrote a new song. Something just for me to sing, alone:

Love's like money,
I ain't never got enough.
My wallet's always empty,
My heart's only full of fluff.

Love's like money,
Better squirrel it away.
Winter's gonna come, one day,
And steal your nuts away.

I used to dream that love was free
But now I see you earn it,
You sell it and you steal it
And in a pinch you burn it
—It's business and you're the boss!

Love's like money,
Even when you're rich
It could all just disappear,
And leave you sleeping in a ditch.

I used to dream that love was free
But now I see you earn it,

You sell it and you steal it
And in a pinch you burn it
—It's business and you're the boss!

Love's like money,
Doesn't matter what you're owed.
It's your job to make it
Out here on the open road ...

(Train whistle blows.

ADDIE and JESSIE appear, with luggage.

ADDIE carries two suitcase—one for EFFIE.)

ADDIE

Let's go, Effie. Train's leaving.

(EFFIE takes her suitcase.)

JESSIE

It'll be so nice to see Ella again ...

EFFIE

We're not going home. We're going on tour.

JESSIE

How can we— ?

ADDIE

We don't have any money left, Jessie ...

JESSIE

We don't have a manager either!

EFFIE

I'll be our manager from now on.

JESSIE

That's absurd! a manager is a man—that's why it's spelled that way!

EFFIE

Not anymore, Jessie. It's the Twentieth Century now. Remember?

10: THE OPEN ROAD.

EFFIE

Pick up the pace, girls! —Pick up those bags, Jessie, they won't carry themselves.

(JESSIE has several bags, in fact, like a pack mule.)

JESSIE

Where are we now ... ?

ADDIE

In Cairo.

JESSIE

As in Egypt?

ADDIE

Illinois actually.

JESSIE

Where's my ticket? ... Has anyone seen my other suitcase?

EFFIE

We'll need more light in here!

ADDIE

—Drop the net! —Raise the curtain!

EFFIE

That's not what the contract said, asshole.

JESSIE

Effie! ... It's like I don't know you anymore ...

(EFFIE runs into the arms of JESSIE:)

EFFIE

"Mother!"

JESSIE

"There, there, my child. There, there. There. Now, rest your head, here, upon my pendulous breasts."

ADDIE

Ladies and—one gentlemen. —Is that a gentleman? I beg your pardon, Sister.

—The human pyramid!

(They do it—JESSIE's always on the bottom.

They break out of it.)

EFFIE

Let's go.

ADDIE

Look, there's a letter here from Ella—

(ELLA appears, wearing some kind of fancy headdress.)

ELLA

Dear my three remaining sisters:

Snow is cold here; Iowa is cold here, in winter. And fall. And spring. Summer is just about right, don't you think?

Thanks for all that spare change you send ...

EFFIE

(To us.)

If you're surprised she can write like this, so are we.

ADDIE

Is that a semi-colon?

JESSIE

Is she getting someone else to write these letters for her? Whom?

ADDIE

That's Ella's handwriting all right: enormous ...

EFFIE

In red crayon.

ELLA

I've been working on my routine.

JESSIE

What routine?

ELLA

Because I know, if only I can get better, if I can find some more talent—*in* me, somewhere—then one day I'll be able to see you all again, to perform with you, out on the open road ...

I miss you all ...

I know I was not so good before. I don't blame you all that much.

(She starts to juggle, some old whiskey bottles.)

ELLA (cont'd.)

Every day now I go out to the barn, and I practice my juggling—some of Pops' old bottles. The ones he kept hidden inside all that wet hay. There's so much wet hay— ! Which is why it hardly matters when I break a few.

(She breaks all of them.)

JESSIE

That sounds dangerous ...

ELLA

(Cuts her finger.)

Shit.

EFFIE

Let's go girls, train's leaving.

JESSIE

—Again?

ADDIE

Oskaloosa ...

(EFFIE's scribbling in her little brown journal:)

EFFIE

Thirteen dollars for deposit please ...

ADDIE

Osceola ...

EFFIE

Eight seventy-four, no make that -five.

ADDIE

Ottumwa ...

JESSIE

Where's that? in Canada?

EFFIE

We're in Dubuque now.

JESSIE

Sioux City.

ADDIE

(Fading away.)

Waterloooo ...

JESSIE

As in France?

EFFIE

What difference does it make where we are, Jessie? We're on stage—we're all over the corn-belt these days!

JESSIE

"We're the best the corn-belt has to offer" ...

EFFIE

We are!

JESSIE

I'm going to take a nap.

(JESSIE takes out a hip flask and swigs.)

ADDIE

(Prompting.)

"My dear sir—"

EFFIE

"My dear sir, I think you're fresh!"

ADDIE

"I think *you're* fresh! Like a summer rain!"

EFFIE

"And you're like a winter drizzle."

ADDIE

"I can't help it! You make me feel damp!"

EFFIE

—"Fresh!"

(EFFIE slaps ADDIE perfunctorily.)

ADDIE

Ladies and—or should I say, nightwalkers and—gentleman farmers:
—The human pyramid!

(They do it again: JESSIE's on the bottom again, of course.)

ELLA

Dear Mis Hermanas:

(Enter ELLA again, with a unicycle, and wearing a dirty army helmet. She's got some mud on her face too.)

ELLA (cont'd.)

Today is spring thaw. Mud is ubiquitous.

EFFIE

"Ubiquitous"?

ELLA

Meaning "everywhere," like God used to be. You should know that, Effie!

EFFIE

I *do* know that but—

ELLA

I've been learning to ride my unicycle.

(ELLA prepares to ride the unicycle.)

JESSIE

Where'd she find a unicycle ... ?

ELLA

I made it. From an old bike with only one wheel left. Hence "uni."

EFFIE

We know what a unicycle is ...

ADDIE

"Hence"?

ELLA

And it's difficult but I think I might learn how to do it well, one day.
And juggle at the very same time.

(She tries to juggle and cycle at the same time: she fails.

She falls.)

ELLA (cont'd.)

—Damn! Damn it all to Hell I swear it is hard work!

JESSIE

Amen, sister ...

ELLA

I think one day you will like my new act, girls. When you come home to visit, I'll show you.

When will you be coming home ... ?

JESSIE

When *will* we, Effie ... ?

EFFIE

(Her book.)

Tulsa. Five flat for deposit please ...

ADDIE

Amarillo.

EFFIE

Three dollars and thirteen cents.

JESSIE

Does anyone else have this rash?

ADDIE

That's not a rash, Jessie. Those are bed bug bites.

JESSIE

—Jesus!

EFFIE

—Jessie! your language—

JESSIE

Oh, blow it out your ass.

(JESSIE takes another swig.)

ADDIE

Salt Lake City.

EFFIE

(Journal.)

Two fifty: "house was small and mean."

JESSIE

These Mormons can be so touchy sometimes ...

ADDIE

It's the polygamy. It makes you grouchy.

EFFIE

Manhattan.

JESSIE

Where?

ADDIE

Kansas.

JESSIE

Oh.

EFFIE

Bellevue.

JESSIE

Hospital?

ADDIE

Nebraska.

JESSIE

Right. —Are you going to eat that meatloaf?

ADDIE

That's not meatloaf, that's an old sponge.

JESSIE

... It's raining so hard.

EFFIE

No that's hail.

ADDIE

And sleet.

JESSIE

It's snowing again ...

EFFIE

Flood.

JESSIE

Lift up your skirts, girls— !

ADDIE

Drought.

JESSIE

—Has anyone seen my medicine?

ADDIE

You mean your corn juice?

EFFIE

Twister!

ADDIE

Dust bowl! —A-choo!

EFFIE

Locusts.

JESSIE

Are you going to eat that honey?

ADDIE

That's not honey, I just sneezed.

JESSIE

Is there a draft?

EFFIE

It's winter.

ADDIE

Summer.

JESSIE

Autumn.

EFFIE

Winter.

ADDIE

Winter.

JESSIE

When is it ever not winter?

EFFIE

These years are racing by—like a train—

ADDIE

Like we're *on* that train—

EFFIE

There's a cow. And another. And another.

ADDIE

It's all moving so fast— !

JESSIE

Is anyone else feeling nauseous?

EFFIE

Is this what life's like, getting old ... ?

ADDIE

Cabool, Missouri.

EFFIE

Twenty-four cents and *(someone throws these onstage:)* two miniature chickens.

ADDIE

Thank you!

JESSIE

My corns ...

ADDIE

Mansfield, Missouri.

EFFIE

One Canadian dime.

ADDIE

—Cheapskates!

JESSIE

Does this feel like a hernia to you ... ?

ADDIE

Licking, Missouri.

EFFIE

Nobody came. Nobody at all. Left Licking, all our bills unpaid.

ADDIE

Missouri ... Missouri ...

JESSIE

(Sounding a lot like "misery".)

Missouri ...

EFFIE

What's wrong with you this time, Jessie?

JESSIE

I'm sweating, all over. I'm hot, I'm tired—

EFFIE

Maybe you shouldn't carry that accordion around with you all the time.

JESSIE

My squeezebox? —I've got to practice.

ADDIE

Maybe it's the change of life.

JESSIE

What change of life?

ADDIE

You know ...

EFFIE

Already?

ADDIE

It *is* getting a bit stale, Effie ... Maybe we need a new act? Something a little more ... contemporary?

(JESSIE plays her squeezebox.

As EFFIE hooks on a very long thick black beard:)

EFFIE

"K-nock, k-nock!"

JESSIE

"Who'sa dere?"

EFFIE

"It is I! The landlord, Tevieh Schmalzagazicht! —Oy gevalt!"

JESSIE

"—Oh sole mio!"

ADDIE

"Turn offa de light and shutupa de face!"

JESSIE

"—He wantsa de rent!"

ADDIE

"How cana we paya de renta! We can nota evena feed spaghetti to our own bambinos and bambinas!"

JESSIE

"We can nota feed our bambinitos because you nevera go to a worka!"

ADDIE

"How cana I go to a worka when I'm Italian? —Oh! I wish I wasa back at a home-a in Sicilia with Mama!"

EFFIE

(Still Tevieh.)

"And for this I went to college? —You know what? forget about it ... "

JESSIE

(On her squeezebox.)

We can not pay the landlord
When his hands go k-nock, k-nock, k-nock.

ADDIE

We can not pay the loan sharks
With the meatballs that we hock.

JESSIE

We can not pay the doctor
After a visit from the stork.

ADDIE

So we blow out all our candles,
Not a flame and not a spark,

JESSIE

And we feed our children garlic
So we can find them in the dark!

(ELLA appears in the barn loft above, wearing an aviator cap, goggles on her forehead.)

ELLA

Dear Gals:

What a hot summer it's been. Jesus! —Jesus H. Christ! Our barn is falling down practically! The barn has become a bastion of broken bottles and rags—

EFFIE

"Bastion"? I know what that means, but—

ADDIE

Why is she yelling so much ... ?

JESSIE

She's been drinking. She sounds drunk.

ELLA

I am finally now so good at juggling whilst riding on this unicycle, that I have decided to string a rope from loft to rafter out here in the barn—

JESSIE

Oh sweet Jesus ...

ELLA

And any moment now I promise you I'll be ready to wheel out across that empty space above our very hard barnyard floor—

JESSIE

She can't do that!

ELLA

—whilst juggling—

EFFIE

"Whilst"?

JESSIE

—She'll die!

ELLA

And yes, I am afraid that I might die ...

So I have taken to fortifying myself with corn juice. I find it gives me strength. No wonder Pops was so fond of the devil drink!—woops.

(ELLA has been climbing up onto the loft railing, reaching out for a piece of dangling rope ... and she almost falls.

JESSIE almost faints: she sits.)

ELLA (cont'd.)

Effie ... ?

Remember that dream I told you about? years ago? That you would get married, out of doors, at night? With a dress like snow, and a veil of snow also ... ?

Well I was wrong about one thing: it's not a wedding. Not a wedding at all ...

(ELLA disappears.

JESSIE, below, picks up her suitcase.)

JESSIE

I'm going home.

EFFIE

They paid to see a show, Jessie.

JESSIE

Who cares about them? —Our sister's about to kill herself!

ADDIE

We'll go home together, when the tour's over. Okay? Just for a rest. —How's that sound, Effie? take a month off—

EFFIE

Whose side are you on?

(Pause. Now ADDIE is hurt.)

JESSIE

We can sell the land, keep the house. Or get a house in town—

EFFIE

(Disgusted.)

In Marion?

JESSIE

In Cedar Rapids, if we want. An apartment, in the city.

EFFIE

Cedar Rapid's not the city.

ADDIE

—What would we *do* all day, Jessie?

JESSIE

Nothing! Can you imagine how nice that would be?

We'd take care of Ella ... listen to the radio, all of us together, to all the acts coming straight to us from New York City. We'd make fun of them for once—it'd be so nice to make fun of somebody else, for once, wouldn't it?

And we'd grow our own vegetables, and fruit. We wouldn't have to dodge them anymore—we'd eat them! And we'd clean up all that mess that Ella's made.

We'd walk up and down that old house in Marion, remembering things how they used to be.

EFFIE

Things were awful in that house.

JESSIE

Then we'd remember it better than it was ...

Instead of living out here, on the open road all the time—

ADDIE

I like it out here, on the open road. We meet so many people—

JESSIE

Who we never see again.

ADDIE

Nobody ever tells us what to do—

JESSIE

Don't you want to fall in love? Don't you want a family?

ADDIE

Why? ... I already have one.

EFFIE

She's lazy. That's all it is. —You've always been this way, Jessie. —*And* pessimistic. You've never *once* believed in us!

JESSIE

Oh, Effie. *(Pause.)* That was impolite.

(Another pause.)

JESSIE (cont'd.)

Tonight, Effie. Because you're my sister. Then I'm done.

ADDIE

—Inmates and guards of Leavenworth Prison—and Warden Johansen, of course:

The human pyramid!

(They do it one more time.

This time JESSIE collapses under the weight of her sisters.

She's squashed flat like a bug. They roll off her.)

EFFIE

Jessie. —Jessie, get up.

(The sound of applause is deafening.)

ADDIE

I'll get a doctor—

(ADDIE exits.)

EFFIE

(To us.)

It was her heart.

(As the protective netting rises up out of view ...

And POPS appears, looking like the old Pops again, whiskey bottles dangling off his ragged clothes, blasted wet cigar in his mouth.)

POPS

There you've gone and killed another one, you murderous little girl. Wherefore all this rage, little Effie? Why?

(EFFIE runs at him, with a murderous rage.

POPS evades gracefully—he's a ghost, he sings:)

POPS (cont'd.)

Your skirts are up above your knees, you're dancin', girl—
Be careful, girl, be careful, please;
Me eyes are like twin stars o' fire, advancin', girl
—O, do be careful! —O, do be careful!

There now, it's up above your waist,
Your pearly goods are all uncased,
They're surely temper'd to my taste
—St. Patrick's Day in the morning!

JESSIE

(Pops up.)

Hi, Pops.

POPS

Hello, me dear.

JESSIE

Is Mother here?

POPS

You know, I haven't thought to ask.

JESSIE

Are we in Heaven, Pops, or Hell?

POPS

They won't tell me that one yet neither!

EFFIE

—How can you even *talk* to him?

JESSIE

He's dead. I'm dead. He's our father.

POPS

Have you not learned your lesson yet, Effie? Have you not figured out what went wrong?

EFFIE

What went wrong? —*You* went wrong! Momma *dying* went wrong—

POPS

(Chuckling.)

Oh now, Effie ... It's almost over now. Can't you see? It's the end of the road for you ... It's time you went home.

JESSIE

I'd like to deliver a little homily before I go: it's called, on "The Importance of Manners in The Afterlife." No exclamation necessary now, naturally. You can chime in anytime you'd like, Pops.

POPS

I wouldn't dream.

JESSIE

(In her usual style.)

"What will the coming life bring? Is there such a thing as life beyond the grave? Whom shall we meet—or meet again—in Heaven, Hell, or *Purgatorio*, as our dago brethren say.

"Well, I don't know about you, but I believe our after-lives will be better than our before-ones. Full of chit-chat and finger sandwiches.

"And we shall be kind to one another at last. Even unto family members, whom we may have hated in life, or felt betrayed or injured by ...

"For if we can not forgive them now, then how shall we ever begin to forgive ourselves?"

(Someone in the audience throws JESSIE white roses.)

EFFIE

—I'm so sorry, Jessie!

JESSIE

Why?

EFFIE

We're no good! I'm no good! —I'm horrible! I was horrible! Just like you were. We were all of us no good at all and I've known it for the longest time!

JESSIE

So have I ... We've all known that, haven't we? The whole world's known that ...

EFFIE

Why didn't you say something? why didn't we ever speak of it?

(JESSIE gives EFFIE one of her white roses. JESSIE disappears.

POPS follows.)

POPS

(To EFFIE, as he goes.)

I'll see you soon, me girl.

EFFIE

I will never forgive you.

(ADDIE appears, carrying their two suitcases:)

ADDIE

Let's go, Effie. Train's leaving, again ...

11: THAT BARN IN MARION.

(Train whistle becomes a heartless plains wind ...

EFFIE looks around her. ADDIE looks to Effie.

EFFIE turns to us, to say something—then forgets what she was about to say.

How much time has passed?

Though the girls are elderly now, the tempo here is quick, fluid, a patter of senility.

ADDIE sniffs the air:)

ADDIE

Smells like snow.

EFFIE

It's winter ...

ADDIE

Again? That's nice.

EFFIE

What is?

ADDIE

What?

EFFIE

Where are we now?

ADDIE

Back home, in Iowa.

EFFIE

It's like we never left ... !

ADDIE

Did we?

EFFIE

What time is it now?

ADDIE

1935.

EFFIE

Exactly?

ADDIE

Give or take.

EFFIE

That's late ... This barn could use some work.

ADDIE

What?

EFFIE

—I said that's nice!

ADDIE

Where's Ella?

EFFIE

Oh, she's dead ...

ADDIE

Did she die out here on that tightrope? Did she fall to her death from way up there?

EFFIE

Oh no.

ADDIE

That's nice.

EFFIE

—That *is* nice!

ADDIE

What is?

EFFIE

We moved home, when Jessie died. We lived with Ella, who died in her bed of old age ...

ADDIE

Old age?

EFFIE

Old age.

ADDIE

That's nice.

EFFIE

—And easy!

We had to burn our furniture sometimes, for warmth ...

ADDIE

(Nostalgically.)

I remember warmth.

We still have our chickens though, don't we?

EFFIE

We ate them. Had to. The Depression.

ADDIE

Depression?

EFFIE

The Depression.

(They both sigh, depressed.)

EFFIE (cont'd.)

Why are we out here again?

ADDIE

You don't know?

EFFIE

Should I?

ADDIE

It was your idea.

EFFIE

Was it? Why?

ADDIE

To rehearse, I think ...

EFFIE

Rehearsal is such a depressing word. Redundant.

ADDIE

What is?

EFFIE

We are.

ADDIE

What are we meant to be rehearsing again ... ?

EFFIE

A job, I think. For a show, in New York City.

(Short pause. Some magic.)

ADDIE

What kind of show?

EFFIE

A nostalgic revue ...

ADDIE

"Nostalgia is a useless emotion."

EFFIE

Who said that?

ADDIE

What?

EFFIE

Who?

ADDIE

—And I agree!

EFFIE

—Me too!

ADDIE

Whatever was I saying ... ?

EFFIE

Who invited us all the way to New York City?

ADDIE

You should know. Some guy.

EFFIE

Some man.

ADDIE

Some schmoe.

EFFIE

—What a timewaster!

ADDIE

I've got the letter here to prove it.

EFFIE

He wrote us a letter?

ADDIE

He phoned you.

EFFIE

What's a telephone?

ADDIE

Who knows?

EFFIE

Who knows?

ADDIE

Should we go?

EFFIE

Would you like to?

(Pause.)

EFFIE (cont'd.)

They'll be kinder to us this time, Addie. I think so ...

ADDIE

How do you know that?

EFFIE

I don't.

ADDIE

Do we need the money? If we need the money ...

EFFIE

Of course we need the money.

ADDIE

That's not why.

EFFIE

No, that's not why.

ADDIE

Will they laugh at us?

EFFIE

I think they will.

ADDIE

Will they cry?

EFFIE

I hope they don't.

ADDIE

—But we're so out of practice!

EFFIE

Are we? At what?

ADDIE

Remembering ... How to sing, and dance. Tell our funny jokes ...

(Pause. Something happens:)

ADDIE (cont'd.)

"I'm only goin' so far as Yahnkers!"

EFFIE

Where'd that come from?

ADDIE

I have no idea.

EFFIE

From the ether.

ADDIE
What do you call a cow with no milk?

EFFIE
Who knows?

ADDIE
Who knows?

EFFIE
—What the Hell?

ADDIE
Look at my fingers! —Like lizards!

EFFIE
That's why we're here? To remember?

ADDIE
What are we remembering again? Tell me one more time ...

EFFIE
Our show. Don't you want to go?

ADDIE
To New York City?

EFFIE
New York City.

ADDIE
All right, Effie. I'll go if you will.

(EFFIE takes ADDIE's hand this time.

They sing the song slowly, in a minor key.)

EFFIE
I ain't never been kissed,

ADDIE
I ain't never been kissed.

EFFIE & ADDIE
We ain't talking cheeks, we're talking hot lips.
No matter how hard we swing these hips,
We ain't never had no lover's kiss.

(A pause.)

EFFIE (cont'd.)

(To us.)

Not a missile was fired. Not a voice cried out in ridicule ...

Some women wept softly. Men hid their eyes in their hands and were thankful for the dark.

ADDIE

Good night, Effie. This was fun.

(She kisses her sister. Lets go of her hand.)

EFFIE

Addie passed away that year.

I moved to Cedar Rapids, where I opened up a bakery and sold only cherry tarts ... and cherry pies ... Anything with a cherry in it, really.

I never went to the theater, or *(with derision)* the movies.

I ran for public office. I lost.

I grew fond of pasta, and ranting in public, often at the same time. I'd tell anyone who'd listen to me the world was going to Hell and here's why.

I kept on writing in this little brown book. A memoir of sorts, that remains unpublished to this day ... in a drawer ... in a desk somewhere in Iowa ...

It hardly explains things anyway, so ... So what?

(Her sisters appear one-by-one, with their lines:)

ELLA

(Pointing.)

It's snowing.

(It's true:

Snowflakes are falling from the rafters, as if the roof has lifted off the barn.

The snow will grow heavier, the lighting blue and wintry.)

EFFIE

And then, one night, or early one winter's morning, as I lay in my bed above the bakery ... I saw in my room a tall man, a Spaniard.

A cavalier, with his knife sheathed by his side ...

ADDIE

I'm not a man, Effie. I'm your sister. Here I am again.

EFFIE

And in the street below I thought I heard his horse chuff and stamp its hooves in the snow.

JESSIE

It's me, Effie! It's freezing out here!

(LIZZIE begins to sing, softly beneath the scene:)

LIZZIE

I'm so lonely for Old Broadway,
I'm so bored by these cornfields and hay ...

(POPS—as their father—appears, standing in the shadows.)

EFFIE

I rose from my bed and followed my ears, out into the hallway and down the back stairs ...

ADDIE

Watch your step—

EFFIE

Out into the street where the snow's falling fast ...

JESSIE

Don't fall, Effie—

EFFIE

Not silently, the snow sounds like rain. —No, like applause, falling on rooftops, past darkened windowpanes ... Steady clapping falling down from unseen hands.

ADDIE

Don't slip in the snow, Effie. Here, hold my hand.

(ADDIE and EFFIE join hands again.)

EFFIE

I was wearing my white nightgown ...

ELLA

Like a wedding dress.

(Pause.)

EFFIE (cont'd.)

Let's see it again.

ADDIE

It's all over now, Effie.

EFFIE

I want to see it—just once more, okay? Can we? Please? —We can.

JESSIE

If you don't come now then we can't go either.

LIZZIE

We won't go, Effie, if you won't come. Come on!

ADDIE

Please, Effie. Show's over ...

EFFIE

Am I ready though?

JESSIE

Aren't you yet?

EFFIE

Have I figured it out this time? what went wrong?

ADDIE

What went wrong?

EFFIE

I don't know. Whose fault was it?

JESSIE

"Fault"?

EFFIE

Was it Pops?

JESSIE

Yes.

EFFIE

Was it the people in the audience?

LIZZIE

Yes.

EFFIE

Was it my fault ... ?

ADDIE

Was it worth it?

(EFFIE looks around her, at the snow; out to us.

Now she looks to her sisters:)

EFFIE

I want to see it again. Just one more time.

(Stage to black.)

END OF PLAY

THE VOYAGE OF THE CARCASS

Characters

BANE Barrington, *commanding* / BILL, *an actor; early 30s*

Elijah (Eliza) KANE, *ship's chaplain* / HELEN, *Bill's wife, a former actress; early 30s*

ISRAEL, *first-mate* / DAN, *a writer* / Bjorn BJORNSEN, *Arctic explorer; late 20s*

Time

A hundred years ago, or so / Today

Place

Somewhere just south of the North Pole / A small theater in the middle of nowhere

Notes

1) When one character starts speaking before the other has finished, the point of interruption is marked / as in:

DAN
The thing, the / air-conditioning.

BILL
I tried.

2) Nonverbal "lines" in the script:

BANE
. . . ?

or

KANE
—!

or

ISRAEL
. . .

etc., should be played as "takes"—of surprise, or confusion, or shock, as the case may be.

3) SMYTHE is a dummy. The more lifelike, the better.

4) MISHKA the sledge dog can (and maybe should) be entirely a figment of BJORNSEN's imagination.

5) An intermission is suggested after Scene Five.

6) There's some mention of Bill wearing a clown nose in this play, but there's no explicit call for it in the various North Pole scenes. From what I've seen, the "clown" business works better without the somewhat clichéd distraction of the bright red foam-rubber clown noses. This doesn't have to be at odds with Bill's use of one in Scenes 5 and 8, as he might just happen to have one lying around—in the trunk, perhaps.

7) The last scene requires some tricky business involving Israel's dead body. (The actor playing Israel is meant to die onstage, remain onstage, then magically appear several minutes later as Bjorn Bjornsen.) Some productions have simply used the "absent" dummy of Bo'sun Smythe and quickly, in the blue-light transition between Israel's death and the beginning of Scene 9, added a few elements of Israel's costume to the dummy to make it clear that a switcheroo had taken place. To embrace the awkwardness of this seems to me to be in keeping with the particular theatricality of this play.

The Voyage of the Carcass received its world premiere with Page 73 Productions at HERE Arts Center in New York City in 2002, directed by Alyse Rothman:

BANE / BILL	Michael Anderson
KANE / HELEN	Rebecca Harris
ISRAEL / DAN / BJORNSEN	Chris Mason

The play received a commercial run in 2006 at the SoHo Playhouse in NYC, directed by Randy Baruh.

BANE / BILL	Dan Fogler
KANE / HELEN	Kelly Hutchinson
ISRAEL / DAN / BJORNSEN	Noah Bean

Acknowledgments

A one-act version of *The Voyage of the Carcass* was created from scratch with a company of actors in August 1998 at Middlebury College in Middlebury, Vermont. The author would like to thank Alexandra Harbold for her participation in the creation of this earlier version.

. . Their normal social relations had been suspended and replaced by a primitive unmannerliness which demonstrated how queer these people had become under the influence of prolonged and trying association with each other . . .

—Frederick Pryce Evans,
Captain of the Nimrod,
on discovering survivors
of a failed Antarctic expedition

When that I was and a little tiny boy,
   With hey, ho, the wind and the rain,
A foolish thing was but a toy,
   For the rain it raineth every day.

But when I came to man's estate,
   With hey, ho, the wind and the rain,
'Gainst knaves and thieves men shut the gate,
   For the rain it raineth every day.

—*Twelfth Night*

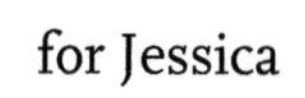

for Jessica

1.

(A foolish man with a large ass in a tuxedo:)

BANE

"Men wanted for hazardous journey. Small wages, bitter cold, long months of complete and utter darkness. Constant danger. Safe return doubtful. Honor and recognition in case of success."

...

That wasn't my advertisement. That was Shackleton's.

Mine was much longer ...

But the gist was the same:

The date was April trois, 1899: with no experience worth mentioning, save a bout with typhoid during the Spanish-American War; no proof to substantiate my plan, save what rumors I'd fished from the mouths of drunken whalers; and no real capital for the venture—save loads and loads of recently inherited cash: I had a boat built and christened *The Carcass*.

A name, I'll admit, not promising of success.

And yet a name I hoped would suit a ship with a hull in the shape of a perfect ellipse, so that when winter pressed in on all sides *The Carcass* would lift upon the ice like the body of some fallen warrior, and drift, higher, higher, into the North ...

It was an amateur's fantasy.

Where others had perished on foot, I would succeed by merely standing still ...

We brought all manner of supply aboard: forty dogs for hunting, and the occasional excursion on sledge; and as pets for the forty men.

—How I loved those dogs ...

I bade goodbye to my friends and to my family; to my fiancé, Eliza Kane—

(Light: KANE in a dress.)

BANE (cont'd.)

—who did not seem to take the parting at all well:

(She hurts BANE in a highly personal place.)

BANE (cont'd.)

... Women are not built like us.

And with my trusted friend Israel by my side:

(ISRAEL, in his own light, burdened with a very large sack of supplies.)

BANE (cont'd.)

—a ragtag band of hardened seamen under me; including my fiancé's own uncle, one "Elijah" Kane as ship's chaplain ...

(KANE slaps on a beard, or some other simple gender-bending device.)

BANE (cont'd.)

... we set sail for the North Pole, with nothing but the highest of hopes ... !

(A cold, arctic wind.)

2.

(Deep inside the hold of The Carcass.

The space is cramped and dirty yet mostly empty. Ropes lie about. A trunk with a lock in it. One entrance / exit high upon the upstage wall, if possible; a rope ladder descends to a table to take meals at.

KANE and BANE sit at this table, threadbare blankets over their shoulders. KANE's clothes are too big for her; BANE is bursting his seams, particularly in the rear. Both "men" are hollow-eyed, their faces like death masks. KANE is reading a big, old book.

A cabin lamp dangles from a length of rope. BANE watches the lamp swing.)

BANE

(Scratching in his journal as he counts.)

Four thousand nine hundred and eighty five.
Four thousand nine hundred and eighty six.
Four thousand nine hundred and eighty seven.
Four thousand nine hundred and eighty eight.
Four thousand nine hundred and eighty nine—

(He keeps counting, as long as it takes for the lamp to stop swinging.

KANE tries to ignore him.

BANE records the final figure in his journal:)

BANE (cont'd.)

Five thousand! *(For example.)* —A new record, Kane!

(She ignores him further.

He walks over to the lamp, pulls it back, lets it swing.

Delighted, he sits again:)

BANE (cont'd.)

One. Two. Three—

(KANE stands and stops the lamp in mid-swing. She sets it still. She sits again and resumes reading.

BANE stands and walks over to the lamp, tries to pull it back without her noticing ...

She notices.

BANE whips out his handkerchief as if to buff the lamp: fog the glass, wipe it clean—he "accidentally" drops the hankie to the ground.

He reaches for the handkerchief—but he can't reach it while holding the lamp ...

What a dilemma!

He stoops quickly for the handkerchief, and the lamp swings free again.)

BANE

(Delighted, sotto voce.)

One. Two—

(KANE leaps for the lamp, stops it swinging. A reproachful glare. She returns to her seat. Resumes reading.

BANE sits.

From his seat, he tries to blow the lamp into motion.

KANE notices.

He's now blowing into his hands, as if for warmth. He blows what sounds like one long, high note on a pitch-pipe.

They double-take, respectively. She goes back to reading ...

BANE fixes his stare upon the lamp and tries to start it swinging by sheer force of mind control. He gesticulates wildly, like a hypnotist. This psychic exertion lifts him from his seat.

KANE notices.

He fixes his cufflinks, such as they are ...

She resumes reading.

BANE paces, lost in thought: What does a man have to do to get a lamp to start swinging?

Absently, he leans his hand upon the lamp. He falls over. —The lamp swings!

KANE leaps to the lamp; stops it.

She glowers at BANE; and this time remains there, holding the lamp still. She lifts her big, old book before her face to read ...

BANE wanders the cabin, playing with himself, his handkerchief, talking to it, stroking it, etc.

He lays the handkerchief scarily over his face and begins to tell himself a story:)

BANE

It was a dark and stormy night, and the Captain said, "Bo'sun, tell me a story." And the Bo'sun said, "It was a dark and stormy night, and the Captain said, 'Bo'sun, tell me a story.' And the Bo'sun said, 'It was a dark and stormy night, and the Captain said, "Bo'sun, tell me a story." And the Bo'sun said, "It was a dark and stormy night, and the Captain said, 'Bo'sun, tell me a story—*(etc.)*

(KANE snatches BANE's handkerchief off his head and blows her nose into it, wetly.

She lays it out flat again on his head and face.

He removes the handkerchief; blots himself; folds the handkerchief into lumpy squares, returns it to his pocket.

He saunters downstage to a pile of refuse, amidst which there exists one haunted umbrella.

KANE is alarmed.

He taunts her with the umbrella. [It's obvious KANE is a superstitious "fellow."] She makes a grab for it, but BANE twirls and dodges, feints and dodges again, all the while threatening to open it.

Eventually, they both have the umbrella; and in the struggle it is opened, then closed, then opened, closed, opened—KANE hurts BANE in a highly personal place.

—She has the umbrella! She closes it. She unlocks the upstage trunk with a key she keeps concealed in her concealed bosom, dumps the umbrella in the trunk, then locks the trunk again.

They catch their breaths, respectively.

They sit down again at the table, as before.

Silence. Boredom ... It's been like this forever.

ISRAEL enters, dragging or carrying or dumping from above the apparently very dead body of Bo'sun SMYTHE.

Both ISRAEL and SMYTHE are dressed like the others—formal wear that's seen better days, loose raggish clothes and clownish shoes.

Neither KANE nor BANE take much notice of ISRAEL, who lays SMYTHE out flat on the table between them and waits for a response.

Then:)

BANE

Good God!

KANE

Thank you, Izzie.

BANE

What has happened to Bo'sun Smythe— ?

KANE

Bo'sun Smythe is dead.

BANE

I can see that! I can see that Bo'sun Smythe is dead! What concerns me now is the nature of his death ...

(KANE ties on a bloodied apron.)

KANE

Write "natural causes."

BANE

He's got an ice pick in his head—

KANE

"Accidental causes" then—what difference does it make?

BANE

There's an actual ice pick in his actual head!

KANE

O that's been there for ages—a childhood injury from which he never fully recovered.

Izzie: the knives!

BANE

(In his journal.)

"Day two thousand five hundred and eighty-two: Bo'sun Smythe is dead."

KANE

Must you always do that?

BANE

"Victim thirty-seven of this our Arctic entombment: now only three remain."

KANE

(To ISRAEL.)

No, you mongoloid, the knives! the meat-carving knives!

BANE

"Bo'sun Smythe was a fine Bo'sun"—

KANE

He was an inept Bo'sun.

BANE

—"always ready with a cup of good cheer"—

KANE
Cup he'd piss in first.

BANE
—"pure in mind"—

KANE
You never heard his confession.

BANE
—"and body too"—

KANE
He handled the dogs roughly.

BANE
... Did he do that?

(KANE nods, grimly.)

BANE
"He was tall"—

KANE
Short.

BANE
Thin ... ?

KANE
Fat.

BANE
A ha! —A ha! A ha, a ha, a ha!

(He does a few steps of a victory jig. ISRAEL knows this dance too—he joins in.)

BANE (cont'd.)
We've been starving for seven years! How could any one of us possibly be fat!

(He sits, triumphant, and breaks a chair.)

KANE
(Scratching ISRAEL, like he's a dog.)
Thank you, Izzie, Izzie wizzie pizzie poo: this knife will do just fine ...

(She takes a shocking scimitar of a knife from ISRAEL, and gives him a serving tray to hold.)

BANE

We should bury him outside in the pack-ice ...

KANE

You had no trouble before.

BANE

When before?

KANE

"When before?" he asks—

BANE

I remember the dogs ... We were forced to butcher the dogs ... And for that I am much aggrievèd—

KANE

Do you want to live or die?

BANE

...

KANE

Then let me do my work.

BANE

(Writing, sotto voce.)

"Things have grown techy. How long can this nacht stute endure? Not only has Bo'sun Smythe died the victim of an 'accidental' ice picking, but Ship's Chaplain Kane has declared open mutiny ... O, I knew the time was nigh. One can only marvel that betrayal has not come sooner: arsenic in the pemmican; a pannikin of pemmican—what is pemmican!? Considering the interminable cold and isolation, bedsheet vision in all directulations undulating icesea and shroud of snow and the bloodred razor crescent moon and—The Age At Which Christ Was Crucified! *(Reads what he's written; shakes his head, tries again:)*

"The Age At Which Christ—"

(KANE grabs his head.)

KANE

You must not lose your mind.

BANE

How old am I, Kane ... ?

KANE

You mustn't fall to pieces: not now.

BANE

—Listen! Do you hear them?

KANE

I don't hear anything—

BANE

The ghosts of the murderèd sledge dogs! They're out there!

(He buries his head in KANE's concealed bosom.

ISRAEL tries to comfort BANE—by showing him his own reflection in a silver serving tray.

BANE freaks.)

BANE

— !

KANE

—Izzie! no!

BANE

— ! — !

ISRAEL

... !

KANE

Outside! —Now!

(ISRAEL exits sulkily.

KANE and BANE alone again ...

KANE still holds the knife, perhaps in an accidentally threatening pose.

BANE gasps.)

BANE

— ! *(Then, in his journal:)*
" ... It is now all too apparent that Ship's Chaplain Kane has murderèd Bo'sun Smythe ... O, the evil that rots the roots of men's hearts!

He doth approach: I feel his foul and bated breath upon my neck—
the steely blade creeps—

KANE

Bane?

BANE

(Wetting himself, perhaps.)

—!

KANE

Care to help me with dinner?

BANE

Yes. —Yes of course ...
    But wouldn't it be quicker with two of us? "cutting"?

KANE

One knife will suffice. You can hold the tray:

(She gives it to him.

And just as she's about to slice into SMYTHE:)

BANE

—Aren't we forgetting something, Ship's "Chaplain" Kane?

KANE

...

(Grudgingly, she prepares to pray. Then, thinking better of praying with knife-in-hand, she stabs it into the farthest corner of the table top.

They kneel.)

KANE (cont'd.)

(Eyes shut.)

O Vague Something Behind Everything:
    We give thanks this day for the meal You have brought to our table.
    We regret that this meal happens also to be Bo'sun Smythe;
but who are we to question Your Big Ideas?
    Thanks all the same, Lord. And if you could get around to it,
we'd appreciate the ice melting soon.
    Jesus H. Christ.
    Amen.

(This whole prayer, BANE's been struggling to free the knife from the table—with no success.

KANE opens her eyes: BANE leaps upon the body of Bo'sun SMYTHE as if in terrific mourning:)

BANE

No, God! No, no, no, no! Not Bo'sun Smythe! Not him! Not him!
Smythe! Smythe! Take me, God! Take me— !

(Etc., until he's freed the knife.

—He's freed the knife.

He leaps from the table, brandishing:)

BANE (cont'd.)

—You!

KANE

What.

BANE

Did it! You Did Done Killed Bo'sun Smythe!

KANE

I did no such thing!

BANE

Liar! —I've seen the way you looked at him: vulture! The way you're looking at me right now, coveting my generous portions—proportions!

KANE

Let's say Bo'sun Smythe was murdered ...

BANE

"Bo'sun Smythe was murderèd."

KANE

Any of us could be the murderer.

BANE

Now you're speaking in riddles, Kane.

KANE

Izzie brought the body.

BANE

He always brings us things.

KANE

Precisely! Don't you think that's odd?

BANE

Not really: he's showing us his affection ...

KANE

But whether Bo'sun Smythe's been murdered or not—that's not really at issue, is it? It was your idea, your "dream" to come here in the first place; and it was your ignorance—your arrogance and naiveté—that's left us stuck here in the ice these past uncountable years ...

"Sailing to the Pole"? —Really, Bane! Whoever heard of such a thing?

BANE

It was quite a popular theory in its day.

KANE

—Idiot!

BANE

Puritan!

KANE

Anglophile!

BANE

Lesbian!

KANE

— ?

BANE

— ?

KANE

—Thespian! —Clown!

BANE

— !

(BANE, obliviously, stabs the knife somewhere into SMYTHE:)

BANE (cont'd.)

I have made mistakes ...

I'll admit as much: I'm "human."

But unlike you, Ship's Chaplain Kane, I have never given up.

I've long questioned your dedication to this our little "undertaking." —You are not much of a man, are you!? One might think you'd signed aboard only to keep an eye on me like some sort of perverse nanny!

And also unlike you, Ship's Chaplain Kane, I came with a porpoise. Purpose. Answered a higher calling; and I have never—not once in seven long years—yes, "seven," I have been counting!—regretted my decision to go, longing for the so-called finer things: luxury, wealth, chocolate ... the love and comfort of my dear Eliza!

—Hang it all, man! I would keep your nice niece waiting another seven years if it meant we'd one day reach the Pole!

(He sets the hanging lamp in motion.)

BANE (cont'd.)

One, two, three—

(KANE wrests the knife from SMYTHE's body.)

KANE

She's not going to wait that long.

(A fierce battle ensues. The playful tone of the earlier umbrella fracas is gone: they're trying to kill each other now.

ISRAEL enters, tries to speak:)

ISRAEL

— !

(He moves to intervene but gets swept into the melee instead.

Together, BANE and KANE manage to pin ISRAEL down and hold him still, knives pressed to his trembling neck.

... BANE and KANE are horrified, respectively, at what they've almost done:)

BANE

We have to leave this place behind.

KANE

Agreed.

(Black.)

3.

(In darkness, we hear the voice of the actor playing BANE:)

BILL

Okay, that's ten.

(Lights rise on the hold of The Carcass *again.*

Everything looks the same, except for a tape recorder that's somehow materialized on one of the chairs.

The actors playing ISRAEL and KANE head offstage in different directions, in grumpy silence.

BILL—a.k.a. BANE—remains.

He's out of breath, sweating, rubbing his chest. He rubs his chest a lot.

He might remove some clothing, and/or some padding.

He crosses to the tape recorder, picks it up, rewinds, presses Play:)

RECORDER

"We have to leave this place behind."
"Agreed."

(Stops it. Places tape recorder back on the chair. Lifts the book from the other chair—the book KANE was reading in the previous scene. Reads title to himself: "Dictionary of Symbols.")

BILL

(Shaking his head.)

Jesus. This ... *(And opens to a random page. Reads. Eyebrows lift:)*
Hm ...

(He sits his giant padded ass down. Flipping through pages, he finds something of interest. Picks up recorder. Presses Record, reads:)

BILL

" ... image of the world of phenomena, for both the theatre and the world are stages. The actors stand in relation to their parts as the Jungian Selbst stands to the personality." *(Stops recording.)*
How true ...

(He stands up. Returns book to the chair. Steps forward, bends, and launches himself into an impressive, steady, meditative headstand.

Enter DAN, the actor playing ISRAEL.

He sees BILL in his headstand. He goes to the book. Picks it up, opens it. Perhaps he notices a very small winged insect moving through the air—or perhaps he's only pretending. The insect lands on the face of the open book. DAN claps the book shut, loudly.

BILL tumbles out of his headstand.)

DAN

Sorry.

BILL

Shit.
—I'm fine.

DAN

It's cold.

BILL

—Hm?

DAN

I said it's—kind of "cold" in here. Can't we, you know, turn it / off?

BILL

What?

DAN

This thing, the / air-conditioning.

BILL

I tried.
You're welcome to try. —It's broken. There's no one here to, you know, fix it ...

DAN

Well, it's better than being hot ...

BILL

What?

DAN

I said, "It's better than being hot." In the summer. You know.

BILL

Yes, Daniel, it certainly is better than being hot ...

DAN

But this is too cold ... *(Re. the book:)*

Whose ... ?

BILL

Whose do you think?

DAN

Hm. *(Closes book, tosses it to the table.)*

Don't like books much.

(He picks up recorder, pressed Record:)

DAN (cont'd.)

How're you feeling?

BILL

(Rubbing his chest.)

Bloated.

DAN

No, about the Play: "the process," thus far:

BILL

Do we have / to?

DAN

Why not?

BILL

We're on a break.

DAN

So?

BILL

So—what?

DAN

"Whatever" ...

BILL

What do you want to know?

DAN

Do you like what we've got so far? Scene One.

BILL

... I don't know ...

DAN

Okay; but what do you "think" about it?

BILL

It's fine I guess ...

DAN

Shit ...

BILL

It's fine. —It has too many props. Do we need this many props?

DAN

I don't know ...

BILL

I fear ...

DAN

What:

BILL

... there are too many—threads to, you know, "tie together."

DAN

Hm.

BILL

A lot of levels, symbols and / inconsistencies.

DAN

Like what?

BILL

Well—why does Bane have a big ass when they're supposed to be starving?

DAN

It's meant to be ironic.

BILL

O.

DAN

He's eaten the sailors. He's eaten the dogs.

BILL

—They've all eaten the dogs.

DAN

—He's eaten more of the dogs.

BILL

Whatever ...

DAN

What's wrong ... ? You can tell me. I'm your friend, aren't I?

BILL

I'm worried: can we do it?

DAN

I don't know. I mean:

BILL

Are we going to / make it?

DAN

I do not know that ...

BILL

I think we can. We / just need to go—

DAN

It just hasn't found its—

BILL

/ "Further."

DAN

"Center." —What?

BILL

Farther—further. / Which is it?

DAN

Which way "further"?

BILL

What's the story here, Dan? What are we meant to "feel"? If you'll pardon the, whatever: "We're leaving the harbor with you; where do you want to take us?"

DAN

I have no idea.

BILL

You should. You should know where you want to take us.

DAN

...

BILL

This is going to be a problem for you. As a writer. In / the future.

DAN

How do you / see that?

BILL

In your future career.

DAN

What "career"?

BILL

It's a problem how you, you know, spin a lot of—plates.

DAN

... I'm young.

BILL

What does that mean?

DAN

"Voice of my generation."

BILL

What?

DAN

You didn't hear me?

BILL

It's my generation too, you know.

DAN

No, you're older than me.

BILL

Three years.

DAN

Three years is / three years.

BILL

—We're the same fucking generation, Dan.

DAN

Look, it's just—"how I see things."
Okay?

BILL

I'm sorry: I don't / follow you—

DAN

The plates: spinning.
I call it, "The Onion Effect."

BILL

Why?

DAN

I don't know. It's just a whatever a / metaphor.

BILL

Whatever, you're the writer ...

DAN

We're all the writer. That's what we're doing here, right? "We" improvise the Play. "We" talk about the Play. We tape record the Play as we improvise it. I'm really just the what do you call it, the—"stenographer" here.
It's like Ouija.

BILL

What?

DAN

The "process." Play. It's like a Ouija board.

BILL

I thought you said it was like an Onion.

DAN

—Ah! but you see that's the genius of The Onion Effect: things can be both an onion and a Ouija.

BILL

It's a collaboration, I'll grant you that. But you're "in charge" of the writing, right?

DAN

Sure.

BILL

It's what we agreed to, right?

DAN

"Aye-aye, captain!"

BILL

What does that mean ... ?

DAN

I'm just the mute guy ...

BILL

What is that supposed / to mean?

DAN

—Nothing: it's just "who I am."

BILL

You think I'm being, what, power-hungry?

DAN

Perhaps ...

BILL

—Cause if you are just say the word, and I'll just I don't know—"hit the bricks."
—I'm just trying to help / you here, Dan.

DAN

—And all I'm saying is: we'll find out. Won't we? We'll find out where this is going "as we go."

Remember how it was in college?

BILL

"In college" ...

DAN

Yes; it wasn't about the destination, right? —It was about the journey.

BILL

... O.

DAN

See?

BILL

Thanks for reminding me: "the journey."

DAN

... You think I'm being what, "pretentious"?

BILL

Persnaps.

DAN

Huh. Okay:

Well excuse me, Mr. Mime ...

BILL

—What did you say?

DAN

...

BILL

What does that mean? what does / "Mr. Mime" mean?

DAN

I just mean, what I meant is—as a Clown, as a "Mime"; you might want to be a little more careful who you call pretentious.

'Kay?

BILL

... Touché.

DAN

Touché yourself.

BILL

—Will they "get it," Dan?

DAN

Who.

BILL

"The audience."

DAN

What audience?

BILL

There will be an audience. One day. God willing.

DAN

I'm not going to dumb it down for anybody!

BILL

It's not about dumb, Dan—it's not a question of dumb, it's a question of "clarity"!

DAN

I don't—

BILL

See?

What:

DAN

I don't see your point exactly ...

BILL

For example: will an audience "get" that—well; will an audience "get" that Kane is really Bane's fiancée in disguise?

DAN

Yes.

BILL

That's it? / "yes"?

DAN

Yes.

BILL

Just by that what, that part in / the beginning?

DAN

"The Overture," yes.

BILL

You sure?

DAN

—Come on, Bill, we're practically handing it to them!

BILL

—But it will be a surprise then to Bane? That he's a "she"?

DAN

That's the general, uh—trajectory.

BILL

—Why?

DAN

Well; it's meant to be ironic.

BILL

—O come on!

DAN

What?

BILL

Everything can't be "ironic" with you.

DAN

Why / not?

BILL

It's a cop-out! You could say that to anything:

"Why brutally dismember a house finch on stage?"

"It's meant to be ironic."

DAN

So what you're saying ...

BILL

Exactly.

DAN

... is, "Why the transvestitism" in the play?

BILL

...

DAN

(Shrugs.)

It's—theatrical. The Elizabethans—

BILL

Everything's theatrical—life is theatrical!

DAN

No, life is sometimes theatrical, at points of, junctures of—

BILL

What:

DAN

Change.

BILL

...

"Change" ...

DAN

Yes.

BILL

Huh ...

So when do you think Bane finds out?

DAN

About Kane? whenever we choose. Later in / the play.

BILL

Whenever I choose because I'm / Bane.

DAN

Yes; I want your input, Bill. Please.

BILL

This is a "journey" / you said—

DAN

It sure as Hell is—

BILL

Like Ouija, you said—

DAN

Like an Onion—

BILL

And as a journey—

DAN

Um hm—

BILL

—we're all in this together so I can give you my "feedback"—

DAN

That's right—

BILL

—as to how my "character" is developing?

DAN

You are in charge of your own character, Bill! I wouldn't have it any other / way!

BILL

Then quit making fun of me, okay?

DAN

...

BILL

Quit making fun of me: in the play.

DAN

... Am I making / fun of you?

BILL

—You're not making fun of me—in what you've written "thus far"?

DAN

I don't think / I am ...

BILL

All this clown'n'mime business? Bane being a "millionaire"?

DAN

You're not a millionaire, are / you Bill?

BILL

No. But you know—my family—.

And while I didn't build *The Carcass,* I did study at Le Coq.

DAN

Le what?

BILL

You heard what I / said.

DAN

I know, but I like how you say it.

I thought you said you went to mime school, anyway.

BILL

Listen: I have a sense of humor. You know that. But for the last time, I am not "a mime." I may have trained with mimes, I may be friends with mimes; I may know how to "walk against wind" and pull on invisible ropes—but I am not a fucking mime!

—And "clown" is very different from "mime": there's no "pretense" in Clown. Clown is honest, and innocent—in all ways altogether different from your average person: hence the need for the nose.

DAN

... Nobody likes a smart clown.

BILL

Har dee har / har—

DAN

As a matter of fact—nobody likes clowns!

BILL

You can joke all you want / Dan—

DAN

—I always have this burning desire to just step on those fucking shoes!

BILL

You know this is my Money.

DAN

What money?

BILL

For the theater. For This.

DAN

I know ...

BILL

All the money I have left. My "inheritance."

DAN

...

BILL

So I have a lot of expectations for this—whatever this turns out to be.

DAN

So do I. —What kind / of expectations?

BILL

—Just so long as you're not / making fun of me.

DAN

What kind of expectations? —I'm not.

BILL

Good.

DAN

—What kind of expectations?

BILL

(Rubbing his chest.)

I feel bloated. Where's Hel'?

DAN

What?

BILL

My wife?
Helen?

(He exits.)

BILL

(Off stage.)

Hon'?

(DAN alone with tape recorder.

He stops it, rewinds, presses Play.)

RECORDER

"I feel bloated. Where's Hel'?"
"What?"
"My wife?"

(DAN stops it. Rewinds. Plays.)

RECORDER (cont'd.)

"What?"
"My wife? Helen? Hon'?"

(Enter HELEN.

DAN quickly presses Record and hides the recorder under SMYTHE.)

HELEN

—Sorry.

DAN

No; I was / just ...

HELEN

Uh huh.
Where's Bill?

DAN

He's bloated.

HELEN

Where'd he go? to the?

DAN

Yeah.

HELEN

... Super.

DAN

Yeah ... "super."
So: he was—looking for you.
Yeah ... *(He picks up the book:)*
This you?

HELEN

It's a Dictionary of Symbols. You know: what everything "means."
I'm a big believer in symbology ...

DAN

Sure ...

HELEN

I thought it might help us. You know: in the writing of this—whatever this Thing turns out to be.

Are you recording / us?

DAN

Yes.

... How does that make you feel?

HELEN

Fine ...

Would you like to know what I think of our journey thus far?

DAN

Sure:

HELEN

Sucks. That first scene like totally blows. And—whatever—nobody's going to get that I'm a "she" disguised as a "he": there'll think it's some kind of gender-blind casting, or we're making a confused feminist statement, or—.

It's not your writing. —Your writing's—. It's me: I'm just really not an actor anymore.

DAN

Yes you are.

HELEN

I'm not. I don't have it in me, anymore.

DAN

Come on! You've got it in you!

HELEN

I don't! Some people have it, and others—don't. Have it.

DAN

Have what?

HELEN

Demons, or—whatever ...

I think I might be just too well-adjusted to be an actor.

DAN

I don't think that's true.

HELEN

Shut up.

DAN

I think you're a great actor, Hel'.

HELEN

—You and Bill were always better than me in college.

DAN

No we / weren't.

HELEN

—You were. Why do you think I don't act anymore?

DAN

That was a very long time ago ...

HELEN

Not that long ...

DAN

I think you are a very good actor, Helen: still.

HELEN

Thank you, Dan. That's sweet.

DAN

...

HELEN

Now. Can I ask you something? before Bill / gets back?

DAN

Sure.

HELEN

About Kane. About my "character"?

DAN

Shoot:

HELEN

Am I man or woman?

DAN

...

HELEN

My character: Kane.

DAN

I know—

HELEN

But. You just looked kind of confused—

DAN

Well, she's a—"lady," I guess. I mean, isn't that obvious?

HELEN

But has she "become her disguise"?

DAN

That's an interesting idea ...

HELEN

I mean, seven years, and she was in love with this man; she was in love enough to go on this—"journey" with him—to support him in this—whatever; why?

DAN

She loved him?

HELEN

She loves him still ...

DAN

Yeah.

HELEN

She believed in him. —She believed in the journey.
But she doesn't anymore...

DAN

... I don't know, maybe / not.

HELEN

People change.

DAN

I've heard of that happening.

HELEN

This is my money, you know.

DAN

... O yeah?

HELEN

Yeah. Bill doesn't have any money left. His trust fund's run dry. I'm his Sugar Daddy. Which is all right, most of the time ...

—This was my birthday present to him: rent a theater in the middle of nowhere; "have fun," get back to basics ... see what we've got left ...

You know?

DAN

...

HELEN

Can I ask you a logistical question?

DAN

About?

HELEN

Well, how did she keep it from everyone? when she had her period?

DAN

Who?

HELEN

Kane.

DAN

O. It's sort of meant to be an unrealistic play ...

HELEN

I get that. I understand that—"magical realism" and all that. But she could do it.

DAN

/ What:

HELEN

Women do it all the time. For instance: I'm menstruating right now.

DAN

...

HELEN

No, I'm not. But you would've believed me if I said yes, right?

DAN

Sure. I mean. Why would you lie?

HELEN

What I'm saying is, keep in mind, when you're writing: how women can keep a lot of things secret ...

DAN

... That's a really interesting idea.

HELEN

—Are you okay? you look kind of fried ...

DAN

—I feel stressed ...

HELEN

You look fried.

DAN

"Fried"? Do I?
It's—

HELEN

Come here: what is it?

DAN

—money.
You know: "Future"—

HELEN

Shh:

DAN

—"Ambition."
—No really I'm fine—

HELEN

You have to "circulate your cerebral spinal fluid." *(She begins rubbing his neck, his head:)*

... I used to have the biggest crush on you in college ... Don't tell Bill I told you—not that he'd be jealous but—.

He's always had this weird competition thing with you ...

DAN

Huh.

HELEN

Yeah. I remember he once said: "Dan's got such great demons."
—He's got a heart murmur, did he tell / you that?

DAN

(Smiling.)
I don't have many demons ...

HELEN

I loved that play you wrote in college; what was it?

DAN

Existenz. —It was just a one-act.

HELEN

Yeah.

DAN

Sucky title.

HELEN

No!

DAN

Sucky play. Just trying to be, I don't know, "Samuel Beckett."
In my own little way.

HELEN

No, after I saw it: I cried.

DAN

No! Really?

HELEN

Yes! And I hate people who cry. In public.

And I went home, and I wrote this six page tone-poem all about—"how I felt" ...

I was going to send it to you ... but then I think I sat down and read it the next day and it didn't seem so—"true," anymore. You know? —It all sounded so stupid and trite and not at all the very beautiful things I was feeling at the time ... *(She stops rubbing his head:)*

There ...

Now: go write us out of this mess ...

DAN

Thanks.

HELEN

Anytime ...

DAN

I'll go get Bane.

HELEN

Who?

DAN

"Bill." —What I say?

HELEN

You said "Bane."

DAN

Did I?

HELEN

Yeah.

DAN

Wow.
"Whatever."

(Exits through stage door.)

HELEN

...

(She stretches her hands ceiling-ward, shakes her arms and legs. Resonates sound in her nasal cavities.

She stands like a man now:)

HELEN (cont'd.)

... !

(Then begins absently touching her hair, her face, her neck, her arms ...

She grabs her crotch as if she had balls:)

HELEN (cont'd.)

Kane!

(BILL reenters, rubbing his chest.)

HELEN (cont'd.)

—What are / you okay?

BILL

I'm fine.

HELEN

Dan said you were / bloated.

BILL

Let's keep going. —I was. I am.

HELEN

How's your— ?

BILL

It's my / stomach—

HELEN

Did you take your / medication?

BILL

—Let's keep going!
    "I'm fine"!
    I was feeling bloated!

HELEN

... I need a break.

BILL

We just took a break—

HELEN

Not if you're / feeling sick—

BILL

I'm feeling great!
    I'm feeling so fucking great!
    Let's just keep fucking going!

HELEN

... You know how I feel about that, Bill ... Your tone. —We've discussed / this.

BILL

Use it, baby ...

HELEN

You don't know when to quit, do you?

BILL

No, why don't you give me a lesson in "quitting."

HELEN

—What does that mean?

BILL

What do you think / it means?

HELEN

I want to hear you say it.

BILL

Nothing. It "means" / nothing.

HELEN

I know what that / means.

BILL

—It doesn't "mean" anything!—it means something that doesn't actually / mean anything!

HELEN

Everything means Something, Bill— !

BILL

No it doesn't! Sometimes "the thing" just is what it is!

HELEN

(Quietly.)

... What's wrong with you?

BILL

... What do you think's wrong?

HELEN

... Your vagina is bleeding. Profusely.

BILL

Let's try and be professional here, okay?

HELEN

—What does that mean?

BILL

Nothing—it's—. You're my wife! —Don't you see how this might get a little bit complicated sometimes—this "situation"?

HELEN

...

BILL

You know how much this means to me ...

HELEN

Yes, I know how much this means to you ... Jesus, Bill!
Where's Dan?

BILL

... Helen: I'm fried.
You know? "fried" ... ?
"I love you" ...
Did you / hear me?

HELEN

Can't we fix this God damned air-conditioning?

(DAN enters with a ball.)

DAN

Anyone for a refreshing game of "ball"?

HELEN

Give:

(DAN tosses ball to HELEN.

With each toss, the players toss off a new word:)

DAN

"blood"

HELEN

"baby"

BILL

"basket"

HELEN

"eggs"

BILL

—What?

HELEN

"eggs"

BILL

—"vomit"

DAN

"water"

HELEN

"sea"

DAN

"no"

BILL

"evil"

DAN

"hear"

BILL

"no"

DAN

"ice"

HELEN

"cream"

DAN

"man"

BILL

"cometh"

HELEN

—"don't"

DAN

"go"

BILL

"any"

DAN

"further."

BILL

—What did we just say?

HELEN

"Don't go any further." *(Throwing the ball:)*
"exploratory"

BILL

"surgery"

DAN

"knife"

BILL

"tape"

DAN

"recorder"

BILL

—"I hardly know her"

HELEN

That's not funny. —"Night"

DAN

"mare"

HELEN

"howling"

DAN

"wind"

HELEN

"and"

DAN

"rain"

HELEN

"and"

DAN

"snow"

(BILL's hands are outstretched: waiting for the ball that doesn't come.

—Lights. Wind.)

4.

(ISRAEL is sulking.

KANE is packing.

BANE is thinking about packing ...)

BANE

Where is my Burberry windsuit? *(His journal:)*
"Day two thousand five hundred and eighty two, continuèd:
"We are going home.
"Am looking for my Burberry windsuit."

KANE

I don't know; where'd you last see it?

BANE

I've never worn it.

KANE

What about the furs we bartered for in Svitzbargen?

BANE

Furs? I'm not a savage! It's Burberry for me or nothing at all!

KANE

Izzie?

ISRAEL

(Sulks.)

...

KANE

Izzie, will you help Kane find the Inuit furs?

BANE

"Windsuit's whereabouts unknown. —Furs of the Esquimeaux—"

KANE

Inuit.

BANE

"—Esquimeaux: conspicuously missing ... "
Has anyone seen my lucky snowshoes?

KANE

We ate them.

BANE

"Snowshoes digested." —Skis?

KANE

Fire.

BANE

Sledge?

KANE

"Sled," Bane.

BANE

—"Sledge"?

KANE

We had no dogs to pull it—

BANE

We've got Israel! He's stronger than forty dogs!
—Right, Izzie? Right, old boy?

(ISRAEL doesn't answer.

BANE attempts a few steps of their victory jig; to no avail.)

KANE

It'll be strange to be home ...
Do you think we'll remember how to talk?
Politely, I mean ...
I'm very nervous to be normal again—with people ...
I wonder if my mother's still alive?

(BANE is writing in his journal.)

BANE

Hm?

KANE

Talking.

BANE

Yes: in moderation.

KANE

What are you writing?

BANE

An inventory. Of everything we don't have ...

KANE

Don't forget your letters ...

The letters you wrote my niece, Eliza?

BANE

I burned them. For warmth.

KANE

...

BANE

It's nice to be leaving, isn't it Kane?

You forget that, don't you? that you have that power—that we all have that power, to just get up and go ... ?

The religious would call it "will."

Most people would call it "will" ...

I don't know what else you'd call it ...

—Regardless! we have it, and we Will set forth at once—south, as far as our feet will carry, or as long as Smythe here will hold together ...

We'll build ourselves some "idgloos," which means "seat-of-ease," in the aboriginal tongue. We'll hunt the mighty "nanooq": legendary "ghost-bear" of the frozen North. —Or perhaps we'll do a spot of fishing—I like fishing—if it is the "okipole": season for manly thrusting of roughhewn spears through ice-holes ...

We shall sew ourselves some sealskin pants ... reindeer jumpers, warm walrus boots ... O yes; we'll look so smashing ...

—Then it's into some peaceful "Esquimeaux" we shall run! near Greenland—or perhaps some modern-day explorers? equipped with modern-day tools and supplies: compasses, vitamins, chocolate; fresh crimson-fleshed sealsmeats ...

They'll be so happy to have found us!

—"Bane Barrington, I presume?"

And I'll say, "Yes. And who might you be, my tall bearded fellow?"

"Bjorn Bjornsen. I heard you speak in '99 at the Royal Geographic Society on the topography of Frans Josef Land."

"O no, Mr. Bjornson, but I'm not British at all!"

"Then why do you speak that funny way?"

"Well you see, Bjornsen, I've lost my mind. You must have mistaken me for another Bane Barrington. I'm Bane Barrington of Barrington Dried Goods, Flushing New York."

"Dried Goods Barrington! Christ, man! We'd given you up for dead!"

"So had I, Bjorn, so had I. But remember: there is the word 'end' inside that larger word 'endurance.' A man can only hold out so long ... There are other people to think about. There are other people's lives at stake ... "

O yes. This is when you know you're truly alive, eh Kane? when you can admit you were wrong ... ?

(BANE begins to cry, a little. Maybe.

This whole time, KANE's been going through her trunk. She comes away from it now, suspicious.)

KANE

Have you seen the camera?

BANE

Do you mean the photographic apparatus? What do we want with the photographic apparatus? There'll be plenty of photographic apparati where we're going—

KANE

Izzie, have you seen the camera?

BANE

Leave him alone—

KANE

Israel ... ?

BANE

He doesn't even know how to work it!

ISRAEL

(Sulks harder.)

... !

(Simultaneously:)

BANE & KANE

—Now look what you've done!

KANE

You're the one who said he doesn't know how to work a camera!

BANE

It's true! He's not mechanically inclined.

KANE

He's smarter than you think.

BANE

Who said he wasn't smart? Whoever said Israel wasn't smart? He's sensitive, that's all ...

Did you know he used to be a dancer? He studied under Minushkakakov in Petersburg ...

KANE

Look at him:

BANE

Poor Minushkakakov, with his all-over matte of body hair ...

KANE

He's angry.

BANE

Of course he was angry: people don't like too much body hair: it reminds us of evolution.

KANE

I'm talking about Israel.

BANE

—Well of course Izzie's angry with us! We almost slit his throat!

KANE

—That was an accident!

BANE

—As was Smythe ... ?

KANE

You know very well I did not kill Bo'sun Smythe!

BANE

Methinks the lady doth protest a lot!

KANE

—Izzie's the one we should be concerned with.

BANE

—Izzie?

KANE

Yes, he is ...

BANE

... ?

KANE

—What's he thinking ... ?

BANE

O, let the man have his privy ...

KANE

He has too much privacy.

BANE

Don't be absurd! How can a man have too much privy? How can any of us have too much privy? A man succeeds in maintaining a modicum of privy in this ice-locked dung-hole, and he's what, a monster?

KANE

A "privy" is an outhouse, Bane.

BANE

Maybe where you come from.

KANE

What kind of name is "Israel" anyway?

BANE

Canadian. His family was from Upper Ontario, which is why he's so at home in this Arctic clime ...

KANE

Why does he never speak? He's got a tongue. Did he ever talk?

BANE

O yes: in Cuba he was the lark of the barracks. He'd keep us up all night with his side-splitting impression of President and Mrs. McKinley.

KANE

Why did he stop talking?

BANE

One day he went off to San Juan Hill. I couldn't go: typhoid, explosive business in the jakes. And when he returned he couldn't talk a lick ...

Must've seen some awful carnage up there; a real wine-dark stain upon his snow-white soul ...

Months later, we were recuperating beachside in the equatorial balm; and Israel handed me a very small white scrap of paper: the first words he'd spoken in months. And do you know what he'd written on that small, white scrap of paper? One word: "The North Pole."

KANE

...

BANE

So you see this trip was as much his idea as mine ...

What is it about wars that make men want to take long holidays together?

KANE

Why did he want to go to the North Pole?

BANE

There's always been something religious in Israel. Mysterious, really. I've always secretly hated him for it.

(ISRAEL moves upstage to an humungous sack stuffed full of personal belongings.)

KANE

He's hiding something.

BANE

You're a suspicious old goat, aren't you Kane? One's bound to think you've got some nasty little secret of your own locked away somewhere—in the trunk perhaps?! The way you cast aspersions ... No wonder you're clergy. Why, you're making him out to be some great sinner when in fact he's just mildly retarded.

KANE

—He's a thief!

BANE

—I hope you have the proof to substantiate such a claim!

(She gives him the key to her trunk.)

BANE (cont'd.)

You're giving me your key.

KANE

Bring me a knife.

BANE

You're not going to knife him are you?

KANE

Bring me a knife!

(BANE moves to the trunk, unlocks it, opens it, peers inside, closes it, locks it, returns the key to KANE.)

BANE

There are no knives inside that trunk.

(She gives him the key again.)

KANE

Bring me a rifle.

BANE

You're not going to rifle him, are you!

(She doesn't answer.

He moves to the trunk, unlocks it, opens it, peers inside, closes it, locks it, returns the key to KANE.)

BANE (cont'd.)

There are no rifles inside that trunk either!

(She gives him the key again.)

KANE

Bring me a camera:

BANE

—You're not going to take a picture of him, are you!

(She doesn't answer.

He moves to the trunk, unlocks it, opens it, peers inside, closes it, locks it, returns the key to KANE.)

BANE (cont'd.)

The camera's not there either. —What are you driving at, Kane?

KANE

Things are missing: important things: snowshoes, boots, furs, goggles, gloves, knives, rifles, camera ...

There is but one key to that trunk; if these valuable accouterments have disappeared, only one other person can be responsible:

BANE

—Smythe!

KANE

No, you idiot!

(They turn on ISRAEL, slowly, so as not to rouse his suspicion of their suspicion.

This whole time he's been taking stolen goods out of his sack and outfitting himself as if for a very long journey:

Snowshoes, boots, furs, goggles, gloves, knives, a rifle, photographic apparatus, etc.)

BANE

We'll need proof.

We must place something of extraordinary monetary value in an open and unguarded place—like the table, right here, next to Smythe ...

We must tempt him, if indeed Israel is the thief—

(BANE places his journal on the table next to SMYTHE.)

BANE (cont'd.)

Then, we secrete ourselves, awaiting the criminal's arrival.

Believing himself alone, the dark-minded miscreant will creep stealthily to the table, and Smythe, where he will then abstract the extraordinarily valuable *object de temptation* from the table—and Smythe—

(ISRAEL takes the journal, unnoticed, and exits calmly during the following:)

KANE

—At which time we spring from our hiding place and apprehend the villain red-handed! We bind him, and question him: Was he acting alone? is espionage at issue? Suspending habeas corpus and all other democratic niceties that have no place beyond the Arctic pale, we argue for prudence and restraint—yet the jury will have none of it! They demand justice:

"We will cut off the criminal's balls! His balls— !"

BANE

Kane—

KANE

His balls— !

BANE

Kane!

KANE

By God we shall have his balls!

BANE

Elijah!

KANE

... ?

BANE

Israel is gone ...

KANE

... Izzie?

BANE

Yes, I'm afraid he is ...

Do you suppose he heard us talking about him?

KANE

Of course he heard us talking— !

BANE

You shouldn't have said that about his balls ...

KANE

Go after him!

(He moves for the exit; then stops himself:)

BANE

—What about the ghosts of the murderèd sledge-dogs?

(She moves for the exit, then stops herself:)

KANE

I'd freeze to death without furs ...

BANE

You can borrow my Burberry windsui—.

...

KANE

...

BANE

(Sitting.)

He'll come back. He has to ...

(KANE sets the lamp in motion.

She sits too.

As lights go:)

KANE

One, two, three ...

5.

(The hold of The Carcass *as a play set again.*

BILL, HELEN and DAN.

BILL is wearing a bright red foam-rubber clown nose.

The tape recorder is playing:)

RECORDER

(HELEN's voice.)

"Well I guess you could say I had a really bad childhood. My parents were always, you know, fighting. It's not really remarkable, I guess, in this day and age ...

"So I used to pretend a lot—like that I was a dancer or—whatever. But then I realized I was just too clutzy for being a dancer, so I thought about—. I used to pretend a lot of things so well that people would think I had head-aches or I'd actually passed out or you know, whatever it was in the ... Thing ...

"You know?

"Yeah. —And, I think, as an only child, I read a lot ...

"O. And I was scared of everything."

(DAN stops it.)

HELEN

God.

DAN

What:

HELEN

Is that me?

DAN

No, it's the / machine.

HELEN

That's not me.

DAN

Not really no, it's the waves—everybody sounds that / way, distorted.

HELEN

God ...

DAN

Yeah ...

BILL

It's a tape recorder, dear. It's artificial.

HELEN

—Why are you wearing that nose?

BILL

What nose?

HELEN

Take that / off.

BILL

It's just my nose: learn to love it.

HELEN

(Handing him the tape recorder.)

Your turn.

BILL

No thanks.

HELEN

You have to.

BILL

I take "the fifth."

HELEN

This is not a game, this is not a, I don't know, congressional / hearing.

BILL

What is it then?

HELEN

A journey / of discovery.

BILL

I'm beginning to really hate that word ...

DAN

Which word? "journey" or "discovery"—

HELEN

It's a collaboration. We need to know why this particular story is important to you. Why "the theatre" is important / to you.

BILL

You mean "Daniel" needs to know why this play is "important" to me.

HELEN

...

BILL

Okay, wait ... hold on ... I've got it ... *(into the recorder:)*
"Eat me."

HELEN

—Bill.

BILL

"Chow My Box"—

HELEN

Stop it!

BILL

What?

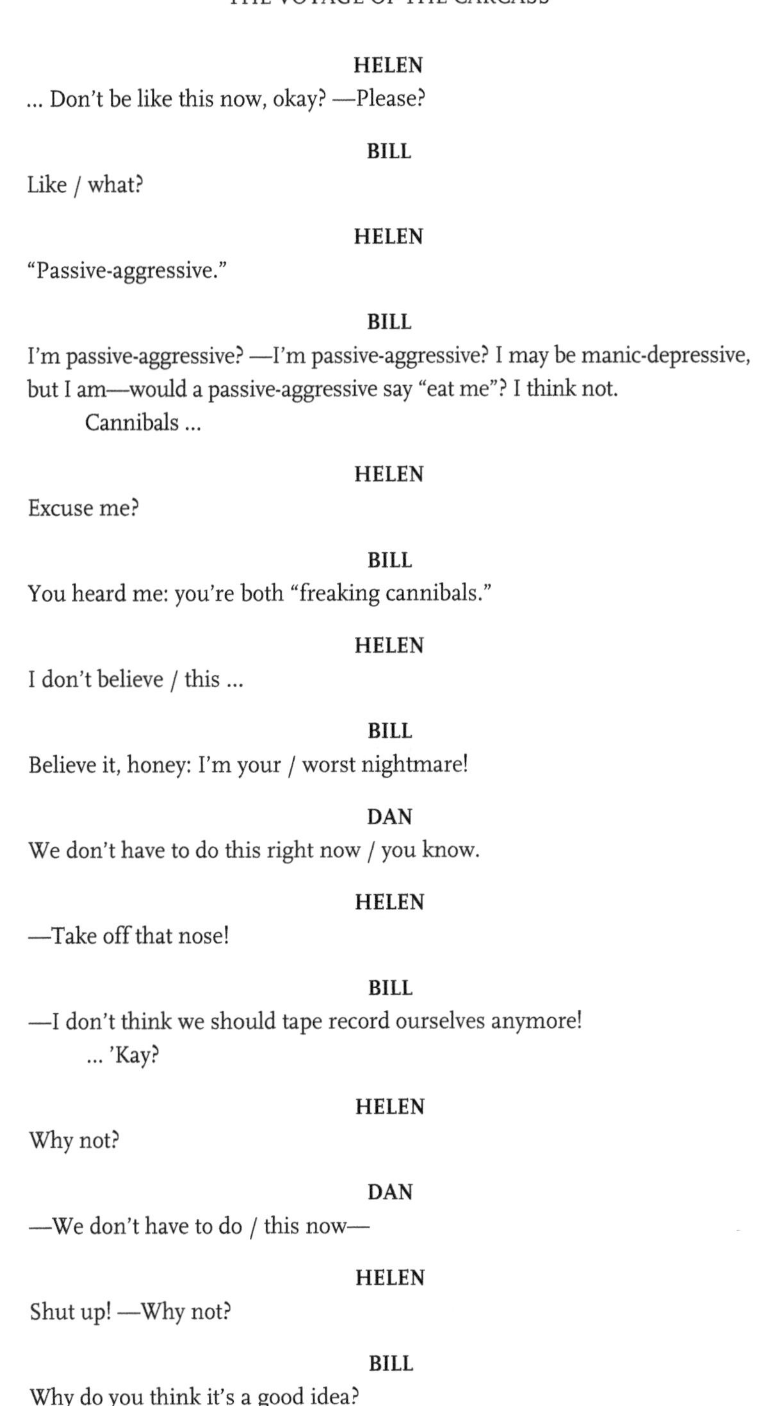

HELEN

... Don't be like this now, okay? —Please?

BILL

Like / what?

HELEN

"Passive-aggressive."

BILL

I'm passive-aggressive? —I'm passive-aggressive? I may be manic-depressive, but I am—would a passive-aggressive say "eat me"? I think not.
    Cannibals ...

HELEN

Excuse me?

BILL

You heard me: you're both "freaking cannibals."

HELEN

I don't believe / this ...

BILL

Believe it, honey: I'm your / worst nightmare!

DAN

We don't have to do this right now / you know.

HELEN

—Take off that nose!

BILL

—I don't think we should tape record ourselves anymore!
    ... 'Kay?

HELEN

Why not?

DAN

—We don't have to do / this now—

HELEN

Shut up! —Why not?

BILL

Why do you think it's a good idea?

HELEN

I think it's helpful. For process.

BILL

"Process."

HELEN

You think that's what, pretentious?

BILL

Persnaps. Yes.

HELEN

—It's material. It's—we're making this play ours and not just Dan's.

BILL

"Dan's" play?

HELEN

That's right.

BILL

—This was my idea to begin / with.

HELEN

—This way my idea, if you could possibly retain anything in that fat selfish head of yours!

—It was my idea, and you agreed, and Dan agreed, and nobody else we asked agreed, if you remember; and because we can't write, Dan is writing the play. —So tell him what he needs to know!

BILL

What's he going to do, write us into the play?

HELEN

We're already in there now, aren't we?

BILL

Are we? I don't see that.

HELEN

You don't see the— ?

BILL

No.

HELEN

—"connection"? between—

BILL

Sorry / I don't.

HELEN

—being stuck in the ice at the North Pole and being stuck here?

BILL

... You feel "stuck" here? *(To DAN:)*

Do you feel stuck here? *(Standing:)*

—I will not Be in this play! —That, "Bane," is not me! I am playing a part! If I thought I was in this stupid fucking play, I would go home and put a bullet in my brain!

HELEN

... Don't say that.

BILL

...

DAN

I'm going to go take / a break—

HELEN

—No.

BILL

No.

HELEN

Stay.

BILL

Yes: stay; you're part of the family now.

HELEN

How could you say that?

BILL

What?

HELEN

You know what you said ...

BILL

I know, but Dan doesn't. Why not share it with the tape recorder, dear? "Collaborate."

Maybe we could get a Oiuja board out, see if your "dad" wants to collaborate ...

HELEN

...

(She exits.)

BILL

(Calling off.)

... Am I in trouble?

(No answer.)

BILL (cont'd.)

I'm in trouble.

(He exits.

DAN sits alone onstage and listens to their argument through the stage door:)

HELEN

—Fuck: you.

BILL

Whoa!—easy with the I don't know "sympathy" here—

HELEN

You want me to be / sympathetic?

BILL

Yes! why not?

HELEN

I'm out of "sympathy," okay? —How long do I have to be sympathetic / to you?

BILL

I'm Unhappy ... !

See ... ?

How does that make you "feel"?

HELEN

What are you so unhappy with exactly? —Let's go over it one / more time.

BILL

This whole—Thing! This—"farce"!

HELEN

Our marriage is a farce to you?

BILL

Not our marriage—the play.

(DAN picks up the tape recorder—it's still recording—and brings it closer to the stage door.)

HELEN

Okay: what's wrong with "farce" ... ?

BILL

—You thought I was talking about / our marriage?

HELEN

—What's wrong with farce, Bill?

BILL

—Farce isn't true!

HELEN

What does "truth" have to do with / anything?

BILL

—Everything's fake, everything's a metaphor now—everything's exaggerated and fantasy and—it's not Clown anymore, it's not honest—

HELEN

Fantasies can't be honest?

BILL

No, fantasies are Advertising— !

HELEN

...

BILL

...

HELEN

It's a living.

BILL

...

HELEN

We'd be starving without it, so—

BILL

I'm just trying to find ...

HELEN

—What, Bill? —What are you trying / to "find"?

BILL

Something I can care about.
Okay?

HELEN

...
I don't know what you mean by that.
I don't know how to respond—.

(A long silence.

They re-enter together.)

DAN

Has anyone noticed— ?

HELEN

Sorry, Dan.

BILL

Yeah / sorry Dan.

DAN

A certain similarity between our play and Shakespeare?

BILL

...

HELEN

...

DAN

As You Like It; Twelfth Night—

BILL

(Rubbing his chest.)

I feel / bloated.

HELEN

—What similarities, Dan?

DAN

The cross-dressing.

BILL

—And?

DAN

The cross-dressing.

(HELEN takes the tape recorder.)

HELEN

"When I was a little girl, I had this watercolor Shakespeare. I still remember what Prince Hal looked like. I wanted Hal so badly. He looked like my father ... I've been told that's means something ...

"My father killed himself when I was thirteen. I'm over it now, but every once in / a while—"

BILL

Turn it off.

HELEN

Why? I haven't even mentioned my / anorexia yet—

BILL

"I don't want him raping your memory!"

HELEN

"I am not being raped! I'm making art!"

DAN

... It's meant to be a collaboration.

BILL

—Then why don't I record you?

DAN

You can. If you want ...

(BILL takes the tape recorder.)

BILL

What are your thoughts on Israel?

DAN

I'm not a very political writer; I wish I was but—

BILL

The "character"—your Character: "Israel." I have some questions about your holy little character, Daniel. —Or should I say your "characters"?

DAN

What are you saying, that I'm what, "Sybil"?

BILL

How come you never talk?

(DAN shrugs.)

BILL (cont'd.)

You listen and you ask questions:

"What's your earliest childhood trauma?"
"When did you first realize you wanted to be an actor?"
"What do you think theatre can do?"
—"How do you spell 'theatre':—r-e, e-r?"

HELEN

What are you so afraid of?

BILL

Mediocrity, projectile vomiting, and psychiatrists.

HELEN

This isn't psychoanalysis!

BILL

Well it sure as Hell isn't clown anymore!

HELEN

What is it then— ?

BILL

A failure.

(He takes off his nose.)

HELEN

Well.

Somebody had to say it ...

DAN

Listen: I've been meaning to tell you guys. Both of you. This seems as good a time as ever, so ...

When I agreed to be a part of this, whatever—"journey," I thought I had more money than I actually do. In fact I'm "bending my butt," so to speak, and I'm still flat broke.

So: I'm not going to burden you both with the nitty-gritty here. Let's just say I have this opportunity to be in Buffalo in three days to appear in *Godspell.*

It's nobody's fault.

... So: *Godspell*: Bye.

(DAN leaves.)

BILL

What the / fuck?

HELEN

He's joking. He has to / be joking—

BILL

This was supposed to be fun—

(DAN re-enters.)

DAN

This was supposed to be fun!

BILL

I'm having fun!

DAN

The fuck you are!

HELEN

—Whoa—

BILL

That's it! Let it out! —You're not having fun?

DAN

Helen: are you having fun?

BILL

—She never has fun!

DAN

You are such—*(he hits BILL in the head with the ball)*—a fucknut!

BILL

You're hitting me with the— ? *(Whipping the ball at DAN:)* "Taste the Ball, bitch!"

HELEN

—Do you want some money?

DAN

...

What? No.

HELEN

To stay. We can give you four hundred—five. Right now. Cash. I can spare it. —I know you're not in *Godspell* in Buffalo. If you had money, we might, you know—work together better.

BILL

Don't give him our / money.

HELEN

—I'll give him my money.

DAN

—I don't need money: I've got Godspell.

HELEN

Just a loan; you're / distracted.

BILL

We're doing this for free—this is volunteer.

HELEN

That's fine, but not everybody is as fortunate as we are.

BILL

—You mean as you are.

HELEN

Yes, as fortunate as I am: the difference being I work for a living.

BILL

...

HELEN

...

BILL

I don't need— !
This fucking— !
Shit!

(BILL exits, loudly.)

DAN

(Re. the tape recorder:)
... Why don't you turn it off?

HELEN

Was it like that the whole time? / on?

DAN

Yeah.
How do you feel about that?

(She picks it up, brings it to him.)

HELEN

... When did you first realize you wanted to be a writer?

DAN

... When I was a boy—maybe five, six years old—my parents took me to Québec ...

We stayed in a Bed and Breakfast run by this exceptionally overweight Inuit woman ...

She was "New Agey" ...

She had Egyptian prints hung over each doorway. You know: "glyphs." The furniture was like stage furniture, and the walls were painted deep red, blood color ...

I remember we were leaving for the night and it was very cold. We'd gotten all the way to the car before I realized I didn't have my mittens: I loved those mittens. My father gave me the key and told me to go back inside and get them myself. I was a big boy now.

My heart was pounding in my stomach, and my neck. The house was dark. I could hear my footsteps resounding in the emptiness ... I opened the door to the room, and there, on my parents' bed, was the exceptionally overweight Inuit woman ... having sex with a very small man.

A dwarf maybe, or a midget.

HELEN

O my God.

DAN

Yeah.

HELEN

That's when you first realized you wanted to be a writer?

DAN

Pretty much.

/ Yeah.

HELEN

O my God.

DAN

I know. Kind of makes sense though, doesn't it?

HELEN

Who was the midget?

DAN

—Hm?

HELEN

Who was—having sex with the Inuit woman?

DAN

You know, I never found out ...

HELEN

Did you tell anyone?

DAN

Not till now. —You're the first.

HELEN

...

DAN

...

HELEN

You are so full / of shit.

DAN

I thought you bought it!

HELEN

Why do you lie so much?

DAN

...

HELEN

(Into the tape recorder.)

... Do you like who you are?

(He kisses her.)

DAN

I just—wanted to do that ...

(He kisses her some more.)

HELEN

Are you kissing me because you're bored?

DAN

No.

HELEN

Because you're angry?

(He kisses her.)

HELEN (cont'd.)

I worry sometimes that I'm a lesbian.

DAN

Okay.

(They kiss.)

DAN (cont'd.)

Come on.

(They exit together.

The tape recorder is still running.

Silence.

Enter BILL, after a while.

He looks around for the others. He sees the recorder, picks it up. Stops it. Rewinds. Presses Play.

As lights slowly fade:)

RECORDER

"Are you kissing me because you're bored?"
"No."
"Because you're angry?" ...

6.

(Music. Something from The Nutcracker Suite, *perhaps.*

ISRAEL enters, snowshoeing to the Pole.

He leaps and steps, through slush and needle-storm, across slick glaciers, over steep crevasses ...

He begins to dance, as if he were still in St. Petersburg ...

...

White light grows—)

7.

(KANE and BANE asleep at either end of the table, SMYTHE laid out between them.

They're each holding one of SMYTHE's hands in theirs.

Suddenly, we hear the sound of a dog being murderèd.

KANE screams, and wakes up.

BANE screams, and wakes up.

They look at each other and scream and continue to wake up.

They look at SMYTHE between them and scream.

They throw SMYTHE off the table and, screaming, pummel and pound him until they're sure he's still dead.

...)

BANE

Did you say something, Elijah?

KANE

I was dreaming ...

BANE

You, Elijah ... ?

KANE

... of the Pole.

BANE

Really? What was it like?

KANE

Izzie was there.

BANE

Izzie?

KANE

Yes ... He was.

BANE

...

(They hear the sound of the dog dying, again—this time farther off.)

BANE (cont'd.)

—Did you hear that?

KANE

I don't believe in ghosts ...

BANE

Those dogs are angry, Kane! We ate them!

KANE

We ate the men, too!

BANE

—Why can't I remember their names ... ?

KANE

Johnson, Clarke, Patterson ...

BANE

Rover, Rex, Socks ...

KANE

Bryant, Jensen, Marshall—

BANE

Quan. Chin-ho—

(Staggered, overlapping:)

KANE	**BANE**
Derby.	Reynaldo.
Hudson.	Rufus.
Hedlund.	Ronald.
Coyle.	Ginger.
Cortiñas.	Darcy.
Garrett.	Delilah.
Lee.	Mephistopheles.
Rogers.	Charlamegne.
Jones—	Jones—

BANE

...

KANE

...

BANE

Was Jones a man or a dog?

KANE

He was definitely a man ...

BANE

—I remember Jones! He gave his hardtack to the dogs, dear old Jonesy—

KANE

He's dead.

BANE

So you say ...

Clarke could make the loveliest ice figurines—

KANE

Clarke drowned.

BANE

Coyle had the most disfiguring hairlip that nonetheless lent him a charming lisp—

KANE

—He ate Garrett, then killed himself!

They're gone, Bane, all gone ...

(BANE sits, dejected.

A *long, depressive pause.)*

KANE (cont'd.)

What kind of name was *The Carcass* anyway? Were you trying to curse us right from the start?

(BANE laughs.)

KANE (cont'd.)

... What's so funny?

BANE

Nothing.

KANE

Say it:

BANE

It was a typographical error! It was meant to read "Caracas," but the painter got it switched ...

Damn foolish name, either way. I've never even been to Peru ...

I've wasted my entire life. That's a sin, isn't it, Kane?

KANE

Do you think you're the only one?

Smythe's wife was demented: they'd lost six children whilst hiking the Swiss Alps.

BANE

I've always said the Swiss were too good to be true ...

KANE

And Izzie—what was Izzie running from?

BANE

I told you: San Juan Hill.

KANE

The point is we've all run away—from something; or someone ...

BANE

—Not you, Elijah. What could you be hiding from?

KANE

A girl.

BANE

Ship's Chaplain Kane, you sly old fornicator you!

KANE

You wouldn't know it to look at me now, but I was once quite beautiful ...

BANE

Do you remember what she looked like, your girl?

KANE

...

BANE

Neither do I. It used to bother me quite a lot, that I could no longer remember her face: I thought, Isn't that odd? how quickly we forget the most important things ...

...
Remember making love, Kane?
Your hand upon a woman's breast ...
—Eh, Kane?
Hands moving beneath a woman's skirt ... Hips, like a bowl of sugar ...

KANE

...

BANE

... Eh? ... Kane?

(She shudders, with desire.)

BANE (cont'd.)

—Kane! —You bloody puritan you!

KANE

What would you say to her? if you saw her again?

BANE

"Hi, Liz. You're not pregnant, are you?"

KANE

It's the gala welcome-home ball; all the world is there—at least all of New York, the papers—

BANE

"Mr. Kane, Mr. Kane: How does it feel to be back in civilization?"

KANE

"Mr. Bane, Mr. Bane: What was it like, coming so close to the Pole only to admit defeat and turn back?"

BANE

"Mr. Kane: Is it true you ate your sailors?"

KANE

"No, that is patently false!"

BANE

—Can we lie?

KANE

What's to stop us? It's our story, not theirs.

BANE

—"And what about Mr. Israel? What can you tell us of his whereabouts?"

KANE

"As far as we know, ladies and gentlemen of the press, Mr. Israel is on his way to the Pole as we speak."

BANE

"You left him behind?"

KANE

"He left us, actually."

"Mr. Bane! Mr. Bane— !"

BANE

No more questions, please! Please!

KANE

The photographic flash is blinding, your head is spinning; amidst the kaleidoscope of who's-who you recognize an old familiar face:

BANE

Mumsy?

KANE

Hello, Banesy ...

(KANE has removed her disguise.)

BANE

Eliza ...

KANE

...

BANE

Where have you been hiding all this time?

KANE

I've been here ... With you.

(He moves to embrace her.

She hurts him in a highly personal place, flips him over, etc.

A band somewhere strikes up—a waltz; it could be simply in their minds, their memories.

She holds out her hand to him as he crawls to his feet.

They try to dance together ... as lights slowly fade.)

8.

(The hold of The Carcass.

DAN alone, looking for his tape recorder.

HELEN enters.)

HELEN

Bill's not coming.

DAN

Where's my tape / recorder?

HELEN

It's his heart. —It's in his head. He's been to eight doctors for this so-called "heart-murmur," all in the past year, and none of them can find anything wrong / with it.

DAN

What?

HELEN

His heart.

DAN

—Have you seen my tape recorder?

HELEN

No. What's it—gone?

DAN

Looks that way.

HELEN

Huh ...
Weird ...

DAN

Yeah: this / bites.

HELEN

Yeah.

DAN

This so totally—bites!

HELEN

... So he said we should, you know, rehearse. On our own.

DAN

Who?

HELEN

"Bill."

DAN

...

HELEN

Yeah.

DAN

Really ... ?

HELEN

Uh huh.

DAN

So ... okay ... What part do you want to "rehearse"?

(He moves to embrace her; she evades.)

DAN (cont'd.)

Sorry—

HELEN

No I'm / sorry—

DAN

No—

HELEN

—it's just—

DAN

I shouldn't—I'm / overstepping—

HELEN

It's not that it's—

DAN

Presuming—

HELEN

"Adultery," and—

DAN

Fine.

HELEN

Fine.

DAN

Fine.

HELEN

...

DAN

"Fines are for people who get caught."

(He picks up the ball.)

HELEN

Sorry, Dan ...

DAN

...

HELEN

(Re. the ball.)

Give:

DAN

(Throwing it to her.)

Take.

HELEN

(Throwing.)

Take.

DAN

(Throwing.)

Take.

HELEN

(Still throwing the ball.)

...

DAN

(Still throwing.)

...

HELEN

(Throwing.)

...

DAN

(Throw.)

...

HELEN

(Throw.)

...

DAN

(Throw.)

...

(She catches ball and holds it.)

HELEN

Whatever. You can't play with just two people ...

DAN

Do you think they sleep together?

In the last scene, or the next-to-last ... Once they find out who each other is—or who Kane is: do Bane and Kane sleep together?

HELEN

Well it would be kind of easy if they didn't. I mean, that's kind of what you'd expect—"not in love anymore," etcetera—

DAN

Are they "not" not-in-love anymore?

HELEN

You mean, are they still "in love"?

DAN

Yeah.

HELEN

Well, not in love but they love each other. —They need each other, I guess.

DAN

That's kind of sad, isn't it?

HELEN

No; it's not.

DAN

Yes it is: it's pathetic.

HELEN

You'll understand when you're older, Dan ...

DAN

So, what, they "fuck" out of pity? for old / time's sake?

HELEN

—Do you have to do that?

DAN

/ What?

HELEN

I'm talking about "mature love" here—

DAN

Mature / love.

HELEN

Yeah.

DAN

Hm.

HELEN

—Are you mad?
You've got nothing to be mad about / you know.

DAN

No. I'm just—

HELEN

What:

DAN

... Bored.

HELEN

Really.

DAN

Yes—I'm so totally bored. —And cold—why is it so fucking cold in this place!

(BILL enters.)

BILL

Hey, I want to read you two something:
"All transformations are invested with something at once of profound mystery and of the shameful, since anything that is so modified

as to become 'something else' while remaining the thing that it was, must inevitably be productive of ambiguity and shame.

"Therefore, metamorphoses must be hidden from view: hence the need for the mask." *(He pops on his clown nose. He closes the book.)*

I've reached a certain—juncture in my life.

HELEN

Bill—

(BILL takes the tape recorder out of his pants.)

BILL

Looking for something, Dano? *(He presses Record.)*

"Bill here: day twenty three of this our 'Artistic Entombment:' "

I'm almost thirty-two years old. I know that's not old by contemporary standards, but let's think what Christ had done by my age.

... I have to go to my 10th college reunion soon ... I wanted to be somebody by then.

HELEN

You are somebody.

BILL

To you I am.

HELEN

Who else is there?

BILL

—Everybody in the entire fucking world!

HELEN

What are you talking about, Bill?

BILL

—I'm talking about the state of American Theatre!

A fucking corpse, that's what it is! A fucking cadaver! Nobody cares—nobody fucking cares / anymore!

HELEN

That's right: nobody cares, so / shut up—

BILL

Shakespeare totally sucks! —Who decided he was good? Hm? A bunch of high school English teachers who figured out that Julius Caesar was cheaper than horse tranquilizers?

Things would be so much easier if I were a woman ...

HELEN

Bill—

BILL

No, wait: if I were a black, quadriplegic lesbian clown ... I would have so much more grant money!

DAN

I'd see that show.

HELEN

You'd never get to Broadway.

BILL

—Fuck Broadway! —And off-Broadway. And off-off-off-Broadway. And the "downtown theatre scene." And "regional theatre." And "festivals," and "workshops." And theatre about "thorny social issues." And theatre about nothing at all but God damned entertainment, packed with quirky character-composites spouting pithy truths about life. In the kitchen. Fuck dramas. And comedies—fuck revivals; above all fuck revivals! Of musicals! Fuck all musicals. And plays based on literature in the public domain. —Fuck the public domain! Fuck the public! —No, I love my public, wherever they may be: fuck the proletariat. Fuck critics, speaking of commie pinko bastards. Fuck the New York Fucking Times and the Star-Fucking-Ledger. Fuck old people. And their fucking little crackling candies. Fuck "subscribers." Fuck suburban housewives from New Jersey and their narcoleptic banker-husbands. —I fucking hate New Jersey so fucking much! —Fuck tourists from Idaho, or Iowa, whichever, doesn't matter. Fuck Disney, of course. Fuck old people, again, one more time. And kids fresh from Juilliard, or N.Y.U., or Brown. Fuck hipsters from Williamsburg. And as much as it pains me to say this because some of my best friends are members but: fuck the gay mafia. And lesbians, if they even have a mafia. Do they? they should. Fuck "Yalies." Fuck trust-fund babies. Fuck actors and writers of all stripes—and mimes. And clowns. Fuck me. Above all fuck me. Above all you must all go ahead and fuck me so hard.

HELEN

Maybe you're just not good enough, Bill.
Did you ever think of that?

BILL

No that's not it.

HELEN

I'll see you guys later ...

BILL

—Where you going?

HELEN

Out.

BILL

Are you scared?

HELEN

Of you?

BILL

I don't know: might say something I shouldn't: "mixed company," that / sort of thing.

HELEN

No Bill, you go right ahead: you say whatever it is you need to say.

BILL

—Because you shouldn't, sweetheart, you know—be scared. I mean, we're just talking politics here. Talking "art"—where's the shame in art? "Government funding for the arts." *(To DAN:)*

Can you believe I married a Republican?

Of course, she wasn't a Republican when I met her; they never are. Now it's just: "If art can't pay for itself, let it die!"

HELEN

Let it die.

BILL

"Let it / fucking starve!"

HELEN

You realize what you're saying.

BILL

I'm finally agreeing with you, honey. —You think I'm what, "selfish"?

HELEN

Yes, I do.

BILL

Hey, I'm not the one quashing dreams here—

HELEN

"Quashing" dreams? —Is that even a word?

DAN

Actually it / is ...

HELEN

How am I quashing anything? I gave you this: this whole—thing: "Theater."

—I paid for this!

BILL

O, so you're my what, "benefactress"? —Hel, you're my wife ...

HELEN

Don't you pull that one on me—don't you dare / pull that—

BILL

Pull what?

HELEN

"I never supported you."

BILL

I didn't say you never supported me. —Did I say she "never / supported me"?

HELEN

Don't you think I'd rather be like you? with "principles" and—Art? That I'd rather wear a clown nose and dedicate my—whatever—to "noble pursuits," and not have to worry about eating and—I don't want to be a child anymore, Bill: I want to have children. I want to stop playing these fucking games, and I want to grow up!

BILL

... You don't think we're grown-ups?

(She moves to take BILL's nose off; he evades.)

BILL (cont'd.)

—That's a problem, see.

HELEN

I've given you everything—my "youth" and—because you've wasted it, you hate me ...

BILL

I don't hate you ...

HELEN

Well you don't love me anymore; that's obvious. Isn't it?

BILL

I don't think you should be talking about love. —This isn't about "love," I don't think.

HELEN

You're right: it's about making a decision.

(She turns to go.)

BILL

Does that mean you've already made your decision?
Because I haven't! made mine!
Not yet— !

HELEN

(Leaving.)

Whatever!

BILL

—Where are you / going?

HELEN

To the North Fucking Pole!

(She's gone.)

DAN

...

BILL

...

DAN

How's your heart?

BILL

(Rubbing his chest.)

Murmuring: "You asshole, you asshole" ...

DAN

You okay?

BILL

—You know we're getting a divorce.

DAN

...

BILL

You know that, don't you.

DAN

No.

BILL

We are: bad idea: marriage.

Don't do it.

She can't understand ideals. Either you have them, or you don't. —What she does have is a certain "pragmatic genius"; she's got reality in her back pocket. She's not willing to suffer, like we are, for our what?

DAN

Are you drunk?

BILL

Aren't you?

DAN

Not yet.

(BILL pulls a bottle out of his padded ass.

He takes a swig; hands it to DAN.

DAN drinks.)

BILL

I don't mean to burden you. These are just my problems ...

DAN

(The bottle.)

Thanks.

BILL

You're my friend ... Right?

DAN

...

BILL

You're so capable of listening ... Other people's problems don't seem to, I don't know—"weigh you down."

DAN

(Shrugs.)

...

BILL

Huh.

DAN

Yeah.

BILL

—Why do I do it, Dan?

DAN

What:

BILL

Act. / The Theatre.

DAN

I don't know. —You love it?

BILL

... Do I?

DAN

Yes.

BILL

Do you?

DAN

O ... "Gee" ...

BILL

—Do you love it?

DAN

"The theatre"? Not in love with it, but I love it.
I have a mature love of the theatre ...

BILL

...

DAN

I guess I don't have such high—expectations. As you.

BILL

Huh.

DAN

Yeah. You don't think that's true?

BILL

—It's the only thing I know how to do: that's all. And it's bad for me, obviously.

When I'm alone out there, out here, doing my headstands, climbing my invisible ladders, whatever, my heart murmurs: "Get out!" which means, "Get out of this fucking room with no windows. Have some kids, teach them how to swim. Go out and live your life before it's too late." —And then my heart flips over on itself, you know, skips a beat—like a warning: I could die out here, on stage, in front of an empty house—.

...

... And yet.

DAN

...

BILL

How do you feel?

DAN

About Helen?

BILL

...

DAN

...

BILL

... About this—our "farce" ...

Talk to me, Dano. I'm doing all the talking here; it's really / exhausting ...

DAN

I like it—the Play.

BILL

Uh huh.

DAN

It's got some—funny bits.

... That part where Izzie puts on all their clothes and the snowshoes—that really gets me.

BILL

We've got to finish it.

DAN

Sure.

BILL

We can't go on like this forever.

DAN

You're telling / me.

BILL

—What happens? How does it end? Do they go home? does the ice melt and they all sail home? Or do they walk out on the ice together and freeze to death? —Do they eat / each other?

DAN

I don't know that yet—

BILL

Come on—work with me / here, Dan— !

DAN

I have no fucking clue!
... Okay?
Back off ...

BILL

What's wrong with you?

DAN

You mean in general, or / right now?

BILL

Why can't you just play / along?

DAN

Why can't you just—"give me some space"!

BILL

Are we dating?

DAN

You don't understand how writers work ...

BILL

I think I have a pretty good idea.

DAN

What does / that mean?

BILL

You just sit there. You don't "do" anything.

DAN

What would you rather I did?

BILL

Talked more. "Shared."

DAN

I'm a better listener.

BILL

But you talk enough—in your plays.

DAN

I'm not talking.

BILL

O sorry: your "voices" / are talking.

DAN

That's right.

BILL

Sorry; just trying to peel back "the Amazing Onion Effect" here, Dan.

DAN

/ Ha ha.

BILL

—You are always talking, Dan! Whether you like it or not. / You're the writer—

DAN

If I ever find myself talking in my own play, I promise: I will kill my self!
'Kay?

BILL

... You've been very hard to work with.

DAN

And you're a fucking walk in the, I don't know— !

BILL

"Park"!

DAN

—Shove it up your ass!

BILL

See: that's your problem right there.
You were very inspiring—in College. I'll say it. You were "heroic." I thought you'd be famous by now. What happened? You've gotten kind of sad.

DAN

...

BILL

It's nice.

DAN

... I don't think—you've got it entirely right.

BILL

Please:

DAN

All this competition stuff: you're creating it yourself.

BILL

Really. You never feel competitive with other people?

DAN

No.

BILL

You never feel "ambition"?

DAN

Not really / no.

BILL

No demons? Dogs howling at your window?

(BILL howls.)

DAN

No: no dogs.

BILL

How come? —I mean, how do you "avoid" it?

DAN

I just kind of, you know—shrug it off:

(DAN shrugs.)

BILL

—None of this stuff bothers you? This—talk about "politics" and "art" and "theatre"?

You don't worry about the larger picture?

DAN

Nope. I wish I did, but—

BILL

So I could say anything to you right now, and it wouldn't upset you?

DAN

Sure. Within reason.

BILL

I know what happened.

DAN

(Re. the tape recorder.)

... Why don't you turn / that off.

BILL

It's a collaboration. We're on a "journey of discovery" here—

DAN

Turn that off / please—

BILL

All I said was I know you "had sex" with my—Helen. Once. She told me. And it's all right. She doesn't love you.

DAN

...

BILL

She was angry—at me. And you happened to be there ...

It's all right: I've made mistakes too ...

I mean you probably did us a favor, in the long run.

DAN

Well in that case, you're welcome.

BILL

... I used to wonder, Why did I suffer all the time and never get any parts and you could just be all cool and detached and write your poetry and shit, and then I figured it out: the reason I suffer is because I'm capable of loving things. People. And you're not.

I don't care if this destroys our—whatever. It's time one of us was honest:

You're a vampire, Dan.

—Parasite.

I just called you a "Parasite," Daniel—

DAN

Loser.

BILL

Cannibal.

DAN

Burn-out.

BILL

Vulture.

DAN

Talentless.

BILL

Coward—

DAN

Clown—. Mime—

BILL

—Fraud. *(They're nose to nose.)*

Hm.

That seemed to work pretty well ...

"Fraud"—

(DAN shoves BILL. They grapple undramatically for a bit, until DAN gets ahold of the stage knife; he "stabs" BILL somewhere in his significant padding, to no effect.

BILL manages to punch him in the stomach; DAN goes down.

Silence.)

BILL

O.

Wow.

(HELEN enters.)

HELEN

—And I'm taking my Dictionary of Symbols with me—. *(She sees DAN:)* What happened / to you ... ?

BILL

Yeah.

DAN

... !

BILL

We had an—altercation ...

(DAN gets up. Moves to the tape recorder.)

DAN

(Picking it up.)

—This!

—Is mine!

HELEN

Where are you going?

DAN

—Buffalo: Godspell.

HELEN

What happened?

DAN

—I'm doing Godspell / there!

HELEN

What about the play?

DAN

I'll finish it! —On my own! —I will go away, and I will write that final scene!
Because it is my play and / not yours— !

BILL

If you put me in this fucking play I swear I will haunt you! I will haunt you till the day / you die— !

HELEN

—Bill?

BILL

I mean it!

DAN

Godspell: Bye!

BILL

You go do Godspell, you prick! I'm going into Advertising, and one day I'm going to have so much more money than you!

DAN

(In the doorway.)

Helen, do you want to come out here for a minute?

HELEN

No—.
/ Bill?

DAN

Helen, we should really talk.
I really need to talk / to you.

HELEN

No. *(To BILL:)* What happened?

BILL

I fucked up... .

HELEN

It's all right—

BILL

I fucked everything up / so badly ...

HELEN

Don't cry—come here:

(DAN exits, with the tape recorder.)

HELEN (cont'd.)

Bill?
Shh ...
What do we do now?

(Transition:)

9.

(BANE and KANE asleep, arms entwined.

Bo'sun SMYTHE is nowhere to be found. Instead, where his body was, only the bloodied ice pick remains ...

ISRAEL is standing in his snowshoes and furs and goggles, etc.

He shivers.)

ISRAEL

I was at the Pole.
It was—.
The snow—. The sky—
Words can not explain ...
I stuck a flag there.
I took a picture with the photographic apparatus.
I couldn't take a picture of myself, so it's just a picture of the snow, which is white, and the sky which is white, and the flag, which is mostly white, on account of the ice and snow and sun ...
I hope it comes out ...
—You really should've seen it: it really was like you think it would be. Flat for hundreds of miles in all directions and then a pucker in the earth like a belly button and that's it:
The Pole.
—Everything was taller there: I was taller there.
The flag was taller there.
The pucker was even bigger than it would've been elsewhere—at the equator, say, or New York.
I could do anything there.
I took off all my clothes.

I pissed my name in the snow—which was difficult because I was dehydrated ...

—Not my real name, which is Isador, but my nickname, Iz ...

"Iz," I pissed in the snow ...

... *(He shivers.)*

I could see right up through the roof of the sky into heaven.

Angels were there, above me.

"Hey Angels! Look at me! —It's me: Isador! I'm at the North Pole!"

—It's not that I'm religious, but I wanted them to understand: to appreciate what I'd done.

But they were wholly unimpressed ...

As if they didn't care.

—After all I'd done for them!

—After all this struggle?

—Do you know what they looked like, those angels up there?

Fat kids.

The paintings are right: angels are just fat kids.

And I thought, What do they know about my life?

What do these fat angel kids know about my life?

They haven't lived ...

So I screamed at the angels at the top of the world: Hey fat kids! Screw you! What do you know about me? What do you know about Isador Jersowitz? I made it to the Pole! I never gave up! I'm one in a million ... !

... *(He shivers.)*

It was white there.

The snow—.

The sky—

I liked it.

I liked it there.

I like it here—can we stay?

... If we could only find more food, things would be just—

(He drops dead.

BANE and KANE take their time waking up.)

KANE

... Good morning, Banesy.

BANE

... Elijah.

KANE

Bane?

BANE

Hm?

KANE

Do you remember last night?

BANE

Of course I remember last night!

Of course I— !

Israel stole our supplies and ran away from home; you heard the mournful wail of the murderèd sledge-dogs for the very first time; we barricaded the door against spectral intrusion—and then we— *(notices ISRAEL:)* was Bo'sun Smythe wearing my Burberry windsuit?

KANE

No.

BANE

—Our Esquimeaux furs over the Burberry windsuit?

KANE

Not that I recall—

BANE

What about my lucky snowshoes? —Goggles? Knives? Compass?

KANE

What about them— ?

BANE

Then who, by God— !?

(BANE removes ISRAEL's goggles and hat.)

KANE

— !

BANE

What has happened to Bo'sun Smythe!

KANE

(Inspecting him.)

—He's frozen ...

BANE

No: Bo'sun Smythe has disappeared ... !

Look: here's the ice pick that was formerly lodged in his skull—

KANE

He's got frostbite all over his body.

BANE

—Where is my journal?

KANE

He's dead.

BANE

Izzie?

KANE

Yes ... He is.

(KANE finds the journal on ISRAEL.)

BANE

He stole my— ? *(He takes it from her.)*

What would he want with— ? *(Opens to most recent entry:)*

"Day two thousand five hundred eighty-three: am at North Pole. Everything here is so."

—He doesn't even write in complete sentences!

(BANE puts his journal away.

Slowly, mournfully, he removes ISRAEL's various accoutrements. He moves to the trunk and dumps them in.

He kneels beside ISRAEL and, after a moment, drives the ice pick through his head.)

KANE

— !

BANE

— !

— ! — !

—What kind of friend steals another friend's journal! *(He spikes him again.)*

It's diabolical— ! *(Another spike.)*

Reading another's private-most thoughts! *(Another spike.)*

Writing in the journal, for Christ's sake! *(Another.)*

And to think I trusted him! A trust unconditional! The one person I trusted in the entire Carcass crew! —Not even you, Elijah—Eliza—Whoever You Are!—not even You inspired such faith!

... And now look at him: he probably stole Smythe; snuck back in here during the night and ate himself to death, the grubscoffing hog— ! *(Spikes, severally.)*

(The whole time, KANE has been un-barricading the exit.

BANE notices, approaches from behind.)

BANE (cont'd.)

Kane?

KANE

— !

BANE

Care to help me with breakfast?

KANE

You mean ... ?

BANE

Shame to let good food go to waste.

(He hands KANE the tray.

He does more horrible things to ISRAEL.)

KANE

Bane?

BANE

Yes, Liz?

KANE

I'm feeling frisky.

BANE

Liz?

I understand last night was quite a pay-off after seven years of confused celibacy, but we can hardly hope to maintain that level of passion—

KANE

You're so handsome in this light: that hand, your pick ...
I think ... I would like ... to kiss you—

(They're about to kiss—she takes the ice pick from him.)

BANE

— !

KANE

—You killed Bo'sun Smythe!

I saw the way you just drove that ice pick into poor Izzie's head: villain! —What did he ever do to deserve that?

BANE

I may have gotten carried away, I'll admit as much; but that prissy little dancer stole my journal— !

KANE

Stay where you are— !

BANE

—All right, let's say I did kill Bo'sun Smythe.

KANE

I already did say that.

BANE

Why would I kill anyone else?

KANE

— ?

BANE

Smythe was always telling me that story:

"It was a dark and stormy night, and the Captain said, 'Bo'sun, tell me a story.' And the Bo'sun said, 'It was a dark and stormy night, and the Captain said, "Bo'sun, tell me a story." And the Bo'sun said, "It was a dark and stormy night, and the Captain said, 'Bo'sun—

He thought it was the funniest damned thing he'd ever heard!

KANE

I don't understand—

BANE

—I don't kill people I love!

And I love you, Liz ...

KANE

You don't love me ...

BANE

Eliza—

KANE

You'll never love me—

BANE

How can you say such a thing— ?

KANE

You can't love anything but the Pole!
I'm going home, Bane; and I'm not going home with you.

BANE

... Does this mean the wedding's off?

(They grapple for the knife.

It's a violent fight, during which both are injured significantly.

But no one wins; KANE *loses a little less: she still holds the knife.*

Wheezing, gasping, panting, BANE *goes to* ISRAEL*'s humongous sack, opens it, takes out a rifle.)*

KANE

You can't shoot me.

BANE

I'm going to shoot myself.

KANE

—You can't do that either.

BANE

Why not?

KANE

There aren't any bullets left.

BANE

Blast— !

(He hurls the rifle to the floor, takes out the photographic apparatus.

He hits himself seriously on the head with it. —Then flashes the camera flash into his eyes, repeatedly.

He's still alive, so he discards it.

While going through the other possessions in ISRAEL's sack—an eggbeater, a rabbits foot, a crazy doll's head, etc.:)

BANE

This isn't me, Liz.

This isn't who I imagined myself to be.

I'm filled with such an awful amount of remorse ...

If only I could move backwards, in time ...

I would learn things differently—how to speak, for one:

I would not sound even remotely British, which was the fault of my nanny—a robust woman whose only other fault was her being from Lincolnshire. —That, and her breath. And the way she used to suck on hard candies ... in public ... for a dollar.

And I would not eat as many sweets—I would not eat at all! I would be thin, and I would not dream so much ...

I would have no dreams at all ...

I would not sleep; and if I slept I would sink like a stone through water ...

I would be reasonable. —I am not a reasonable man, Kane! People see me and they think I must be a Man to command an expedition to the North Pole, but I am really just a child still ...

(He beats himself with the eggbeater.

Suddenly: dogs without.

A real live sledge-DOG—or not—comes trotting in, over the barricade, starts eating ISRAEL.

Enter after him a tall, bearded, Nordic-looking fellow who pushes through or steps over the barricade with ease.

He's played by the same actor who played Israel.)

BJORNSEN

—Mishka, heel!

MISHKA

... !

BJORNSEN

Mishka!

(The dog keeps at ISRAEL.

BJORNSEN kicks MISHKA.)

MISHKA

—!

BJORNSEN

Good dog.

Bane Barrington, I presume?

BANE

How do you know my name? From the Royal Geographic Society lecture on the topography of Frans Josef Land?

BJORNSEN

No.

BANE

From the Royal Geographic Society lecture on the topography of the Upper East Side?

BJORNSEN

No, that's not it either: Smythe told me.

BANE & KANE

—Smythe?

KANE

—He's alive?

BJORNSEN

That's right: Bo'sun Smythe, the one whose six children were all butchered by the Swiss.

KANE

Who are you?

BJORNSEN

My name is Bjorn Bjornsen, Arctic Explorer.

My men and I have been camped not far from you for many months now. Perhaps you have heard our dogs howling mournfully in the night? But we had yet to discover your ice-locked Carc-ass. Until last night; when a man with a hole in the back of his head somnambulated into our camp ...

Naturally, we set our doctors to work on him right away, stanching his wound, fortifying him with copious supplies: fresh crimson-fleshed sealsmeat, vitamin C, Chocolate—the usual.

There have been a great many advances in exploratory technology since you disappeared, Barrington.

For one thing, people have given up thinking they could sail to the Pole.

Aha!

Aha ha ha!

...

Aha ha ha ha ha ha ha!

Dear me. —Mr. Bo'sun Smythe was very sore on that point; he harbors a great deal of resentment towards you, Barrington. But, after a good hot meal he cooled off, expressing a sincere remorse for his ill-will, considering the uncivilized conditions you've all been living under ...

My gravest sympathies to you both. I know what hell seclusion can be. I used to be a nun. Did I say nun? I meant fisherman.

KANE

Smythe is alive ...

BJORNSEN

O yes. And very lucky to be so.

Said he was above on the Carcass deck, chipping away at a great block of ice—as is his pastime—that, and storytelling—when due to the frost and bitter cold he let slip the ice pick, which came to a remarkably balanced resting position upon its handle, pick pointed straight up.

So that when Smythe reached down and lost all muscle control in his lumbar region—owing, again, to the frost and bitter cold—he fell flat upon the upturned pick like a pumpkin on a stick at a peasant wedding.

... You'd be surprised: accidents like that are quite common. *(Noticing ISRAEL:)*

Did he fall on an ice pick too?

BANE

Several times, yes.

BJORNSEN

Criminal. I don't know why we bring those things on board. *(He notices KANE.)*

My, what a handsome Ship's Chaplain you have. What's his name?

BANE

Liz.

BJORNSEN

Well, Liz ... shall we off?

We have a wonderful Inuit cook we've christened Nathan. He does astonishing things with pemmican.

—Mishka, heel!

(He exits after MISHKA, who's run off dragging ISRAEL's carcass, perhaps.)

KANE

We're saved.

BANE

Kane? —Liz?

KANE

... ?

BANE

Before you go—before we go—I want you to know:

I'm going to change when we get home. I'm through with all this polar exploring. From now on in it's going to be a regular job for me. And lots of money. And a family, if you'll have me.

KANE

...

BANE

How about it, Liz. Will you have me?

(A moment together.

She goes.

BANE alone, with his journal.)

BANE

...

...

"Bo'sun Smythe ... is alive. A perplexing helix of events. I am at a loss for—"

(He has an idea—tears out the last several pages of his journal, and begins again:)

BANE (cont'd.)

"Day two thousand five hundred and eighty-two: Smythe dead. Israel not well. The starvation and cold are too much for him. He lies feverish in his bunk, calling out inarticulately to the night for his Anya. Whoever she was.

"Day two thousand five hundred and eighty-three: Israel worse. Kane has a hacking cough to wake the dickens.

"Day two thousand five hundred and eighty-four: Israel gone. Read Prayer for the Dead over Body. Discussed Existence of God and Origin of Species with Ship's Chaplain Kane. No conclusions reached.

"Day two thousand five hundred and eighty-five: there is something in my chest. A rattle. Dog in the woods. Eliza—" *(He scratches that out.)* "Elijah dying fast. Neither of us have the strength to bury poor Israel.

"Day two thousand five hundred and eighty-six: things worse. No turning back. Must stay the course."

KANE

(Off.)

—Bane? Are you coming?

BJORNSEN

(Farther off.)

—Mishka! heel!

BANE

"Day two thousand five hundred and eighty-six, continuèd: Kane gone. I barely have strength to write.

"Day two thousand five hundred and eighty-seven: am worse.

"Day two thousand five hundred and eighty-eight: cold. White ... "

KANE

(Farther off.)

... Bane?

... I can't wait for you forever!

(BANE puts the journal in the trunk, and locks it. He places the ice pick on the table. He considers the photographic apparatus, then takes it with him.

...

The empty hold of The Carcass.

The sound of dogs, a sledge, receding in the distance as lights slowly fade.)

END OF PLAY

THE DEAR BOY

Characters

James FLANAGAN	65
JAMES Doyle	17
RICHARD Purdy	37
ELISE Sanger	29

Time & Place

Scene 1: After school, late December, 1990; Scarsdale Public High School, Scarsdale, NY. Specifically, we're in Flanagan's office.

Scene 2: A party at a bar in the city, later that night.

Scene 3: An apartment (not her apartment), still later that night.

Scene 4: Flanagan's office, early the next morning.

Notes

1) A slash "/" in the script indicates overlapping dialogue.

2) Nonverbal "lines" in the script:

FLANAGAN

... ?

or

FLANAGAN

...

should be played as beats; most often as pauses.

3) Dialogue in quotes and parentheses, i.e. ("Yes.") or ("No."), indicates a nonverbal response.

The Dear Boy was written with the support of the University of the South (Sewanee) and the Tennessee Williams Fellowship in Playwriting.

The play received subsequent development with Atlantic Theater Company, Roundabout Theatre Company, Geva Theatre Center, and Primary Stages.

The Dear Boy received its world premiere production in 2005 from Second Stage Theatre, Carole Rothman, Artistic Director, directed by Michael John Garcés.

Creative Team

Set Design	Wilson Chin
Costume Design	Amela Baksic
Lighting Design	Ben Stanton
Sound Design	Sunil Rajan
Casting	Tara Rubin Casting
Press	Richard Kornberg & Associates
Production Stage Manager	Rachel J. Perlman
Stage Manager	Stephanie Gatton
Associate Artistic Director	Christopher Burney
General Manager	C. Barrack Evans
Production Manager	Jeff Wild

Youth has an end: the end is here.
It will never be. You know that well.
What then?

—*Joyce*

for my brother

1A.

(Tall, effete, brownsuited; cheeks like crabapples and the rest gray pallor so that he seems one almost always chapped by wind and rain and on winter days [like this] outright pneumonic; when he smiles he bares his Celtic teeth; when he speaks he drapes his weight on one leg back as an actor plays to the balcony, his eyes cast up, as if searching a high, dark shelf for something very small, very valuable, very lost:)

FLANAGAN

My dear boy.

What were you thinking?

You're no James Joyce. You're not even Will Faulkner. —You're seventeen! Not a saint, though I know you think you are. I know your type: mother's milk, father bereft, half-repressed literary tendencies—O yes, I know who you are ...

I am not a kind teacher ... I'm not cruel, either. Am I a good teacher? I like to think so, on my good days, and we all have our good days—even you, my dear boy, though you're not a very good student ... Too shy to be a hooligan; not a clown though you can be quite sharp: my "brown suit would suit a mortician better"? —And what was that crack you made about the St. Paddy's Day parade?, that I would be up front this year marching with the interlopers ... ?

I understand: I accept: I take your disdain upon my back as a kind of penance, my cross to carry, a question wrought from God: What to do with the likes of you ...

... The others don't see it ... They bring your name up whilst brightening their coffee with a dollop of cream: O yes, Jimmy Doyle—isn't he sweet?

And darkly I reply, Pass the sugar, Ms. Kane ...

Because you see you lie—you do; you lie well, I'll grant you that. —I know you didn't read past the crime in *Crime and Punishment*, and yet you deserved every bit of that B minus—you did!—and that's your *talent*, my boy! You have that most Irish of gifts of being most convincing when least informed. And while I can't fault you your arrogance—it's the privilege of the young, that is, the ignorant—I've often wondered, in the cocoon of my commute, suspended in my car inside the Henry Hudson Bridge, or reading late at night in my apartment above the shoe factory—yes?; I often feel I want nothing more before I retire than to teach you a lesson.

But a lesson about what?

...

I could teach you how to write.

You are not ungifted as a writer.

You write as one speaks, though not as you speak yourself.

You seem to channel another voice, another person's voice altogether, and this voice seems to be that of a middle-aged, overly chatty housewife. It's a nifty trick, considering your prose speaks not of normal housewifely concerns, but rather darker things, things you've no business knowing ...

Is she your mother?, this voice? Never mind ...

Our first assignment had been to write in the style of William Faulkner. My mistake. Because the story you wrote, that first story you gave me back in—September was it?, made no sense to me at all. In fact it struck me as alarmingly schizophrenic, at least latently so: windows were said to "breathe," trees "watched" or "wept" or actually spoke, if I'm not mistaken, from time to time, in oracular fashion (there is no other word)—*in italics*, of course, thank you so very much.

Further, your main character, a young woman (of all things!) manifests an untoward fascination with feces, and in particular one steaming pile that flops out the backside of a nearby black carriage-horse, tethered to the bottom of your page one ...

My dear boy ... Have you ever even *seen* a horse?

The time throughout, one almost needn't note, is the present.

The incident with the feces is the only occurrence in this twenty-plus-page opus that might possibly be misconstrued as plot. And indeed the horse itself may not have been there at all, may have been an illusion, an equine specter haunting the streets of the young madgirl's mind, as she wends her way to a clinic in "the city" for an "abortion," by the way, though who can be sure of anything in the dark falling light of your prose ...

My dear boy this is not stream-of-consciousness but drowning.

Your sentences are overly long—some overspill a page; punctuation is perverse: parenthetical after (within!) parenthetical threaten to swallow sense—what sense there is—like a whale its own tail, like a snake eats itself unto abstraction, the words slithering and slippery and venomous—that's the word, yes: your prose is *poisoned*, my boy, capable of poisoning, reading your words like digging in a graveyard at night ...

...

—I gave you a B minus.

And without a single note of encouragement, your twenty-two single-spaced pages stark naked of notes, I dropped the B minus down to your desk as if the story itself might soil my hands.

... You suffered silently, but I knew I'd stung your pride.

...

Or so I thought.

Until today.

Until I read this—your most recent retaliation:

A story meant to be told in the style of James Joyce—again, my mistake. —It's longer than the first, thank you very much; but there had been a twist: "Write about a hero of yours" ...

I return these twenty-six typewritten pages to you as you have given them to me: the margins, again, white and dumb. There is no grade this time. As I drop the other childrens' stories down to desk—heartwarming tales of grandmothers blessed with endearingly wise dementia; precocious entertainments of eligible aunts, wily cousins, cigarsmoking coaches—I watch out the corner of my eye as you open your story to the very last page, only to discover there a single, scrawled, page-sprawling question mark. *(He makes the symbol in the air:)*

?

And beneath the symbol an invitation:

1B.

(Skin pale, translucent temples; scattershot of acne spoils the pallor; shoots of rough beard blemish sideburns and upper lip; severe Irish cheekbones—two, asymmetrical; punched up nose, tipped out ears, cowlicks unruly despite too much hair gel; skinny, embarrassed, heartbreaking if not aggravating; a varsity jacket [soccer] with white thread enstitched "Jim":)

JAMES

(Knocks.)

...

FLANAGAN

(Writing; not looking.)

... James:

Have a seat. *(Still writing and not looking.)*

One moment, please; I'm just now at the end of something ...

(JAMES strands himself at the window: blue winter light, sun low already.

FLANAGAN lays aside his pen.)

FLANAGAN (cont'd.)

It's good for them.

JAMES

...

FLANAGAN

The trees: if you cut the limbs in winter, they grow back better in the spring.

JAMES

(As if impressed.)

Wow.

FLANAGAN

I noticed that image—all over your story: trees with their limbs cut off.
I knew where you'd got it from.

JAMES

...

(As he stands to close the door:)

FLANAGAN

(Offering.)

Sit down, please, James.

(JAMES does sit; withdrawn, almost regal; he crosses his legs in the macho manner.)

FLANAGAN (cont'd.)

(Sits again, he pulls his chair beneath & neatly under.)

I suppose you know why you're here.

JAMES

You asked me to come.

FLANAGAN

...

JAMES

In my story. The question mark.
You told me to come / here—

FLANAGAN

Yes. *(Smiles; hides teeth.)* That's true: I did ask you to come. To see me in my office.

And do you know why?

JAMES

("No.")

FLANAGAN

We have a problem here, don't we James.

JAMES

Do we ... ?

FLANAGAN

Don't we?

JAMES

... What kind of problem?

FLANAGAN

What kind of problem ...

JAMES

I don't know if we have / a problem ...

FLANAGAN

You don't know ...

JAMES

No. Not really.

FLANAGAN

—Do you enjoy class?

JAMES

This class?

FLANAGAN

Let's start there / yes.

JAMES

Sure.

FLANAGAN

Why?

JAMES

(Shrugs.)

I don't know ...

I like books. I like English. It's my favorite language.

FLANAGAN

You like *reading*.

JAMES

Sure.

FLANAGAN

And writing?

JAMES

Who doesn't?

FLANAGAN

(Leaning in across desk.)

Then why aren't you happy here, my boy?

JAMES

...

FLANAGAN

You seem all right in class, in person; it's in these stories you write I think I see someone who's deeply, deeply disturbed ...

JAMES

... I'm not disturbed.

FLANAGAN

You're not ... ?

JAMES

I'm happy.

FLANAGAN

(Sits back.)

... Do you have a girlfriend?, what's her name? I've seen you with her: short hair, petite; *quite* striking. —Does she read your stories?

JAMES

(Shrugs.)

Sometimes.

FLANAGAN

Does she like them ... ?

She would have to like them, wouldn't she, if she likes you ...

(He smiles; hides teeth.)

JAMES

(Looks away.)

...

FLANAGAN

Do you like *me*, James?

JAMES

(A hesitation; a smile.)

... What do you mean?

FLANAGAN

Do you like me; your teacher.

JAMES

Why wouldn't I *like* you, Mr. Flanagan?

FLANAGAN

Because I don't like your stories. Very much.

JAMES

(A moment; he shrugs.)

... They rejected Jesus too.

FLANAGAN

I beg your pardon?

JAMES

They rejected Jesus; in his home town.

FLANAGAN

(Sits forward across desk.)

—And do you consider yourself Jesus in some way?

JAMES

(Shrugs.)

Who doesn't?

FLANAGAN

This—is fascinating. Do you think this town *rejects* / you— ?

JAMES

(Strongly.)

—I don't know why you don't like my stories, Mr. Flanagan.

Okay ... ?

I don't care ...

FLANAGAN

That's not what I asked, my boy ... *(Tight smile; hides teeth.)*

—And it's not that I don't like your stories. I *do* like them—I like what it is I think I see you're trying to pull off. —It's *ambitious.* — It's *precocious.* But I can't say I *understand* them. —And you do want me to understand you, don't you? It's important to you that I understand ... ?

JAMES

I guess.

FLANAGAN

Then help me, James. Help me understand this your latest masterwork.

What's it called / again?

JAMES

"Saint James."

FLANAGAN

—Saint James! Of course! —That's my name too, you know.

JAMES

"Saint—"?

FLANAGAN

"James," yes ... Aha ha.

... I understand you better than you think: both of us Irish, yes?, or Irish-American, God help us; both with our—artistic dispositions, living lives surrounded by gratuitous wealth—in a culture *very* different from one we can claim to understand, or appreciate. —It's natural we'd feel put / upon.

JAMES

I'm not Irish.

FLANAGAN

You're not?

JAMES

No.

FLANAGAN

I see ...

Well it must be very difficult, then, with a name like "Doyle," never being Irish; always *correcting* people ...

JAMES

(Looks to window.)

...

FLANAGAN

Is "Saint James" an autobiographical title, do you / think?

JAMES

It's a church—

FLANAGAN

Is it / now ... ?

JAMES

—an Episcopal church I used to go to as a kid.

FLANAGAN

(Smiling darkly.)

That long time ago ... ?

JAMES

...

FLANAGAN

Are you Episcopal then, James?

JAMES

(The window.)

...

FLANAGAN

—What does that title *mean* then, do you suppose: "Saint / James"?

JAMES

(Shrugs.)

I don't know.

FLANAGAN

You don't know what your own title means?

JAMES

Not really / no.

FLANAGAN

You should know what your own title means. —You should know what you're writing before you've written it down—else the world will tear you apart. —Your *intentions*, you see?

JAMES

(A minor explosion.)

—Who cares about the fucking title? —I don't care about the title ...

FLANAGAN

(Cowed, momentarily.)

... Who cares indeed ...

... Let's push on then, shall we? Let's forget the title and discuss the story / proper:

JAMES

Fine ...

FLANAGAN

Fine. —What does it mean?

JAMES

—Jesus ...

FLANAGAN

Hmn ... ?

JAMES

—I don't know.

FLANAGAN

—"You don't know" or you don't / care?

JAMES

—I wrote it, it came out of me, I had to say it—

FLANAGAN

—But what did you end up saying? That's what I'm asking you here —what does your story say, about life?, about poor put-upon "James"?, about the other characters in your imagination ... ?

JAMES

What did I end up "saying"?

FLANAGAN

—Exactly!

JAMES

—Who gives a shit?

FLANAGAN

(Sighs; he watches the boy intently.)

...

JAMES

... Okay?

God ...

FLANAGAN

I don't mean to upset you, James ...

Lord knows the last thing I want to do is to upset you here today ...

I am a fair man. —Let's take this one step—let's back up a step then / shall we?

JAMES

Fine with / me.

FLANAGAN

Fine ... What was the original assignment?

JAMES

—Write a story.

FLANAGAN

Yes, and— ?

JAMES

In the style of "James Joyce."

FLANAGAN

And:

JAMES

Write about a hero of yours.

FLANAGAN

—Why do you say it like that?

JAMES

Like what?

FLANAGAN

With a "sashay" in your voice ...

JAMES

(Shrugs; smiles.)

...

FLANAGAN

—Do you believe in heroes?

JAMES

...

FLANAGAN

There are "heroes" ready to die for you now, liberating Kuwait—. You may very well be drafted in the spring—you may find yourself fighting for your country—*then* I promise you you will find out about heroes ... !

(His pointing white finger quivers in the gloom ...

The room is growing dark.)

JAMES

...

FLANAGAN

(Pulling his finger back.)

... And who have you chosen as the hero of your story, "Saint James"?

JAMES

...

FLANAGAN

You know I like to read these stories to my wife ...

(He crosses his legs behind and beneath the desk.)

FLANAGAN (cont'd.)

I like her to see what my students are up to. And I can tell you right now I would not dare show her this story—*would not dare.*

JAMES

(The window, again.)

...

FLANAGAN

(Almost gently.)

My dear boy: whatever would make you write a story about me?

JAMES

...

FLANAGAN

Hmn ... ?

JAMES

It's not you—

FLANAGAN

Is / it not?

JAMES

—in the story—I made that up: it's fiction.

FLANAGAN

(Uncrossing his legs.)

—But no, I don't think that's true: I think you're hiding from that—behind—"fiction"—.

Do you have it with you please? Let's look at it together.

(JAMES hesitates; then unzips the knapsack at his feet and withdraws a dirty, stapled cone of paper.

He drops it on the desk.

FLANAGAN slides it toward himself, uncurling the pages against the tabletop as he goes, hands trembling delicately ...)

FLANAGAN (cont'd.)

... "James"—

JAMES

What.

FLANAGAN

—your titular character—do you find that word amusing, Mr. Doyle?

JAMES

(Smirking still; he looks away.)

...

FLANAGAN

—James is more a cipher than a boy, isn't he?—more your Steve Dedalus, which is more *Ulysses* than *Dubliners* / any day—

JAMES

I've read *Ulysses.*

FLANAGAN

Have you?, that's special. *(Thumbing through pages:)*

Stephen—"James," sorry—goes to Scarsdale Public High School ... hates school ... has an English teacher—this is rare—named "Mr. Flyswatter."

(He looks up.)

JAMES

...

(FLANAGAN pretends to swat a fly upon his desk.

He smiles; hides teeth; looking back to story:)

FLANAGAN

... Flyswatter wears brown suits. Every day. "Like a mortician" ... *(Up again:)*

Morticians wear black, Mr. Doyle: the better to hide the blood, I think.

JAMES

...

FLANAGAN

(Rolls the story shut.)

—Let's stop playing games now, shall we?

JAMES

... I'm not playing a / game—

FLANAGAN

Who's "Flyswatter" then? You whipped him up out of your what, your / imagination?

JAMES

(Shrugs.)

Maybe.

FLANAGAN

(Reads.)

" ... a pretentious accent, half-English, half-Irish, all Nothing ... "

JAMES

...

FLANAGAN

" ... the hands of a spinster and the eyes of a lecher ... "

JAMES

(The window, again.)

...

FLANAGAN

... ?

JAMES

It's not you.

FLANAGAN

That's a relief, my wife will be glad of it ... *(Skimming again:)*

... Teaches Honors English twelfth grade, Joyce Faulkner and Virginia Woolf ... lives alone in a garret above a shoe factory in the Bronx—this is all quite funny, Mr. Doyle, *very* creative! —How Dickensian! —Have you ever even *been* to the Bronx, my boy ... ?

—And what are these decomposing shoes on page one supposed to be a symbol of?, impotence? ... Harms your case of lechery, I'd wager.

—Whatever could you find funny in what I'm saying?

JAMES

I'm not / laughing—

FLANAGAN

(Almost smiling too.)

Yes you most certainly / are—

JAMES

I'm just—

FLANAGAN

What:

JAMES

—nervous. I guess.

FLANAGAN

Good. *(He turns to a specific page:)* —And the worst part, Mr. Doyle ... the worst thing you could have possibly said about me is right here in your story on page sixteen I believe into seventeen where you describe Mr. Flyswatter's "internally treasured"—your phrase—memory of his dead uncle ... The very same memory I shared with you and the class in a story of my own only a week ago today.

JAMES

...

FLANAGAN

... Now you know, James, I like to complete these assignments in advance of the students. It gives me great sense of sympathy. Not all teachers would risk losing face so. But if I am going to ask my students to bare their souls, I shall bare mine first.

So when I thought to write about a hero, the first person I thought of was my uncle, who died in the Second World War, at the age of eighteen; and I hold this memory of him quite dear to me.

—And you have stolen that memory and put it in your story in the old and addled brain of "Mr. Flyswatter," trumping up disgusting if not *incestuous* innuendo—

JAMES

It was in there already.

FLANAGAN

... ?

JAMES

The story you read in class: it had "innuendo" in it.

FLANAGAN

... My dear boy ... I don't pretend to understand what it is you think / you're saying—

JAMES

You went camping with your uncle. You were twelve, you fell asleep. When you woke up it was late and the moon was full and you looked down from the "dying fire to the water's edge"—your sentence—and you saw him stripping off his clothes ... The surface of the water was like a mirror. And he "slipped his body through."

FLANAGAN

...

JAMES

I didn't add anything to / your story—

FLANAGAN

(Astonished; confused.)

—That was a memory of his death—a *premonition* of it— !

JAMES

...

FLANAGAN

—Do you know anyone who's died, Mr. Doyle ... ?

JAMES

—I thought it was beautiful.

FLANAGAN

...

JAMES

That's why I stole it ...

FLANAGAN

... So you / admit—

JAMES

I took it, but—Flyswatter isn't you: it's a story.

FLANAGAN

(Recovering, somewhat.)

... Let's pretend then, for a moment, for the sake of argument—let's say this story which will on page sixteen into seventeen devolve into something quite dark and then page twenty-five, I believe, is it?, darker still—let's pretend for the time being that your story is as you say "just a story." It has nothing whatever to do with either you or / me.

JAMES

Fine.

FLANAGAN

Fine: plot.

JAMES

What?

FLANAGAN

—Exactly! —Where's your plot, my boy? Throw theme out the window—what's really going on here?

JAMES

I don't know—

FLANAGAN

—The eternal rejoinder!

JAMES

—I can't spew it out just like that—it's *complicated*—

FLANAGAN

Life is complicated— !

JAMES

—*Exactly*— !

FLANAGAN

—You're afraid of making sense? Are you? Don't you want to be understood?

JAMES

—I don't care who gets it—okay? I don't care if it "makes sense" to everyone in the entire fucking world—I'm not *writing* for them.

FLANAGAN

—Who's "them"?, your readers? —There won't be any readers, Saint James, until you *start making sense* ... !

JAMES

...

FLANAGAN

So tell me: I want to know: what's *really* going on here ... ?

JAMES

...

FLANAGAN

—This follows this follows—

JAMES

No.

FLANAGAN

"No."

Why not:

JAMES

I don't want / to.

FLANAGAN

—You don't want to or you don't know how / to?

JAMES

I know how—

FLANAGAN

—Then why won't you— ?

JAMES

—I don't even have to be here, you know—with the door closed—.

FLANAGAN

...

JAMES

(The window.)

...

FLANAGAN

(Suddenly quite gentle.)

... I'm confused ...

That's all; I'm your reader, and you've got me wondering. And lost; lost and wandering in a darkness of your own making. And I need to know what all this darkness is for ...

JAMES

...

FLANAGAN

(Waiting.)

... ?

JAMES

... There's this guy—

FLANAGAN

A boy: how old is he?

JAMES

Seventeen. He lives with his mother.

FLANAGAN

—Where's his father?

JAMES

Gone.

FLANAGAN

Does he have a / father?

JAMES

He did at one time ...

FLANAGAN

But not anymore ... Is he dead?

JAMES

He could be.

And it's winter—in the story—the beginning of winter, like now—and it reminds the boy of another winter when his father abused him.

FLANAGAN

...

JAMES

...

FLANAGAN

And the boy remembers this abuse—in the story? —He remembers it in graphic detail— ?

JAMES

That's the / idea ...

FLANAGAN

—But, you see, this is where I get lost, James—this is precisely where I can go no further with you: I understand he has this memory—we all have these memories—but do we need to see them in such *graphic* detail ... ?

JAMES

Who's "we"?

FLANAGAN

The readers.

JAMES

I have readers now?

FLANAGAN

Why not?

JAMES

—Absolutely.

FLANAGAN

Absolutely / what?

JAMES

You need to see the memory in such graphic detail.

FLANAGAN

Why ... ?

JAMES

It's more honest that way.

FLANAGAN

My dear boy, do you know what "fiction" means ... ? *(Smiles, failing to cover teeth:)*

There are ugly things in life. No one will quarrel you that point: people—children are hurt ...

But it is not the business of art to replicate the ugliness of life.

JAMES

Hold a mirror up to life.

FLANAGAN

...

JAMES

That's *Hamlet.*

FLANAGAN

Thank you ... But you should know that Shakespeare said a lot of stupid things. He's like the Bible that way. —And the Devil can cite scripture for his own purpose.

JAMES

...

FLANAGAN

That's *Merchant of Venice.*

Now: mirrors notwithstanding, this story, like all your stories, is a lie—wait, yes, *you are lying,* because you don't yet know what it is you ought to be writing about! You're borrowing other tragedies—other people's suffering, out the newspaper, off TV—simply because, and I hope you don't mind me saying but it's painfully obvious to anyone who cares to see, that you don't want to write about yourself because you have nothing yet to write about!

JAMES

—How do you know I don't have anything to write about?

FLANAGAN

Well do you?

JAMES

...

FLANAGAN

Do you, James ... ?

JAMES

(The window.)

...

FLANAGAN

(Slumps slowly back in his chair; sighs.)

...

JAMES

... Can I turn a light on in / here?

FLANAGAN

No ...

JAMES

...

FLANAGAN

... I find this time of day, this time of year ... the shortest day of the year ... it's very *sad*, isn't it ...

—And beautiful ...

I find sad things quite beautiful, don't you?

JAMES

...

FLANAGAN

—So the boy lives with his mother—

JAMES

Forget it—

FLANAGAN

—it's winter—

JAMES

I don't want to talk about it / anymore—

FLANAGAN

No no no no please!—this boy remembers—the abuse at the hands of a father is remembered by "Saint James" in graphic detail—*(Flipping through pages.)*

—Now where are we now?, in the story?

JAMES

I have soccer practice.

FLANAGAN

Soccer season's over, Mr. Doyle, even I know that ...

JAMES

...

FLANAGAN

(Flipping through pages, he murmurs.)

... and by way of Howth Castle and Environs ...

JAMES

(Quietly.)

... What are you even / *talking* about?

FLANAGAN

—we come to the climactic confrontation between Flanagan and James.

JAMES

—You said Flanagan.

FLANAGAN

Did I? imagine that ...

I look down at the page in question: page twenty-five stoneface of text no paragraphs quotes one breathless interminable *("sentence"; he breathes.)*—

I don't understand a word of this.

JAMES

How many times have you read it?

FLANAGAN

(Exploding.)

—You're arrogant, you're conceited, you hate your father *terrifically*— ! It's *lovely*, really ... !

JAMES

...

FLANAGAN

(Calmly, eyes back in the page, as if posing a normal question.)

Why does James kill his teacher, do you think?

JAMES

...

FLANAGAN

On page twenty-five—no, twenty-six, here: he kills him with a gun, I presume—it's / unclear.

JAMES

It's a handgun.

FLANAGAN

... And where does he / get this— ?

JAMES

It's his father's.

FLANAGAN

—His father's around?

JAMES

Sometimes.

FLANAGAN

Why does his father have a gun?

JAMES

His father has lots of guns: because his father is a cop.

FLANAGAN

An Episcopal cop ... ?

JAMES

...

FLANAGAN

And where does he keep this gun?—James:

When he comes to see his teacher in the office after school; does he keep the gun in his jacket ... ?

JAMES

It's in his bag. With his books.

FLANAGAN

...

JAMES

...

FLANAGAN

May I see it, please ... ?

(JAMES hesitates, leans forward, unzips the bag at his feet, digs around, comes up with a handgun.

He lays it gently on the desk between them.)

FLANAGAN (cont'd.)

(Rubbing his face.)

...

(JAMES sits back calmly, breathlessly, eyes on the gun.)

FLANAGAN (cont'd.)

... What are we going to do about this, James ... ?

JAMES

... I don't know ...

FLANAGAN

You don't—.

JAMES

...

FLANAGAN

... Would you like to kill me ... ?
—I ask you that in all sincerity—

JAMES

(Shrugs.)

Sure.

FLANAGAN

Why?

JAMES

Because you hate me. You hate all your students. Especially the boys.

(JAMES turns his gaze to the window.

FLANAGAN is speechless, shaken ...

After a moment:)

JAMES (cont'd.)

I've got to go—

(He stands abruptly and reaches for the gun on the desk.

—But FLANAGAN is quicker: he takes the gun first.)

FLANAGAN

(Still seated.)

I'm sorry I can't let you have / that—

JAMES

It's my father's / gun—

FLANAGAN

—I can't give it back to you / now, James—

JAMES

I promise / I won't use it—

FLANAGAN

(Hugging the gun to himself.)

—I'm sorry James but my hands are tied— !

(For a moment it looks like JAMES might cry.

Then as if he might try to wrest the gun from FLANAGAN.

But just as quickly he's become disinterested ...

He opens the office door.)

FLANAGAN (cont'd.)

... James?

(The boy turns around.)

FLANAGAN (cont'd.)

(Changing his mind.)

Will you turn the light on as you go ... ?

(JAMES does so, as he exits.

FLANAGAN sits, breathing, gun in hand.)

2.

(Scarecrow thin, strawhaired and redbearded, bespectacled [his beard is much too neat]; an Oxford-style, pinstriped shirt beneath maroon or red suspenders; his hands are small and childlike; when he speaks he belies the softest Southern drawl, his keen gray eyes in the audience almost always, ranging, merciless:)

RICHARD

(Shaking his head.)

... Whatever were you thinking, James?

FLANAGAN

(Somewhere else entirely.)

...

(A party at a bar in the city, a few hours later.

Music and conversation, though we can't hear it.

A table behind the two standing men.)

RICHARD

... James?

FLANAGAN

... ?

RICHARD

What*ever* could you *possibly* have been thinking ... ?

FLANAGAN

(Tall glass of water with a large lemon slice.)

About what, Richard?

RICHARD

(Gin and tonic, drinking liberally, one in each hand.)

Charles.

FLANAGAN

What about Charles / exactly?

RICHARD

Couldn't you tell when you hired him he's a drug addict?

FLANAGAN

(A hesitation.)

He hasn't had a problem in years, he's a very *gifted* / teacher—

RICHARD

Well he's coked up tonight—that's all I'm saying. Have you seen ... ? Diane's doing damage control like it's 1978—hi there, Diane! Happy Chanukah, dear! —*Love* those shoes!

FLANAGAN

(One hand in his suit jacket pocket; he lifts his glass to:)

Diane.

RICHARD

It's embarrassing; that's all I'm saying ...

FLANAGAN

I haven't noticed anything / amiss—

RICHARD

He's trapped; he can't see it now but that's how it is: suicide—a form of it, addiction. —You look faboo, Charles! —*Sha-zah!*

FLANAGAN

(Raises his glass; a nod to:)

Chuck ...

RICHARD

(Smiling through it all.)

... I feel sorry for him ... That's *all* I'm saying ...

FLANAGAN

...

RICHARD

—I feel sorry for *all* of them.

FLANAGAN

Whom, Richard ... ?

RICHARD

The new ones, mainly ... *Elise* ... They have no idea what they're really in for.

FLANAGAN

Who's Elise?

RICHARD

You know Elise.

FLANAGAN

No, I don't think / I do.

RICHARD

You hired her, James.

FLANAGAN

Did I ... ?

Well that doesn't mean I know her, does it? *(A pretense of a chuckle.)* You don't mean Ms. Sanger, do / you ... ?

RICHARD

Where is she?, she promised me she'd be here ...

(His eyes survey the room; he sips from one of his two drinks.)

FLANAGAN

... Richard, I'd like to tell you something: something—*happened* to me / today—

RICHARD

Have you heard about Fritz ... ?

FLANAGAN

Fritz.

RICHARD

DeLong. —Isn't that the most *perfect* name ... ? Liz says he used to be an underwear model. *(Smiles.)* Who knows, maybe I've bought his brand before; maybe I'm wearing him right now. —Evening, Fritz! Happy holidays, 'hon ...

(His gaze follows wherever Fritz goes ...)

FLANAGAN

(The glass, the nod to:)

Fritz.

RICHARD

(Smiling still.)

... It's so damned hypocritical, that's all I'm saying ...

FLANAGAN

Modeling underwear?

RICHARD

(Missing this.)

We see each other every day, every God damned day for nine months out of every twelve, but we only ever really *talk* to each other—*really* talk to one another—honestly, out of school, like this, at a bar, in the city, like normal human *people*—what, once a year ... ? *Maybe?* Tonight ... ?

FLANAGAN

I suppose it's somewhat hypocritical, Richard; that depends on your definition of hypocrisy—

RICHARD

Nobody cares! That's all I'm saying: nobody ever really gives one good God damn shit about anyone else—not *really*—no matter how long we've *worked* together—nobody here really *likes* each other ...

That's a problem ...

Don't you think?

(He drinks.)

FLANAGAN

I like you, Richard.

RICHARD

Do you? That's good.

FLANAGAN

(Slyly, kindly.)

On occasion.

RICHARD

... Well thank you, James ... Thank you. *(He looks at him.)* That surely means the world to me ...

(He drinks some more.

And starts in upon his second glass.)

FLANAGAN

Will you go to Sewanee for Christmas ... ?

RICHARD

Can't face it—the South, of course, but my parents in particular. —I know I should be grateful they're still here, but ...

FLANAGAN

...

RICHARD

—You know: they don't even look at me with pity, or fear, like everyone else. They don't even *look* at me ...

... They used to call him my "friend" ... "How's your friend's health?" ... I think they're relieved they don't have to ask anymore ...

(He smiles; drinks.)

FLANAGAN

(His water.)

...

RICHARD

... And they're both so God damned old it's sick ...

FLANAGAN

Will you be alone, then ... ?

RICHARD

(Darkly.)

Don't worry about me, James, I'll survive. *(Drinks.)*

FLANAGAN

Because you can come to my place, if you'd like. For Christmas Day.

RICHARD

(Astonished.)

...

FLANAGAN

Would you like that?

RICHARD

James ...

FLANAGAN

... ?

RICHARD

You've never invited me to your place / before ...

FLANAGAN

—I know, but—

RICHARD

I didn't even think you had a "place." —Or if you did have a place I just sort of assumed you kept some kind of dark, oleaginous secret locked away in there ...

FLANAGAN

I don't think I even know what that word means, "oleaginous" ...

RICHARD

James! I'm surprised: it's "oily"—slimy, to you. And don't try changing the subject on me:

I'm *flattered* ...

FLANAGAN

Just think about it, that's all ...

RICHARD

—Why?

Why this sudden, random act of kindness ... ?

FLANAGAN

It's a depressing time of year for everyone, Richard. —Why just this afternoon I had an experience with a student of mine—

RICHARD

James Doyle: I saw him go into your office ...

FLANAGAN

(Continuing.)

Yes; and—

RICHARD

Cute kid—very tortured look: just my type ...

(He drinks.)

FLANAGAN

Yes. Well; I wouldn't know anything about that but—he did something / quite shocking—

RICHARD

(Spilling some.)

—I'm just so God damned *sick* of it all! —That's all I'm saying, James ...

FLANAGAN

(Alarmed.)

Sick of *what*, Richard ... ?

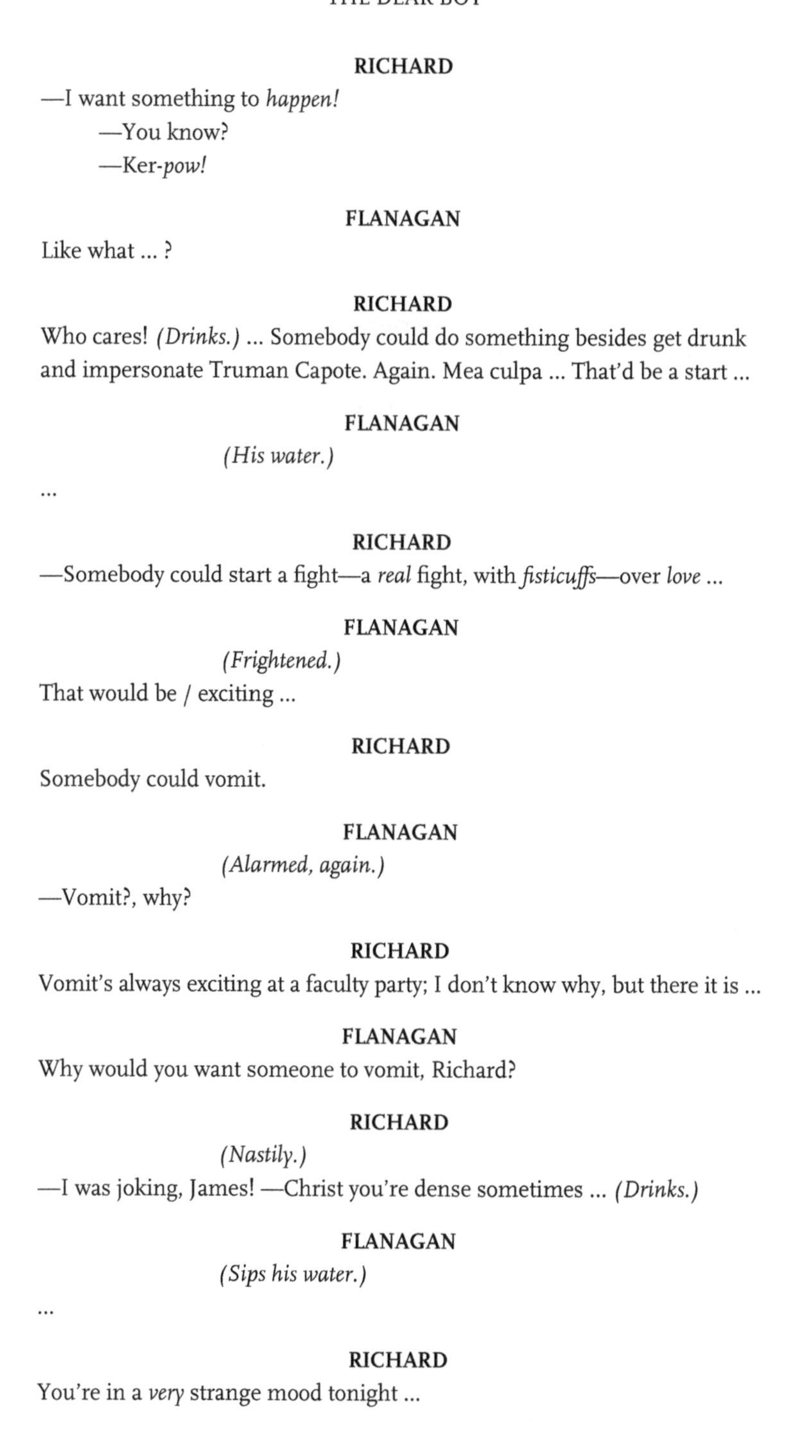

RICHARD

—I want something to *happen!*
—You know?
—Ker-*pow!*

FLANAGAN

Like what ... ?

RICHARD

Who cares! *(Drinks.)* ... Somebody could do something besides get drunk and impersonate Truman Capote. Again. Mea culpa ... That'd be a start ...

FLANAGAN

(His water.)

...

RICHARD

—Somebody could start a fight—a *real* fight, with *fisticuffs*—over *love* ...

FLANAGAN

(Frightened.)

That would be / exciting ...

RICHARD

Somebody could vomit.

FLANAGAN

(Alarmed, again.)

—Vomit?, why?

RICHARD

Vomit's always exciting at a faculty party; I don't know why, but there it is ...

FLANAGAN

Why would you want someone to vomit, Richard?

RICHARD

(Nastily.)

—I was joking, James! —Christ you're dense sometimes ... *(Drinks.)*

FLANAGAN

(Sips his water.)

...

RICHARD

You're in a *very* strange mood tonight ...

FLANAGAN

I'm in a strange / mood ... ?

RICHARD

I've been trying to provoke a response from you the past fifteen minutes.

FLANAGAN

Have you?

RICHARD

Yes; you don't think I was talking just to hear myself talk, do you?

FLANAGAN

The thought had crossed my mind ...

RICHARD

(Stung.)

James—.

FLANAGAN

I've had a rather difficult day today, Richard ...
You see / that boy—

RICHARD

Is Charles guilting you? Is he putting pressure on you? —Christ Jesus, everything has to be a martyrdom with that man. —*I'm* the better teacher; I *love* to teach; I love children. He wants to be a novelist or some such bullshit ... but—*I'm* committed, *I* give of myself, day in, day out—I'm the supervisor on five extracurricular activities this year—*five!*—including our nationally award-winning literary magazine, *Idée Fixe*, thank you very much. While he assists—*assists*, mind you—girls J.V. field hockey, and I think we both know where that's all going to end up—.

FLANAGAN

(Sips.)

...

RICHARD

(Some composure now.)

... I've given my whole life to this school ...

FLANAGAN

I know that, Richard ...

RICHARD

(Looks at him.)

—Do you?

FLANAGAN

...

RICHARD

That's good ... *(He drinks. Quieter:)*

... It's his wife, anyhow: she's the one with the Ferdinand-and-Isabella Complex: Chair in English and a Chair in Spanish, push out all the Jews and Moors. —Well, she's Jewish, but you know what I'm saying ... *(His eyes:)* See those shoes?, red leather high-tops ... ? *Really?* ... She must've bought them special for the occasion. They make her look like a diabetic elf ...

FLANAGAN

A what?

RICHARD

Well *look* at her ... !

FLANAGAN

(He sips his water some more.)

...

RICHARD

(Breathes heavily: a sigh.)

...

FLANAGAN

... You've got nothing to worry about, Richard.

RICHARD

(Won't look at him.)

...

FLANAGAN

I've made my decision ...

RICHARD

Have you? That's good ...

FLANAGAN

You know how I feel about the situation.

RICHARD

So it's a "situation" now ... ?

FLANAGAN

I don't like to keep secrets from you—

RICHARD

—And I'm grateful for that, James. —Grateful, for our many confidences over the years—

FLANAGAN

But I can't announce anything until I've received approval from the Board.

RICHARD

... "The Board."

FLANAGAN

The Board of / Education—

RICHARD

I know who the fucking "Board" is, James ...

FLANAGAN

...

RICHARD

—You said it was a done deal: you said it was your / call entirely—

FLANAGAN

It *is* a done deal, but I don't want to step on any toes—

RICHARD

—For Christ's sake James step on a few toes!—for *once* in your *careful* little life! *(Recovers:)* Hi Liz, happy Kwanza. Is she Pakistani ... ?

FLANAGAN

... I don't see why you're so angry / with me ...

RICHARD

I'm not angry, James. I'm not. —Do I seem angry to you?

FLANAGAN

...

RICHARD

You're leaving ... You're leaving this—*graveyard* behind—

FLANAGAN

(Put off.)

You think / our school is like a graveyard ... ?

RICHARD

(Continuing.)

—who cares what anybody *thinks*?

FLANAGAN

(Sips his water.)

...

RICHARD

Make a *statement* of some kind ... !

FLANAGAN

(Short.)

Yes; I certainly should ...

(He puts his hand in his suit jacket pocket ...)

RICHARD

(Drinks.)

...

FLANAGAN

(His pocket.)

Do you really find me too careful?

RICHARD

(Sighs.)

... James—

FLANAGAN

Is that what you— ? You said: I don't step on any / toes—

RICHARD

I'm sorry I said anything about you—I can't handle this / right now—

FLANAGAN

—You think I've been too careful—in my life—. You've *always* thought that about me—

RICHARD

—Let's not talk about what I may or may not have always thought about you.

—Okay?

—Not everything's *about* you, James ...

Let's just forget everything I said ...

FLANAGAN

(His water.)

...

(Enter ELISE: young, petite, kinetic; a pretty round face and long black hair; a Jewess-hippie-intellectual in a shortish skirt, sexy high heels; some make-up, dramatic eyes, lightly perfumed; she carries a Manhattan in her small white hand:)

ELISE

(An apology.)

I'm late.

RICHARD

Does the father know?

ELISE

(A joke?)

... ?

RICHARD

I'm joking: about your period.

ELISE

You're just jealous I get them.

RICHARD

(Pleasantly.)

Cow.

ELISE

Queen. —What time did you get here?

RICHARD

Darling, I'm *always* here ... *(He drinks.)*

ELISE

I had some trouble getting here. *(Smiles; eyes dart to FLANAGAN, and away.)* I always have trouble getting places. On time. —I took the wrong subway—

RICHARD

Don't you know the subways by now?

ELISE

Yes ...

—I mean, I know the subway to Grand Central like the back of my hand—

RICHARD

Cliché.

ELISE

(For FLANAGAN; without looking.)

—We have this thing; it's a game: he says I use clichéd expressions too much ...

RICHARD

You do.

ELISE

(He's right.)

Anyway, I ended up in Harlem.

RICHARD

—My God; when?

ELISE

Just now. Tonight.

RICHARD

O no dear you don't want to end up there ...

ELISE

They were really very helpful, though.

RICHARD

Who was, dear?

ELISE

... ?

RICHARD

Who was really very helpful to you?

ELISE

The African-Americans.

RICHARD

I know, it's a mouthful to say, isn't it ...

ELISE

And this really very elderly African-American woman turned me right around on the platform and put me back on the downtown express:

"This ain't yo' stop," she said.

Isn't that *amazing* ... ?

FLANAGAN

Quite.

ELISE

—In this day and age ... ?

RICHARD

They're just as afraid of you as you are of them, the African-Americans. Small Jewish-American girls frighten them most ...

(She smiles briefly at FLANAGAN.)

RICHARD (cont'd.)

You two know each other, don't you?
... No?
Elise, this is James / Flanagan—

ELISE

We know each other, Richard ...

RICHARD

Are you certain ... ?

FLANAGAN

—Yes; I believe I hired Ms. Sanger nearly six months ago.

ELISE

—Has it been that long ... ?

RICHARD

—I know, doesn't time just *slay* you?

FLANAGAN

(Gallant & stiff, he offers her his hand.)

How do you do, Ms. Sanger?

(She takes it.

With her other hand, she waves away his formality:)

ELISE

You can just call me "Elise."

FLANAGAN

(His hearing, perhaps.)

... ?

ELISE

Elise! —I'm only twenty-nine ...

FLANAGAN

Are you? Congratulations!

ELISE

What for ... ?

RICHARD

—That's her age, James: she's saying she's too young for "Ms."

FLANAGAN

O ... Well you don't look very much like a "Ms." anyway, Ms. Sanger. —You're much too fetching in that skirt! *(He laughs, lips tight.)*

ELISE

Thank you—. *(To RICHARD:)* I think ...

FLANAGAN

(Sips water, lifts eyebrows at his own humor.)

... !

ELISE

... Where's your tie, Mr. Flanagan?

FLANAGAN

(Hand to neck; another joke?)

O—my— ? —It's gone!

ELISE

(Smiling, charitably.)

I've never seen you without one before ...

FLANAGAN

I know, but you see: I took it off.

I suppose you could say I felt like a change tonight—a change of—*wardrobe!*

RICHARD

(Drinks deeply; says softly.)

... Good Christ ...

ELISE

Well you look very handsome tonight without it, Mr. Flanagan.

FLANAGAN

—There's no very good reason not to call me "James," Ms. Sanger, is there?

ELISE

Okay: *(She smiles.)* "James." —And you can—call me Elise.

FLANAGAN

I know.

ELISE

—What do you know ... ?

FLANAGAN

You've already instructed me as such, haven't you—to call you "Elise," Elise.

ELISE

Have I? —"instructed" you ... ?
You're *very* funny ...

FLANAGAN

... Does that surprise you?

ELISE

Yes. It does.

RICHARD

... This is really very sweet, Elise: you've drawn him out of his shell.

ELISE

—Cliché.

RICHARD

Touché. —I was testing you / anyway ...

FLANAGAN

(Butting in.)

—Yes!, it certainly is silly, how "careful" I've been, always wearing my tie ... around my neck ... But have no fear, it's not far off, my tie: *(He pats it.)*— it's right here in my suit jacket pocket ... !
And I've still got my brown suit! *(Another joke?)*

RICHARD

(Sighs; drinks.)

...

ELISE

(Smiles, but looks to RICHARD again for help.)

I'm sorry ... I—don't think I / get that.

FLANAGAN

—I am still wearing my brown-on-brown *(A la the French:) ensemble!*

RICHARD

—He's feeling very sorry for himself, that's all ...

FLANAGAN

I'm feeling very *funny* tonight, that's all it is, Richard!—strange and funny and—*anything* could happen! *(Imagining castanets in his hands:)* —Cha-cha!

RICHARD

(Ignoring him; to ELISE:)

You look sluttish tonight ...

ELISE

And you look depressed; as usual ...

RICHARD

It's true ... You know I've lost five pounds this month?

ELISE

...

RICHARD

It's the stress ...

ELISE

(Relieved.)

—O; I know—all those *papers*: why do we make them *write* so much?

RICHARD

I don't mind that; I like grading: it makes me feel smart.

No, it's the pressure—you know, *change*, in the department ... I don't handle change well ...

FLANAGAN

Yes, but he does like vomit!

RICHARD

...

ELISE

(Looks between them, almost laughing.)

... Have I missed something between you / two?

FLANAGAN

He likes to see high school teachers vomit! —*Cha-cha!*

RICHARD

At parties ...

FLANAGAN

—Yes, at *parties!*

RICHARD

... He's angry with me about something, I don't / know what—

FLANAGAN

I'm not angry, *Dick!* I'm really not!

ELISE

You're not going to lose your job, Richard, if that's what you're worried about. Is that what you're worried about?

RICHARD

I don't know—what do you think I'm worried about, Elise?

ELISE

You're tenured; you're here for life.

—Isn't that right, James?

FLANAGAN

Right-o, Elise ... !

ELISE

And besides, James isn't retiring for another six months—

RICHARD

—Yes. But change must be in place ... And as you well know, Elise, there are rumors floating about that the Chair of English may very well go to Charles. To Chuck. To Chaz. Because he is a married man. Because "the Board" likes their men hitched. —Or confirmed in their bachelorhood at least—right, James?

FLANAGAN

(Sips water.)

...

ELISE

...

RICHARD

(His second drink is empty now.)

—Who's ready for more?, I am ...

ELISE

I'll go—

RICHARD

No no I'm going—*(He takes her glass.)*—you see?, I'm gone ...
(He turns back:)

What are you having?

ELISE

Manhattan, please.

RICHARD

Of course you are—cliché!

(He's gone.

A *moment here of "What to say ... ?")*

FLANAGAN

(Smiles; hides teeth.)

...

ELISE

... Are you sure you don't want a drink?

FLANAGAN

No thank you: I'm an alcoholic.

ELISE

... O.

FLANAGAN

Thank you, though. *(Smiles; teeth.)*

ELISE

Sorry.

FLANAGAN

—Why ... ?

ELISE

I should've guessed.

FLANAGAN

Could you have ... ?

ELISE

... ?

FLANAGAN

Could you have guessed that about me? That I'm alcoholic?

ELISE

... Well; you're not drinking; you're drinking a very large glass of water, with a rather large slice of lemon. I noticed. —I'm drunk myself— *(She laughs.)*—a *little,* drunk—. —I had this party I had to go to, out in Brooklyn? It's the last night of Chanukah / and—

FLANAGAN

(Interested.)

Is it?

ELISE

Yes.

FLANAGAN

(With great sincerity.)

How wonderful for you!

ELISE

(Smiles.)

... Really? You think so ... ?

FLANAGAN

And what happens on this the very last night of Chanukah, Ms. Sanger?

ELISE

... I'm not sure I understand what you're / asking me—

FLANAGAN

Is there something very *special* that's meant to occur on this, the very last night of Chanukah, the Festival of Lights? *(Smiles tightly; waits for her answer:)*

ELISE

... No. Not really.

FLANAGAN

Ah.

ELISE

—We light a candle. The last candle—of eight. —We can spin a dreidel if we want—are you making fun of me?

FLANAGAN

—No!

ELISE

I'm—. Okay. —You're not making fun of me just a / little bit?

FLANAGAN

—God, no! —I *adore* the Jewish people!

ELISE

...

(Another terrifically awkward moment passes here ...)

FLANAGAN

Have you seen Diane's sneakers? Diabetic elf.

ELISE

(Laughs—too loudly.)

—Excuse me?

FLANAGAN

She looks like a pixie with diabetes. Don't you think? Because she's rather heavy.

ELISE

—That's terrible!

FLANAGAN

Terrible but true ...

ELISE

... I had no *idea* you were funny, Mr. Flanagan ...

(He smiles painfully, lips tight.)

ELISE (cont'd.)

(She smiles back at him.)

...

FLANAGAN

(His eyebrows, again; sips his water.)

...

ELISE

Would you like to sit / down?

FLANAGAN

—No.

ELISE

O—

FLANAGAN

—I'd rather not, you see.

ELISE

That's / fine ...

FLANAGAN

—I've been sitting all day, you see ...

ELISE

I see.

FLANAGAN

—But you may, of course—sit—if you'd prefer ...

ELISE

... I do prefer. Thanks.

(She sits.

A moment; then:)

FLANAGAN

And now, I think I will join you ...

(He sits too.

She smiles a bit confusedly at him.

He smiles and hides his teeth.

She kicks off one of her heels, absentmindedly; begins jangling her foot beneath the table ...)

ELISE

I wasn't going to come tonight ...

FLANAGAN

—Why on earth not?

ELISE

Didn't think I'd have much "fun," I guess. I mean—can I tell you this? I don't think that I really belong here ... with these people. You know? And none of them really like me very much. They *resent* me somehow. I don't know why ... Even Richard doesn't like me—he likes to make fun of me. He's my friend, but—.

Look at them all ... They're all such incredible *losers* ... And I mean that in the kindest way possible ... Trying to talk, drinking *a lot*—some of them even think they can dance; which they can't ... Poor souls ... It's all so unbearably sad ...

... They all have that rusty, dusty, musty-dirty-earth-thing going on—don't they?—that look they get ... ? I don't know what—"geraniums"—that's what they're like ... *yeah* ... *(She smiles to herself.)* ... Teachers are like really very old geraniums ... —And it's not so much that whole dirt-thing because that would be far too "outside," far too healthy a connotation, but—: Teachers are like plants that have not been watered in a very long time ... —And you know how they get, these house plants, that have not been watered: they slowly, inexorably, *die.* —They desiccate and they *die.* —But for a long time they still *look* alive. Until you touch them, and then *(A crumbling sound.)—ffsssssssst ...*

FLANAGAN

(He waters himself: i.e., sips.)

...

ELISE

I wasn't talking about you, you know.

FLANAGAN

(As if with nonchalance.)

... Do you know that a student tried to shoot me today?

(She puts her shoe back on.)

ELISE

You're joking.

FLANAGAN

No: a student tried to shoot me, with a handgun. —He wanted to anyway: he didn't fire the gun / obviously.

ELISE

O my God—*(Laughs, covers mouth.)*—I'm sorry.

FLANAGAN

—Yes, it's surprising, isn't it?—at *our* school ...

ELISE

—Did you call the police?

FLANAGAN

Of course not.

ELISE

Why not?

FLANAGAN

—I don't want to get him in trouble, I suppose—.

ELISE

He had a gun, James—he brought a gun to school—

FLANAGAN

In his rucksack, yes.

ELISE

In his what?

FLANAGAN

Rucksack.

ELISE

Did he take it out of this "rucksack" of his?

FLANAGAN

Of course he did; that's how I knew he / had it.

ELISE

—And he pointed it at you.

FLANAGAN

He placed it on the table between us ...
He was testing me somehow ...

ELISE

And then what happened?

FLANAGAN

He told me—he said he thought I hated him. —That I hated all my students. —Which is of course patently untrue ...

ELISE

...

FLANAGAN

And then he looked as if he might cry ...
—And then he left.

ELISE

My God ...

FLANAGAN

Indeed.

ELISE

Why doesn't stuff like that happen to me?

FLANAGAN

—I beg your pardon?

ELISE

You *know?*

FLANAGAN

(An offended tone.)

Ms. Sanger:

ELISE

I know, but you know what I'm / saying ...

FLANAGAN

—I hardly think / you should—

ELISE

I *know* but—it's *exciting*, right?
—Who is it?

FLANAGAN

I don't think I should be telling you / this ...

ELISE

—What if I have him in one of my classes?

FLANAGAN

He's a senior.

ELISE

So?

FLANAGAN

If you don't have him now you won't have / him ever—

ELISE

—How do I *know* I don't have / him now?

FLANAGAN

—You can't have him now because he's mine!

ELISE

...

FLANAGAN

—He's *my* student ...

ELISE

... You can't let him get away with it ... It's a call for—a cry—. I mean, he could shoot someone else. He could shoot himself.

FLANAGAN

O no he won't do that.

ELISE

—Why not?

FLANAGAN

Because I have the gun.

(He smiles, a bit wildly, shows teeth.

She smiles too.

He leans in conspiratorially:)

FLANAGAN (cont'd.)

... With me, right now; right here in my suit jacket pocket ... *(He pats his pocket proudly; whispers:)* ... wrapped inside my tie.

ELISE

...

(She reaches her hand out slowly, touches the gun through his suit jacket pocket ...

A moment, then:)

ELISE (cont'd.)

... How old are you, Mr. Flanagan?

FLANAGAN

Fifty-nine.

(She smiles; continues to watch him closely; brazenly.

He meets her gaze, her smile; he obstructs her view of his mouth.)

ELISE

Do you want to go someplace else with me?

(RICHARD returns.)

RICHARD

Manhattan for the Manhattanite—

ELISE

(Getting up.)

You can keep it: I'm going—

RICHARD

You just got here—

ELISE

I know.

RICHARD

—Are you going too?

FLANAGAN

(Standing also; bewildered.)

It looks that way, now doesn't it ... ?
—Is everything all right with you?

RICHARD

Of course ... Why wouldn't everything be *all right*, James? Is there a reason why something should be not *all right* / with me... ?

FLANAGAN

—We'll talk on Monday, okay?

RICHARD

Monday's Christmas Eve, James.

FLANAGAN

We'll talk after Christmas—we'll talk in the new / year.

RICHARD

(Quieter; pulling him aside.)

I wanted to talk to you tonight. —I *needed* to talk to you—.

ELISE

I'm going to go get my coat ...

(She's gone.)

RICHARD

She's a slut. She's my friend but—her boyfriend dumped her last summer. He was sleeping with a friend of theirs, and ever since she's been on some kind of rampage.

FLANAGAN

Richard—

RICHARD

She fucked Charles and Fritz—not at the same time but both in the very first month of school. It's pathetic. —I'm not your fairy godmother, James, but if I were you I'd wear a condom. —Assuming you get that far.

FLANAGAN

(Quietly.)

For Christ's sake / Richard—

RICHARD

You surprise me, James ... really, you do; I wouldn't think she'd be your type ...

FLANAGAN

—Is this about Charles? About the / Chair?

RICHARD

(Explodes.)

—I don't know yes *maybe it is about the fucking Chair— !*

FLANAGAN

All right / calm down—

RICHARD

—You can tell me, James. I'm not a child: everyone's talking. —I just heard Diane at the bar telling Liz they've been talking to Charles. Is that true?

FLANAGAN

...

RICHARD

We don't have to dance around it all night; we can tell each other what's really going on: if they don't want me they don't want me—they don't want me, do they?

FLANAGAN

No.

RICHARD

...

FLANAGAN

They do not want you, Richard. They do not want to give you the Chair.

RICHARD

Why?

FLANAGAN

You know why ...

RICHARD

I know but I want to hear you say it.

FLANAGAN

They're worried about the children.

RICHARD

...

FLANAGAN

Their concern is that / the children—

RICHARD

—I'm not contagious—

FLANAGAN

You know what it is I'm trying / to say—

RICHARD

—So I'm a pedophile now, too?

FLANAGAN

They're worried that the children might become—confused. —That it would be an *obstacle* to / their learning—

RICHARD

—I don't make a secret of it now, James—I'm teaching *now*—

FLANAGAN

That's right: you have tenure.

RICHARD

...

FLANAGAN

... Richard ... Things were different when you weren't *talking* about it so much ...

RICHARD

People were dying—people *are* /dying—

FLANAGAN

I understand about / all that—

RICHARD

—You'll talk to them, right? You'll convince them.

FLANAGAN

...

RICHARD

Unless you feel the same way.

(As ELISE returns with her coat:)

FLANAGAN

Let me help you on with that, Elise ... *(He does.)*

RICHARD

—Everyone! *(Clapping hands.)* —Everyone, listen up: Dick Purdy here in the Anguish Department. Mr. Flanagan and I would like to make a brief announcement. —Actually, I'm the one making the announcement, as you can see, because it's *about* our dear old Mr. Flanagan: he has a few problems with me. Always has. There are certain things he does not *like* about me, does not *approve* of entirely—and I think it's time we get this prejudice out in the open before the shit really hits the fan which it will once I sue. Which I will most certainly do. Once James—sorry, "the Board," gives the Chair of the department to our colleague here, Charles. —You've got something on your nose, Chuck—there, it's gone: —Mr. Charles Komisky, ladies and gentlemen!, our new Chair of the English Department ... Instead of me ... Though I have been here twice as long, and I care *deeply* about our students, their minds—and literature—not to mention *Idée Fixe*—thank you, thank you. —And why will Charles get the Chair? For no reason other than he is a straight white male and *I am most emphatically not.* Straight. As you all know. As some of you disapprove of. Or fear. Or *claim not to "understand"* ... Which is all very hypocritical given how many of our greatest writers have been gay, straight and all flavors in between: consider *Moby-Dick.* —But we must protect the children! says Mr. Flanagan, our patron saint of innocence. —We must *save* the children!—from *confusion!* They are not to understand the dark, oleaginous world of men; which means "slimy"; —whereas I dissent. And this is how I will teach them next year when Mr. Flanagan is gone, even though I will not be the Chair and I don't care if it gets me fired—there but for the grace of tenure go I—*I will teach the children everything there is to know about life!* Because they need to know. Whether they want to know or not. I will let them see for themselves that I, for example, am a homosexual, as they've *long* known. And I will let them know what it's like to *be* a homosexual, in this day and age, to be prejudiced against, to watch your friends and your loved ones—.

And Charles here the Chair will let them know what it's like to be addicted to a controlled substance. Namely cocaine. And married to a shrewish megalomaniac with disconcertingly boyish features. For example. —And Fritz, Fritz DeLong, wherever you are, and if that is your real name, you can tell them what it was like to be an underwear model during the halcyon days of the early- to mid-1980s. —And Liz here will clue us all in on how it feels to be racially ambiguous—right, Liz?

And Mr. Flanagan ...

What can our dear old Mr. Flanagan teach us all about life? I know he's leaving—right now—with Ms. Sanger—do y'all know Ms. Sanger?—say hello, Elise; now say goodbye. —But were he to stay on another year: what does Mr. Flanagan know about life? What has he *learned* from his sixty-five years on this earth? Well I don't know about you but I know a thing or two about him, and I don't know if any of you are going to believe this—it's *incredible*—

(With his free hand, and from out his suit jacket, FLANAGAN has removed the gun:)

FLANAGAN

Richard:

(RICHARD turns to see the gun drawn shakily in his face.)

FLANAGAN (cont'd.)

Not another word.

(Dark.)

3A.

(In darkness, climbing stairs, giddy and out of breath:)

ELISE

I can't believe what you did— !

FLANAGAN

I know but it felt so good— !

ELISE

—Did you see his face?

FLANAGAN

I've never seen him at a loss for words; I didn't think it possible—

ELISE

Everything stopped! Everyone just shut up!

FLANAGAN

We really should keep these guns in the classroom, don't you think?

ELISE

—Is it loaded?

FLANAGAN

You know, I haven't even / checked—

ELISE

—Don't look now!

(He cries out:)

FLANAGAN

— !

ELISE

Are you all right ... ?

(She reaches out, with her hand, to steady him in the dark ...)

FLANAGAN

I'm fine; I fell—I almost fell ...

(If we could see, we'd see him pull away from her.)

FLANAGAN (cont'd.)

... Is it always so dark inside your building?

ELISE

(The sound of keys; she's disappointed.)

It's not my building ...

(She opens the door; light grows:)

3B.

(Books everywhere, as if the walls are made of books.

A kitchen table, two chairs.

FLANAGAN heads straight for the books in the downstage "wall," head held horizontal to read the titles off the spines.)

ELISE

The people that live here are writers.

FLANAGAN

Are they? Where do they teach.

ELISE

They don't; they're poets. —They're both poets, believe it or not ...

FLANAGAN

How romantic ...

(She spills her keys across the tabletop.)

ELISE

... Do you want a drink?

FLANAGAN

(Looks up.)

... ?

ELISE

Sorry. I forgot.

FLANAGAN

—No actually I would.

I tell people I'm an alcoholic, you see, because it seems to put their minds at ease. —They expect it of me, somehow ... —While the truth is I simply prefer not to. *(He tries to laugh.)* Except on very special occasions.

ELISE

Is this a very special occasion ... ?

FLANAGAN

(Trying for suave.)

We shall see. —Won't we.

(She smiles—a little—moves to a cabinet or shelf.)

ELISE

Wine?, or Scotch?

FLANAGAN

Please.

ELISE

Which; both?

FLANAGAN

A glass of wine would be fine ...

—A *bottle* of wine would be *divine* ... !

ELISE

... I don't think I have a full bottle ...

FLANAGAN

I'm just being—humorous—.

Let me see here ...

(He studies the titles of the books.

She uncorks an already opened bottle of cheap Merlot, pours it into two shallow glasses.)

ELISE

(Bringing his glass to him.)

... I don't have any clean wine glasses ...

(He takes it.

She watches him awhile.)

ELISE (cont'd.)

(As if disappointed.)

... You weren't going to kill him, were you ...

FLANAGAN

Whom?

ELISE

Richard. He deserves it, you know ...

FLANAGAN

No; of course / I wasn't—

ELISE

You pulled a gun on him.

FLANAGAN

I wanted to frighten him, that's all—to shut him up.

ELISE

Why?

FLANAGAN

(The books, again.)

...

ELISE

(Flirtatiously.)

You're going to get in trouble ... You've done a very bad thing, Mr. Flanagan ... *(She smiles.)* You can not pull a gun in public and then just walk away. There'll be hell to pay come Monday.

FLANAGAN

Monday's Christmas Eve.

ELISE

You could be arrested.

FLANAGAN

—Let them do their worst / to me!

ELISE

They might look for you here, you know ...

FLANAGAN

(Trying for playful.)

Will they? Tonight?

ELISE

Maybe.

FLANAGAN

Do they know where we are?

ELISE

It's not hard to figure out.

FLANAGAN

—Do they know where you live?

ELISE

That's not hard to figure out either ...

(He contemplates his drink.)

FLANAGAN

Then we must hurry up, Ms. Sanger. Mustn't we.

ELISE

(Smiling.)

Hurry up with what exactly, James ... ?

FLANAGAN

...

(He returns his attention to the books.

She watches him some more.)

ELISE

... See anything you like?

FLANAGAN

... ?

ELISE

Books.

FLANAGAN

—No: I'm afraid I'm not a fan of most modern literature. Word-salad.

ELISE

(Entertained, perhaps.)

Word what ... ?

FLANAGAN

That's what it's like for me: art for art's sake—like a salad, made of words.

ELISE

As opposed to ... ?

FLANAGAN

—How do you mean?

ELISE

Art for what's sake then— ?

FLANAGAN

—O, for God's sake, I suppose. *(Smiles tightly.)* For the sake of humanity ... *(He raises his glass:)*

Sláinte! *(Pronounced "Slan-cha.")*

ELISE

Excuse me?

FLANAGAN

Irish. Gaelic. —"Cheers"—bottoms up!

(She raises her glass, too.)

ELISE

(Approximating.)

Sláinte!

FLANAGAN

Indeed ...

(They drink. He clears his throat.

He returns to the books; so she sits down ...

She kicks off her heels, places a bare foot up on the corner of the table ...

He notices.)

FLANAGAN (cont'd.)

... It's remarkable, really, to see so many books inside one room ...

ELISE

They're everywhere. Every wall-space is covered: the bathroom, bedroom—I'll show you—

FLANAGAN

—No, thank you. *(He glances at her foot again.)*
—But *thank* you. This is fine for me now ...

(The books again; he sips furtively at his wine.)

ELISE

... They had them instead of children ...

FLANAGAN

O yes I can see that—

ELISE

Instead of braces or bicycles or college: they bought books.
I like that, I think ...
I don't know if either one of them had a problem with fertility or what—

FLANAGAN

You speak of them as if they're dead.

(He looks up at her.)

ELISE

Well it feels that way, doesn't it?
When I moved in here, at the end of summer, I had this feeling like they were here, always—with me ... You know? ... Like ghosts.

FLANAGAN

(Mild alarm.)

Ghosts?

ELISE

Don't worry: they're in Paris. As far as anyone knows ...
I mean, isn't that *perfect* ... ?
They send me these postcards once in a while. They're friends of my parents ...
—But: it was like I had broken into their apartment, you know?, while they were gone, and I was pretending to *be* them; both of them ...
... It was a very confusing time for me last summer.

FLANAGAN

I imagine it was / that ...

ELISE

I kept having this one recurring dream, a nightmare, where they'd come home unannounced.

FLANAGAN

You're paying rent here, aren't you?

ELISE

... ?

FLANAGAN

—You're paying rent on this place?

ELISE

Of course I'm paying / rent—

FLANAGAN

Then you have nothing to be ashamed of, my girl.

ELISE

(Short.)

—Who was saying anything about shame?

FLANAGAN

... I'm sorry ... I misunderstood ...

ELISE

(She's playing with her keys.)

...

FLANAGAN

(Head bends to books again.)

...

(She gets up: pours herself more wine.)

ELISE

(A challenge.)

I thought you said you were fifty-nine.

FLANAGAN

(Head up.)

Did I?

ELISE

Before: Richard—*he* said / you're—

FLANAGAN

—O. You see, I lied about that too ...

ELISE

... Why?

FLANAGAN

(Shrugs.)

Vanity, I suppose ...

ELISE

You don't strike me as very vain, Mr. Flanagan ...

FLANAGAN

You'd be surprised, Elise. *(Smiles: teeth.)* —And I don't *feel* sixty-five.

ELISE

You don't act sixty-five ...

FLANAGAN

Don't I ... ?

ELISE

("No,") you're not old enough to retire, I don't think ...

FLANAGAN

Amn't I?

ELISE

(Smiles; perhaps charmed.)

—What *is* that?

FLANAGAN

What.

ELISE

That word: "Amn't"— ?

FLANAGAN

"Amn't," yes—

ELISE

Is that really a word?

FLANAGAN

It's a contraction, actually—

ELISE

(Sitting again.)

—Are you English?, or Irish? —I never could figure that one out ...

FLANAGAN

I'm neither. —I'm American.

ELISE

All right: but where are you *from?*

FLANAGAN

The Bronx.

ELISE

As in Bronx, New York ... ?

FLANAGAN

I live in Manhattan now ... But I grew up in the Bronx. —I was Irish, from Ireland, as a boy.

ELISE

And you never outgrew the accent?

FLANAGAN

I should hope not!

ELISE

... It's almost more English than Irish ... More an English-public-school-kind-of—Eton, or—"Harrow," is it ... ?

FLANAGAN

Pretentious, you mean.

ELISE

...

FLANAGAN

You think I speak in a less than truthful manner?

ELISE

I don't know if it has anything to do with being "truthful," James ...

FLANAGAN

(Back to the books.)

...

ELISE

... Are you married?

FLANAGAN

No, no, no ...

ELISE

—The students think you are.

FLANAGAN

That's because I tell them I am so.

ELISE

Why do you lie to them?

FLANAGAN

(Straightening up.)

It's a performance, isn't it? You're playing a part. Most teachers are villains, or they are clowns: both are the teachers without talent; their appeal is wholly low-brow.

But those of us who are burdened with more—sophisticated tastes: we create subtler personas, full of shadow and light, mystery, and more often than not a wife.

ELISE

...

FLANAGAN

No one really trusts a male teacher anyhow, Ms. Sanger. Much less a bachelor.

ELISE

Why do you think that is?

FLANAGAN

You're very curious about me tonight, aren't you?

(She smiles, as if shyly.

He drinks the rest of his wine, sets it down upon her table.)

FLANAGAN (cont'd.)

... And you? *(With great courage, effort:)* Are you—seeing someone ... at the present time?

ELISE

(A long exhalation.)

... I was ... For a long time: six years. —Not married though, thank God ...

We broke up. —It was mutual. —We outgrew each other. —We changed. I love him dearly, but—will you *listen* to me?

FLANAGAN

... ?

ELISE

—I'm so fucking *full* of clichés! It's like a fucking first *language*—I know absolutely *nothing* about life ... !

FLANAGAN

I think you know a great deal. That's why I hired you.

ELISE

—I'm not talking about literature, James ...

FLANAGAN

... Would you like some more wine?

(He takes her glass; careful not to touch her hand.

She watches him as he pours.)

ELISE

... How do you do it?

FLANAGAN

How do I do what ... ?

ELISE

You teach: and you love it. And when you don't love it you at least feel proud. You've got a martyr's pride ...

Because I'll tell you something: I'm good at it. Teaching. The kids *love* me—and I can't *stand* them. —I hate them—the *kids*—I hate "kids" ... And the children at that school can all eat shit for all I care: I mean, this *attitude* they have— ? They look down on you as a matter of course, as if it's somehow *polite* of them to condescend to talk to you, because *you don't live there*—you can't *afford* to! —So I constantly feel this need to shock them, you know? To break them of their smug little complacencies—about life. I flirt with the boys; I wear low-cut blouses, leather minis. I'm a bitch to the girls; I confront them with symbolic gang-rape in *Lord of the Flies*—and they are *shocked!* —Thank God *something* shocks them!, for a moment, for a few days, they're confused, and violated ... Why would she do this to us? What's Miss Sanger trying to *say* ... ?

But they get used to it, don't they ...

They've started to laugh at me already: "O, that's Miss Sanger" —they don't use the word *Ms.*, it's like their mouths are congenitally incapable of forming the sounds required—"That's our *Miss* Sanger for you: it's because she's *so young* ... "

Don't get me wrong: it's me: I'm an artist—a novelist; by nature. That's what I wanted to be in the first place, when I got out—of college. I went to Brown? I wrote a novel as my senior thesis. It's not that good: too long—it's trite—Richard read it; he had *lots* of notes ... It's not organic just yet, let's just put it that way; but it's a start ... It's about a place, in case you're wondering, very much like Brown: there's a murder, yadda yadda yadda ... I haven't given up on it just yet ... But once you grow up, and by "up" I mean twenty-six, -seven, you find you've got to pay your rent, right? You've got to get health insurance. You have *got* to get a life, so—wake up! You know? Get married!, have kids quick before your ovaries dry up like a, like what? ... fruit is so—*fuck!* ... Anyway: and then you've got to find time to be inspired and isn't that just about the most depressing thing you've ever heard ... ?

FLANAGAN

You're not a teacher.

ELISE

...

FLANAGAN

That's simply not who you are.

ELISE

That's the nicest thing anyone's said to me in a very long time ...

FLANAGAN

...

(She smiles up at him as she drinks deeply of her wine ...

He moves himself to the bookcase again.)

FLANAGAN (cont'd.)

—Once. —For a long time when I was young I had that certain ambition of which you speak. I gave myself one year—I was younger than you; and after months and months of sitting at my desk in a state of complete and utter constipation—*artistic* constipation—I suddenly realized: I had no talent. For looking at myself. I find it boring.

ELISE

And frightening.

FLANAGAN

—No: boring. —Indulgent; I'm not unique.

ELISE

You are. Everyone's unique if you're patient enough.

FLANAGAN

You say that because you're young.

One of life's great tragedies, Ms. Sanger, is to grow old and realize that while everyone is indeed an individual, no one is unique.

ELISE

I don't know if I believe that ...

FLANAGAN

(He shrugs.)

You don't have to: it's true.

You'll see ...

ELISE

What did you write about when you were young?

FLANAGAN

Nothing worth reading, I can assure you—

ELISE

Tell me:

FLANAGAN

I wanted to be the next James Joyce. Or Will Faulkner. —No, Joyce: the Irish-American Joyce of Scarsdale! ... That was my privatemost ambition ... When I first came here to teach—I was twenty-three years old—I was obsessed with that place; this town: *Scarsdale* ... There were not so many Jews then. —It was Episcopal: a blue-blood town. This was '49 into '50—Joyce was still quite shocking then—and I wanted to write a novel like *Ulysses*, but instead of Leo Bloom one day in Dublin, it would be—well, me: one day in Scarsdale ... And all our young James Flanagan need do all day was exactly what I did:

Take the seven-fourteen local from Grand Central, empty as it would be in the morning, as it always was, the armies of suburban businessmen in their gray flannel suits, drab trenchcoats and black wool hats waiting up north on their southbound platforms, gazing down along the tracks, *into* the city ... —Uptown to Harlem we'd ride, to 125th Street and farther still, up, into the Bronx, and Melrose, Tremont, Fordham, Botanical Gardens ... The cars fill up with blacks and hispanics—women mostly: nurses, cooks, maids—all the way to Fleetwood, and Bronxville; where the train begins to empty out again: maids and cooks and nurses; the odd merchants and clerks off in the middle-class burgs of Tuckahoe and Crestwood ... And up farther still till we reached Scarsdale ... Bright, clear, sun-filled *Scarsdale* ... Where I disembark neck-deep in a rabble of hired hands ... They look at me strangely, almost as if with pity; if I drop something they call out their name for me: *Sugar*, you dropped yo' scarf! ... And across the platform the late men wait for their late train ... reading the *Times*, the latest Cheever in *The New Yorker*, scratching a line or two of original poetry in the margins of their day books ...

The walk from the station—you know it too: up over East Parkway, down Spencer Place, past the delicatessen where I buy my second cup from the ex-con behind the counter; a packet of cigarettes—I smoked in those days; —and up higher still, up out of the village past the old homes in their crescent-shaped lanes—homes built by the city-rich over a hundred years ago, for the wives and children to escape the immigrants and typhus from the horse dung in the summer in the city ... There has been a murder in that house: someone killed his wife with a hammer while she slept. In that house there has been a child's death, by illness or by accident; adultery in that house; bankruptcy, alcoholism, drug-addiction ... A starvation of affection ... That house is haunted. That one is empty now. —But that one there is happy. That one is full of children ...

... Up the hill and round the bend at the soccer fields, up over that stagnant brook past those black willow trees, perpetually pruned ... I climb the stairs to my office in high heartbeat just to write it all down ... *(With pride:)*

Instead I'd prepare my lesson.

(A moment.

He drinks.

He turns to look at the books again.)

FLANAGAN (cont'd.)

Tell me of their poetry, Ms. Sanger.

ELISE

My poetry?

FLANAGAN

(Turning.)

—You write poetry?

ELISE

Not anymore. —I thought, when you said—your head was / turned.

FLANAGAN

I meant the poets who live here. —They that haunt you, Elise. What's their poetry like:

ELISE

I don't know how to describe it ... Sort of like a—word salad?

FLANAGAN

Ah. *(Smiles tight.)*

ELISE

Yes—*(She smiles too.)* and morbid, too. —I don't like it very much ...

FLANAGAN

I don't either ...

ELISE

—I think you would, actually.

FLANAGAN

—Do you find me morbid, Ms. Sanger?

ELISE

Well, I'd say you're very *serious* sometimes, Mr. Flanagan.

FLANAGAN

Yes, but not morbid; not *depressive.* —I think to have a surfeit of self-pity is a grave, grave sin. —I have great capacity for lightness and mirth.

ELISE

(Smiles.)

"Mirth"?—are you sure ... ?

FLANAGAN

Yes; you might even say that I am lightsome.

ELISE

I would not say that—I don't think I even know what that word really means ...

FLANAGAN

—It means exactly what it says: I have great light inside of me.

ELISE

(She's still smiling.)

...

FLANAGAN

As do you ...

(He smiles in return, showing his teeth.

She sips her wine.)

ELISE

(A secret.)

... I found some letters in a box. Would you like to see them?

FLANAGAN

...

ELISE

They're love letters the poets wrote each other years ago, when they were young. —Sexual letters, some of them ... *(Mock disdain:)*

Filthy stuff, really.

FLANAGAN

... In what way filthy?

ELISE

(Shrugs.)

The usual ... *(She smiles:)*

And a few *not* so usual ...

FLANAGAN

...

ELISE

... They're sweet. —And kind of heartbreaking, too. —People do the most disgusting things to each other when they're in love ...

FLANAGAN

I wouldn't know about that.

ELISE

O come on James—

FLANAGAN

I wouldn't ... !

I suppose you'd find me rather prudish, if you knew me, when it comes to that sort of thing ...

ELISE

What sort of thing?

FLANAGAN

—Sex things.

ELISE

There ... Was that so hard to say, Saint James?

FLANAGAN

... What did you call me?

ELISE

... ?

FLANAGAN

"Saint James"— ?

ELISE

Everyone calls you that: the teachers—. I thought you / knew—

FLANAGAN

No ...

ELISE

—I was teasing.

FLANAGAN

Were you? Why?

ELISE

Why was I teasing / you ... ?

FLANAGAN

—Why do they call me by that name?

ELISE

It's the way you carry yourself: your hands ... The way you walk down the hallway: "Saint James."

FLANAGAN

(Quiet, at first.)

O ... *(Barks:)*
Ha!

ELISE

(She laughs too.)

... You're not mad?

FLANAGAN

No ... I may in fact be "mad"—that is, a little off-kilter tonight, Ms. Sanger—but you're right. —You are *absolutely* right! Road to Calvary, that's how I've been ...

(She watches him, closely.

He drinks some more—finishing off his glass.)

FLANAGAN (cont'd.)

Bring me those letters, please; I'd like to read them now.

ELISE

Really?

FLANAGAN

Why shouldn't I ... ?

ELISE

—You seem—

FLANAGAN

What:

ELISE

—nervous.

FLANAGAN

I am not / nervous— !

ELISE

You are! —You're afraid they'll be too sexy.

FLANAGAN

—Too what?

ELISE

Sexy! pissy! / filthy!

FLANAGAN

—Is that what you think I'm / afraid of?

ELISE

—You *are* afraid! I can tell from here!

FLANAGAN

My dear girl I can assure you I care less what those letters have to say on the subject of "sex."

ELISE

...

FLANAGAN

... I'm curious, that's all.

ELISE

In one letter she says she wants to make love to him with another woman ...

FLANAGAN

...

ELISE

—You see?—you *are* / afraid!

FLANAGAN

—It's a question of taste, my girl! —*Morality* is a question of *taste!* ... And so I simply do not care to speak lightly of that sort of thing. —It's simply an *opinion* of mine: I think we all might be a great deal better off were we all a bit more repressed. Shame is a wonderful tool—for good. And I'm talking about the world here: think of all we might be avoiding, right now, as a culture: —and I know it's not very popular these days, or for the past twenty-, thirty-odd years—*but:* there'd be no AIDS, yes?, fewer undesired pregnancies, divorces, molestations. What I'm saying is simply how I feel: "repression" has got a bad rap since Freud. And that's one *very* big reason why I won't read anything written after the First World War.

—My God, we're obsessed with deviance!—a Godless culture running around with its head and pants cut off. The papers, on TV: you see a new story every day—about *priests*—. Did you know, last month, the priest from my parish was accused of molesting a young man—a boy, really, seminary, *years* ago; and this kindly old man walked down to the river—just last month this all came out, in the press, you can read it— and he threw himself into the water—.

—Right into the *filthy* waves ... !

...

And that boy today who came into my office—he'd been abused.

—I'm sure of it now ...

ELISE

...

FLANAGAN

(Gentler; an apology, perhaps.)

—And I'm not saying people should never have sex—they *should.* And it does not have to be a dreary affair; it can be quite beautiful, Elise ...

—Because a little repression goes a long way in making it that much more rewarding when one finally *does give in*—.

ELISE

...

FLANAGAN

(To the books.)

I said I know it's not / popular ...

ELISE

—Do you really feel that way?

FLANAGAN

About sex?

ELISE

About life.

FLANAGAN

(Quietly.)

... You think I'm an old maid ...

ELISE

(Smiles.)

... A what ... ?

FLANAGAN

An uptight, dried-up old—it's all right if you think that about me. I think that way about myself / sometimes ...

ELISE

I don't think any bad way about you, James ...
Why don't you sit down now; okay?

(A moment.

Then he does sit down: lowers himself discreetly into the chair opposite.

He keeps the suit jacket on.)

ELISE (cont'd.)

... Take your jacket off now, please ...

FLANAGAN

... Shall I?

ELISE

Yes. You shall:

(He takes his suit jacket off.

—And, turning, drapes it over the shoulders of the chair.

The gun clunks ominously in the suit jacket pocket.

She flinches.

He smiles, takes greater care ...

... Long pause here as he arranges himself torturously without his suit jacket on ...

ELISE *watches: he's wearing a light brown shirt ...*

She reaches out to him—to remove a thread?

He kisses her.

Awkwardly. Forcefully.

...

She pulls back.)

FLANAGAN

... ?

(She kisses him now. Gentler.

They begin to caress each other; awkwardly.

After a moment or two:)

ELISE

... You don't remember me, do you.

FLANAGAN

... From when?

ELISE

Scarsdale. Sorry.

FLANAGAN

...

ELISE

I grew up there. —My parents still live there. *(With a sigh, as if disappointed:)* Both of them, still married ...

FLANAGAN

(He pulls away farther.)

...

ELISE

You don't remember me, I know you don't.

FLANAGAN

—Did I have you as a student?

ELISE

("Yes.")

FLANAGAN

—When?

ELISE

I don't know—eleven, twelve years / ago ...

FLANAGAN

Why wasn't— ? Why wouldn't you tell me this before ... ?

ELISE

—When before?

FLANAGAN

—When I interviewed you, last summer—

ELISE

I *did* tell you. —I mean it was on my résumé. Did you even read my résumé?

FLANAGAN

—Does Richard know?

ELISE

I don't know. I think so.

FLANAGAN

You *think*— ?

ELISE

Do you remember this poem I wrote?

(He looks at her, full in the face.)

ELISE (cont'd.)

The assignment had been to write a poem about someone you loved, and then lost. —"Loved and lost." And you wrote about your uncle—how he died in World War Two. —And I wrote this poem about my brother: my younger brother had died a few years before that. An accident ... I couldn't write about it yet—well, or honestly. So I made a kind of free-verse rhyming thing, about a crow. And snow. Those two words rhymed a lot. And how the crow flew from a high branch to the snow on the dead grass, then up again, into the sky ...

You called it trite ...

You gave it back to me, in class: "Heartfelt," you said, "but trite." I had to go home and look that word up in my parents' dictionary just to find out what you meant about me ...

FLANAGAN

...

ELISE

And then you asked Brian Sloan to stand up and read *his* poem. —Do you remember Brian Sloan? He's a plastic surgeon now; married, two kids. —And, anyhow, in heroic couplets he'd written this really very treacly poem about a grandmother who'd suffered a stroke ... "Poignant," you said, to the class, "and *true.*"

What I remember most about Brian was how he used to tease you in class; and you used to tease him right back. To flirt. The rest of us thought there was something somehow weirdly, vaguely sexual going on—we never *said* that, out loud, but we *felt* it ... And then one day, later, after all that business with the poetry, I came to class early and you and Brian were there, discussing *To The Lighthouse*; and Brian was sitting on his desk, with his legs up under him. Like this, you know, like he used to—in a really very childlike position—almost feminine, really. —And you *also* were sitting on your desk! In *exactly* the same way!—You didn't think his poem was any better than mine; you liked *him* more. You wanted to be his friend.

FLANAGAN

(Shaken.)

...

ELISE

Do you remember that— ?

(He kisses her again—aggressively.

After a moment of shock, surprise, she begins to kiss him back.

They continue kissing, groping. He gets his hand up under her shirt. Fondles her, hands shaking terrifically ...

She takes one of his hands and places it on her thigh, under her skirt. His hand moves higher.

She unbuttons his shirt ... His pants ... Her hand goes into his pants.

A moment.

... They both have stopped kissing.

... He stands:)

ELISE (cont'd.)

James—

FLANAGAN

I have to get all the way uptown / and—

ELISE

Sit down, James, it's all right—

FLANAGAN

—No—no, I do not think it is all right, Elise—you see, because: I do not think I should have come here in the first place—

(In throwing his coat over his shoulders, throwing his arms through his coatsleeves:

The gun spills out across the floor.

They both flinch: will it fire?

He bends to pick it up.

He holds the gun for a moment—too long.

He looks at the gun in his hand ...)

FLANAGAN (cont'd.)

... Did you really think I was a pedophile? ... Is that what you really thought of me?

ELISE

No—I didn't / mean that—

FLANAGAN

You said that: —"all the children"—all the children thought this thing of me *(An explosion:)—a disgusting thing about me—* !

ELISE

...

FLANAGAN

(Holding the gun, still; quiet again.)

Are you angry ... ?

Is that why you asked me to leave that bar with you—because you are still angry that I did not understand an adolescent poem ... ?

ELISE

...

FLANAGAN

Because I was under a false impression here, Ms. Sanger—it's not your fault. *(He smiles, lips tight.)* Tonight, when Richard was about to say something in front of all those people that I did not want him to say—do you know what it was he was going to say? About me? He was going to say something *true* ... He's the one living person who knows this one true thing about me ... He knows what is true without knowing the reason for it; —and somehow I feel I ought to tell it to you now. Both what is true, and why. —Or perhaps I should save that for another day ... when we both know each other better. —Because I like you, Ms. Sanger, I do ... *Elise* ... What a great adventure it has been simply for me to be here with you tonight. To stand here in your presence, in a beautiful young girl's apartment, in someone else's apartment that is also your apartment, browsing through books and talking—enjoying such wonderful conversation, even when we have felt compelled to discuss quite serious or morbid things. I have never been with a woman. In all my adult life. I have never been on intimate terms with a single other human being in all my sixty-five years. Because of one incident in my youth.

How cliché, *you* might say, Ms. Sanger ...

...

I am sorry I did not understand your poem.

(She stands still, not knowing what to do.

She holds out her hand—for his hand, or for the gun, perhaps.

After a while, he takes the gun and replaces it gently in his pocket.)

4.

(Next morning.

He stands at his desk, dressed as he's been all night; he's put his tie back on.

Sunlight grows in the window, all throughout the scene.

He takes the gun from his pocket, lays it gently down upon the desk, beside James' story ...

He sits down.

He stares at both the story and the gun ...

After a while:)

FLANAGAN

I know you're there.

(JAMES appears in the doorway, out-of-sorts.)

JAMES

I saw your car in the teacher's lot ...

FLANAGAN

Were you waiting for me?
Why?

JAMES

...

FLANAGAN

It's Saturday, James—

JAMES

Can I come in?

FLANAGAN

Of course you may, my boy ...

(JAMES comes in, but remains standing near the door.

FLANAGAN leaves the gun right where it is.)

JAMES

Why didn't you call the police?

FLANAGAN

... ?

JAMES

Last night—

FLANAGAN

I don't remember. I still might. I'll have to, won't I.

JAMES

—Why didn't you do it in the first place?

FLANAGAN

I don't know. —I suppose I wanted to give you another chance.

JAMES

A chance for what ... ?

FLANAGAN

...

JAMES

—Can I sit down?

(He does.)

JAMES (cont'd.)

Look: if my father finds out the gun's gone he's going to kill me—

FLANAGAN

—You told me all this / yesterday—

JAMES

(Strongly.)

—Why do you always just *assume* you know *everything* about *everyone* ... ?

FLANAGAN

(Covering the gun with his hand.)

...

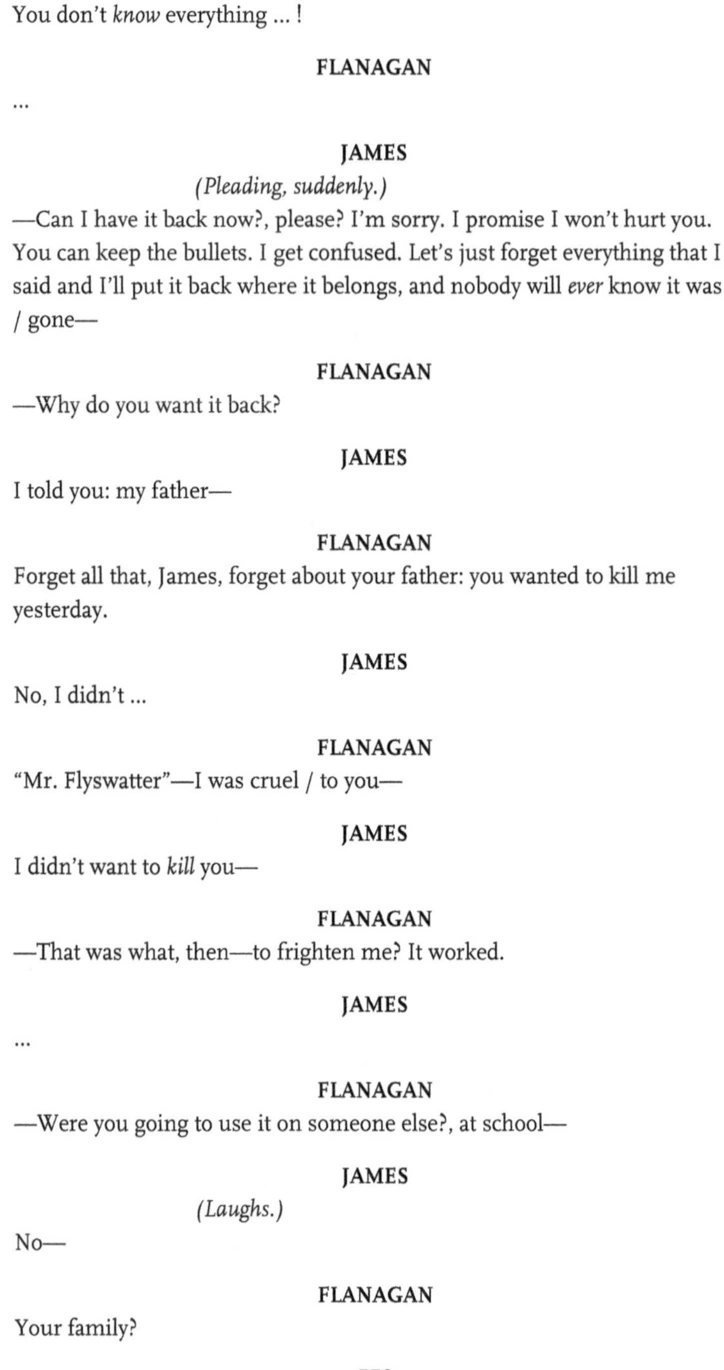

JAMES

You don't *know* everything ... !

FLANAGAN

...

JAMES

(Pleading, suddenly.)

—Can I have it back now?, please? I'm sorry. I promise I won't hurt you. You can keep the bullets. I get confused. Let's just forget everything that I said and I'll put it back where it belongs, and nobody will *ever* know it was / gone—

FLANAGAN

—Why do you want it back?

JAMES

I told you: my father—

FLANAGAN

Forget all that, James, forget about your father: you wanted to kill me yesterday.

JAMES

No, I didn't ...

FLANAGAN

"Mr. Flyswatter"—I was cruel / to you—

JAMES

I didn't want to *kill* you—

FLANAGAN

—That was what, then—to frighten me? It worked.

JAMES

...

FLANAGAN

—Were you going to use it on someone else?, at school—

JAMES

(Laughs.)

No—

FLANAGAN

Your family?

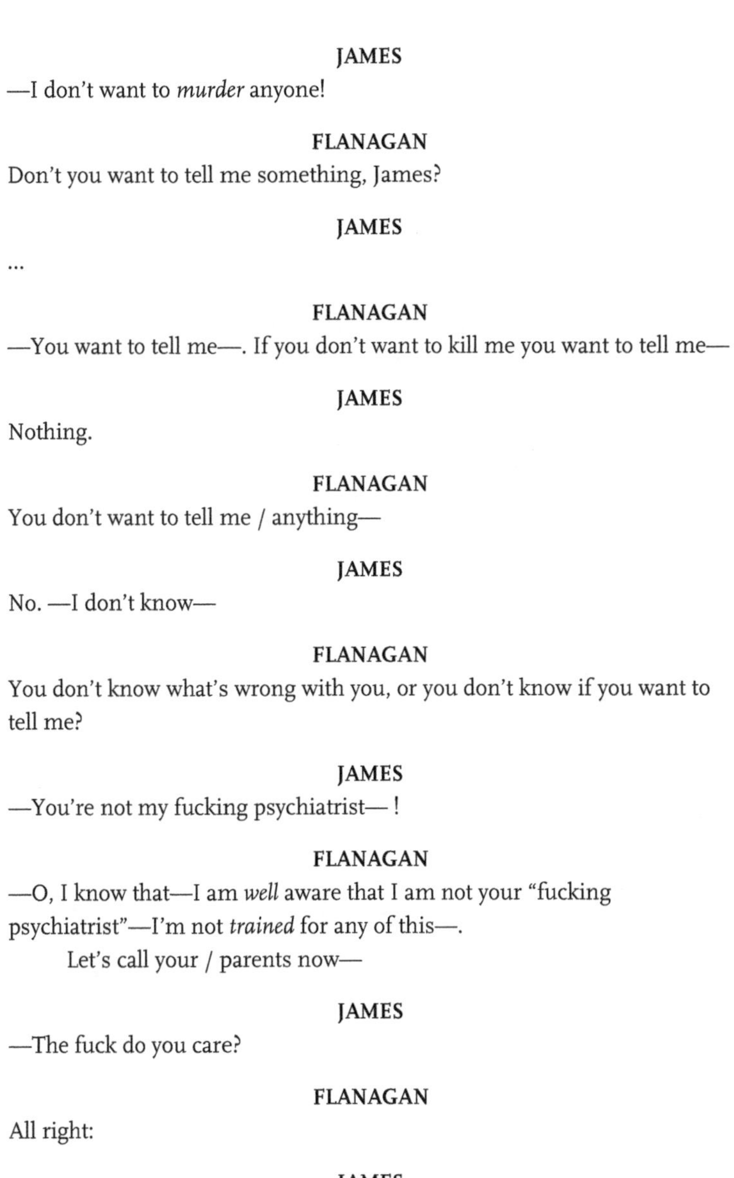

JAMES

—I don't want to *murder* anyone!

FLANAGAN

Don't you want to tell me something, James?

JAMES

...

FLANAGAN

—You want to tell me—. If you don't want to kill me you want to tell me—

JAMES

Nothing.

FLANAGAN

You don't want to tell me / anything—

JAMES

No. —I don't know—

FLANAGAN

You don't know what's wrong with you, or you don't know if you want to tell me?

JAMES

—You're not my fucking psychiatrist— !

FLANAGAN

—O, I know that—I am *well* aware that I am not your "fucking psychiatrist"—I'm not *trained* for any of this—.

Let's call your / parents now—

JAMES

—The fuck do you care?

FLANAGAN

All right:

JAMES

(Standing.)

—You let me leave here yesterday and you did not think twice—. Call the police if you think I'm a danger to myself.

FLANAGAN

Are you a danger to yourself?

JAMES

(The window.)

...

FLANAGAN

James?

JAMES

I could do it other ways if I wanted—.

I could eat a bottle of aspirin. *(He gestures out the window:)* I could hang myself on one of those fucking cut-up trees—.

FLANAGAN

—Is that what you want to do? Do you want to harm yourself?

JAMES

...

FLANAGAN

James:

JAMES

... Sometimes.

FLANAGAN

Good:

JAMES

What?

FLANAGAN

Why:

JAMES

—Why what?

FLANAGAN

Why do you want to kill yourself?

JAMES

(He laughs.)

...

FLANAGAN

Do you know ... ?

JAMES

I know—

FLANAGAN

—Is your life so terrible ... ?

JAMES

—Why do you *say* it like that?

FLANAGAN

Like what?

JAMES

—I can't take it anymore ...
Okay?

FLANAGAN

—You're going to have to be a bit more specific than that, James. —What exactly "can't you take"?

JAMES

Everything—

FLANAGAN

"Everything"?

JAMES

—Life—

FLANAGAN

Life? You can't take "life" anymore— ?

JAMES

—Why are you *laughing* at me?

FLANAGAN

I'm not—I'm simply—. You're going to have to be patient with me on this one because, frankly, this is where I begin to lose sympathy for you; this is *precisely* when I begin to become quite *angry* with you, if you'll forgive me. —If you're going to kill yourself, if you're not going to give yourself at least the *opportunity* to let life prove to you that you are wrong, that life has *something* to offer—that there are people out there in this world who *will* love you, to *some* degree, in *some* way, one day—then you ought to know *why*.
So tell me:

JAMES

...

FLANAGAN

(Quietly, very gently.)

Tell me, James ... You're in pain ... I will listen to you now ...

(The boy begins to cry, almost soundlessly.)

FLANAGAN (cont'd.)

... Listen: what you said to me, yesterday—. About my story ... and *your* story; when you made reference to mine—. —I want you to know that you were right. You were *absolutely right about me* ...

JAMES

...

FLANAGAN

James: has your father interfered with you before?

JAMES

(Looking up.)

... ?

FLANAGAN

Has he abused you— ? Has anyone abused / you— ?

JAMES

(Short laugh.)

—I've never been molested.

FLANAGAN

...

JAMES

That's *your* story.

FLANAGAN

(Slumps slowly back in his chair.)

...

JAMES

(Wiping his eyes.)

...

(FLANAGAN watches JAMES for a long time.)

FLANAGAN

I was wrong about your story ... *(His fingers lightly brush the pages on the desk.)*

I was re-reading it when you came in: it's not bad. It's good. It shows ... potential.

And it would be a shame, in my opinion, after forty-two years of teaching, to see you splatter the brains that could write these words all over the walls of this room. Or any room, for that matter.

JAMES

... It's shit.

FLANAGAN

—It's *not* shit—it's *your* story— ! *(He pushes it across the desk.)*

Pick it up and read it out loud and I will show you *exactly* where I see such promise ...

JAMES

(Wipes his eyes; nose.)

...

FLANAGAN

Go on:

(JAMES picks up the story.)

FLANAGAN (cont'd.)

When you are ready, my boy:

JAMES

(Coughs; wipes nose.)

... "Saint James: Portrait of a Hero," by—me.

(A fragile laugh is shared.)

JAMES (cont'd.)

"At the station the sun is angry. The wet tiles of the train station roof gleam and chortle in the morning sun. The snow shrieks and the crows taunt him. James walks through this sea of commuters, these fat men like beetles in their dark wool coats. Watch where you're going! somebody shouts, and James thinks, *They crucified Jesus, too* ... He lives near the station, in the slums of this rich town. His mother lies in bed late into the morning. His father—*where is his father?* ... James packs his bag, slips into the morning rush and walks through this sea of people who know nothing about him, nothing of his life or of each other, on his way to school and the sun at least loves his heart—"

FLANAGAN

—There.

JAMES

... ?

FLANAGAN

That's good, isn't it? ... That's *very* good: "The sun at least loves his heart."

JAMES

...

FLANAGAN

You may continue, dear boy.

END OF PLAY